Keiko   Suenobu

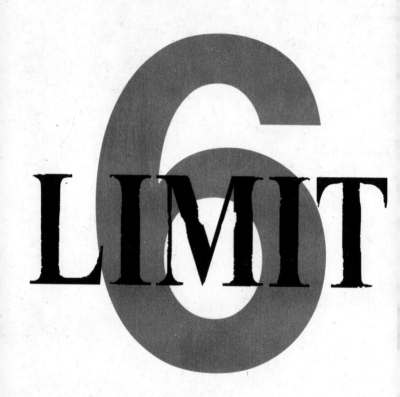

VERTICAL.

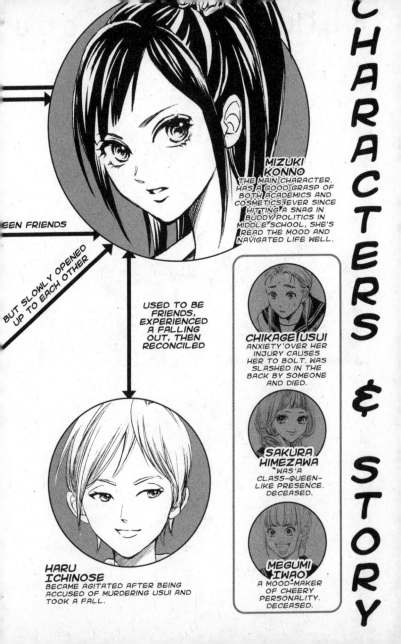

MIZUKI KONNO
THE MAIN CHARACTER. HAS A GOOD GRASP OF BOTH ACADEMICS AND COSMETICS. EVER SINCE HITTING A SNAG IN BUDDY POLITICS IN MIDDLE SCHOOL, SHE'S READ THE MOOD AND NAVIGATED LIFE WELL.

EEN FRIENDS

BUT SLOWLY OPENED UP TO EACH OTHER

USED TO BE FRIENDS, EXPERIENCED A FALLING OUT, THEN RECONCILED

CHIKAGE USUI
ANXIETY OVER HER INJURY CAUSES HER TO BOLT. WAS SLASHED IN THE BACK BY SOMEONE AND DIED.

SAKURA HIMEZAWA
WAS A CLASS-QUEEN-LIKE PRESENCE. DECEASED.

MEGUMI IWAO
A MOOD-MAKER OF CHEERY PERSONALITY. DECEASED.

HARU ICHINOSE
BECAME AGITATED AFTER BEING ACCUSED OF MURDERING USUI AND TOOK A FALL.

ASHAMED OF HAVING RIDICULED HER

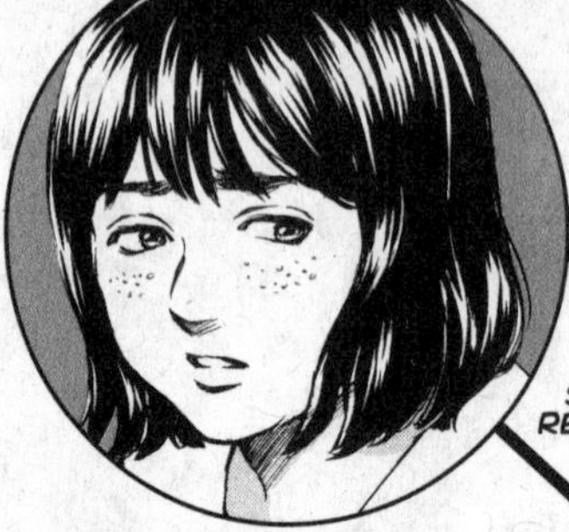

SLOWLY OPENING UP TO HER

STRONG REVULSION

ARISA MORISHIGE
WAS A SUBDUED PRESENCE IN THE CLASS AND WAS BULLIED. AFTER THE ACCIDENT, SHE REVERSES HER STATUS AND REIGNS OVER THE OTHERS, BUT HER HEART IS WAVERING NOW THAT KONNO BELIEVES HER.

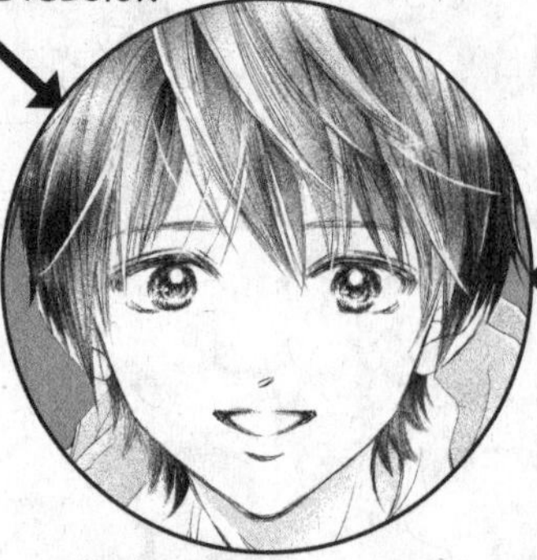

HAV

HARUAKI HINATA
HIS POSITIVE ATTITUDE HAS GIVEN THE OTHERS COURAGE. HOWEVER, HE ACTUALLY KILLED USUI AND HAS BEEN CONTINUOUSLY LYING TO HIDE THAT FACT.

A SUDDEN BUS ACCIDENT. THERE ARE ONLY FIVE SURVIVORS, ALL GIRLS. KONNO'S PERFECT, ORDINARY LIFE THAT WASN'T EVER SUPPOSED TO CHANGE COMPLETELY CRUMBLES AWAY.

ALTHOUGH THE SITUATION INITIALLY IMPROVES WITH THE APPEARANCE OF THE ONE AND ONLY BOY, HINATA, USUI IS DISCOVERED DEAD, AND HARU, SUSPECTED OF BEING THE PERP, FALLS DOWN A CLIFF. HOWEVER, HINATA WAS THE ONE WHO HAD KILLED USUI. HAVING COME TO THAT REALIZATION, KONNO DIRECTLY CONFIRMS IT WITH HINATA BUT IS ALMOST KILLED. KAMIYA ALSO SUFFERS A SERIOUS WOUND TO THE BACK WHEN SHE TRIES TO COME TO KONNO'S AID. DESPAIRING AT BEING PAST THE POINT OF NO RETURN, HINATA CHOOSES DEATH—?!

AT ODDS AT FIRST

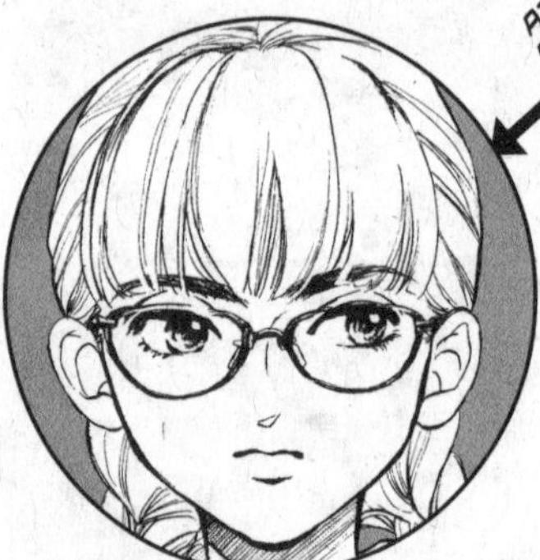

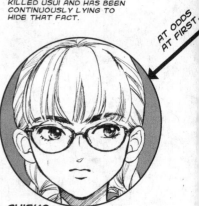

CHIEKO KAMIYA
HAS AN ABUNDANCE OF KNOWLEDGE REGARDING NATURE AND RESCUE. WAS SLASHED AND WOUNDED IN THE BACK BY A SICKLE-WIELDING HINATA.

contents

Scene.20
Before Dawn
5

Scene.21
Carry, My Voice
44

Scene.22
The Final Decision
83

Last Scene.
Onward, Towards Tomorrow.
123

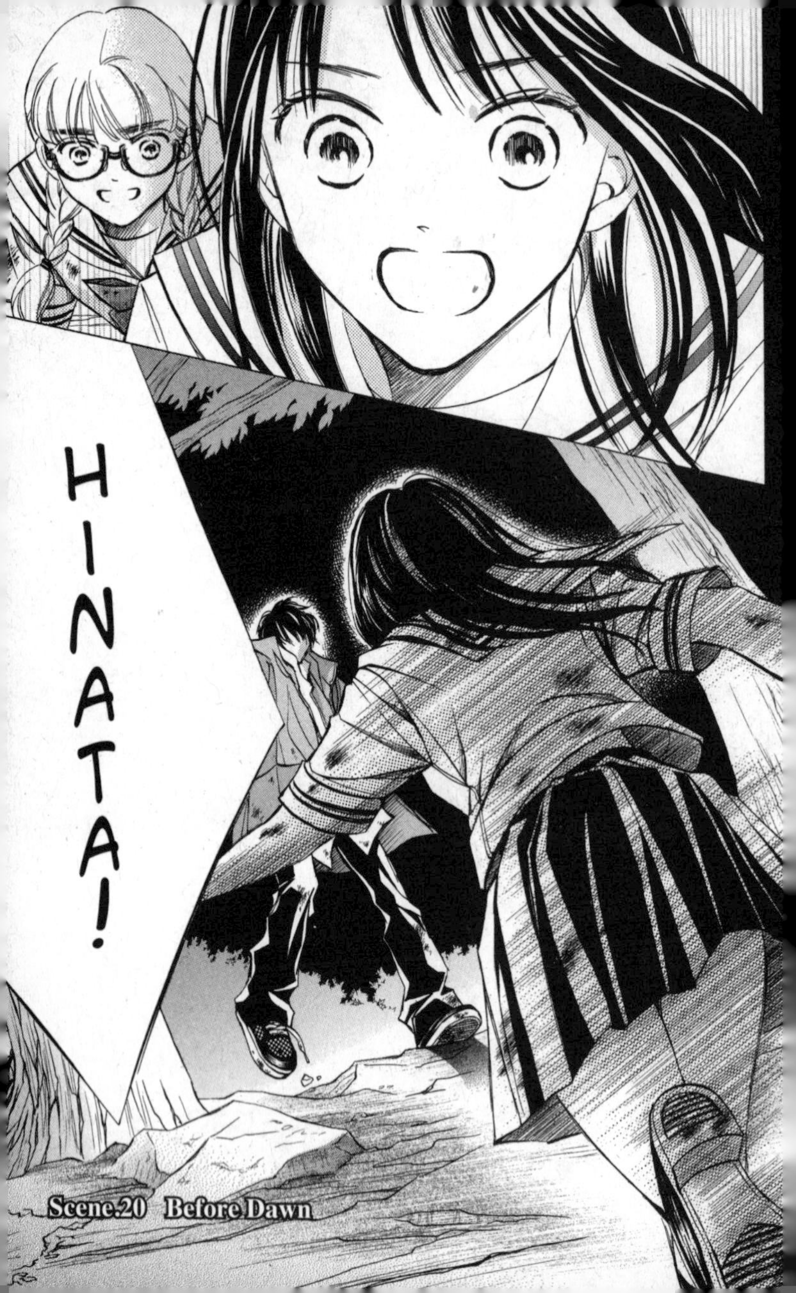
HINATA!
Scene.20 Before Dawn

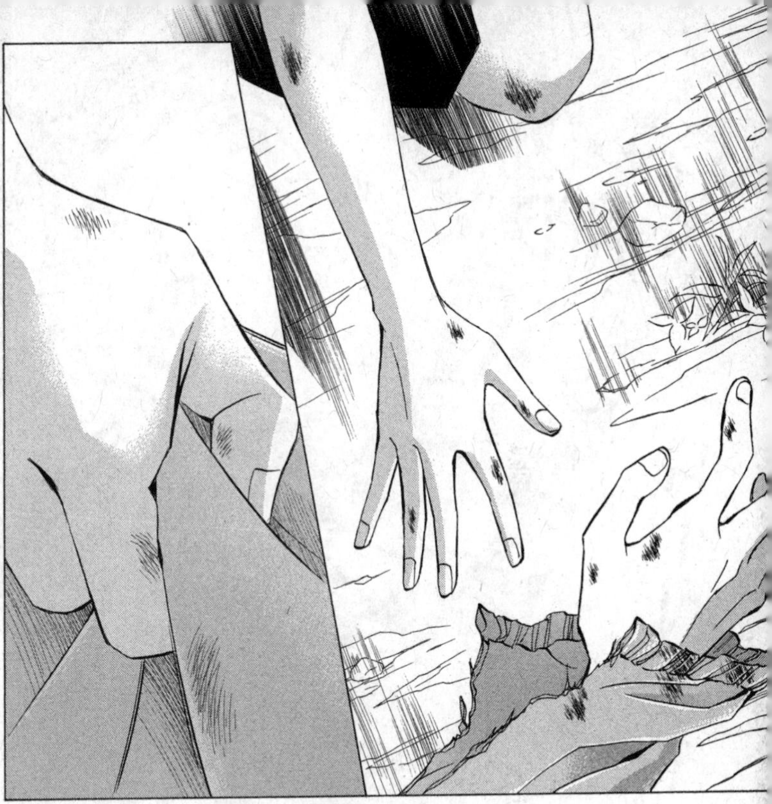

LIMIT

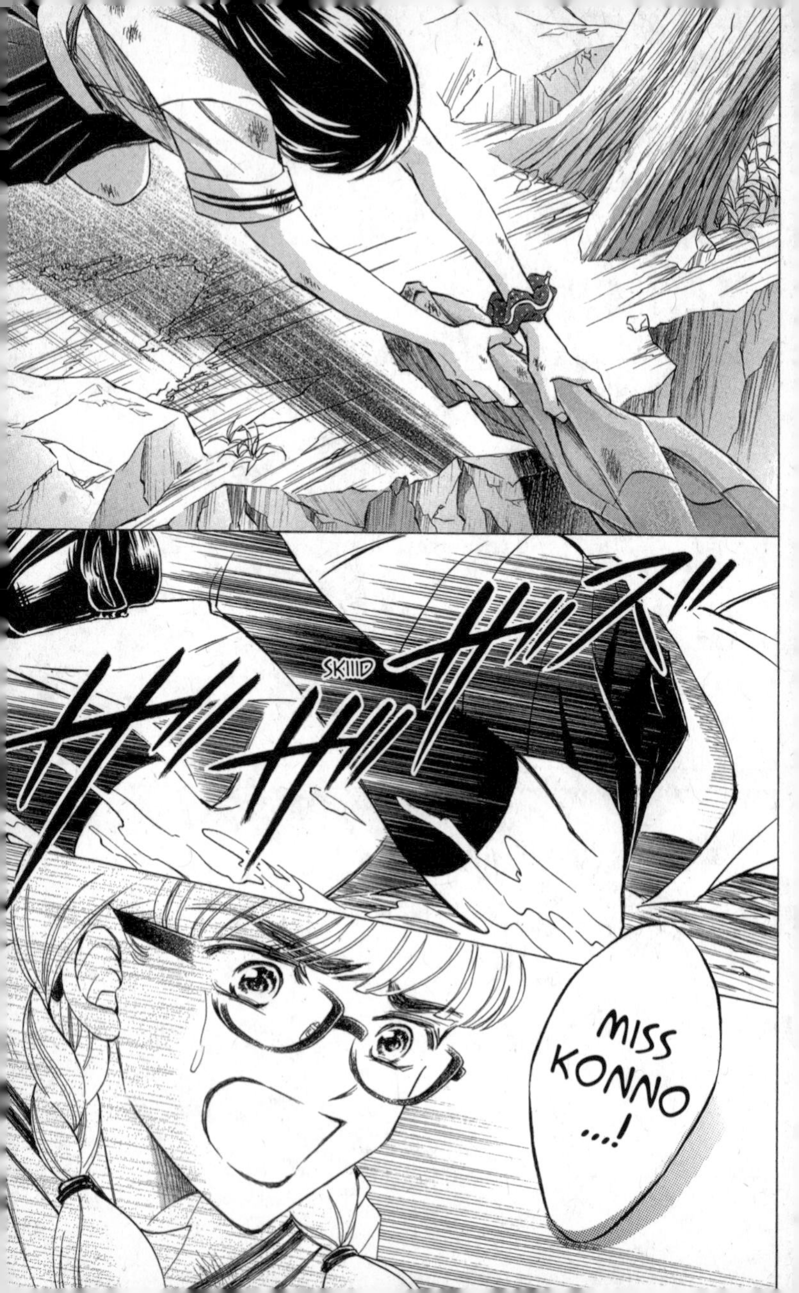
SKIIID
MISS KONNO ...!

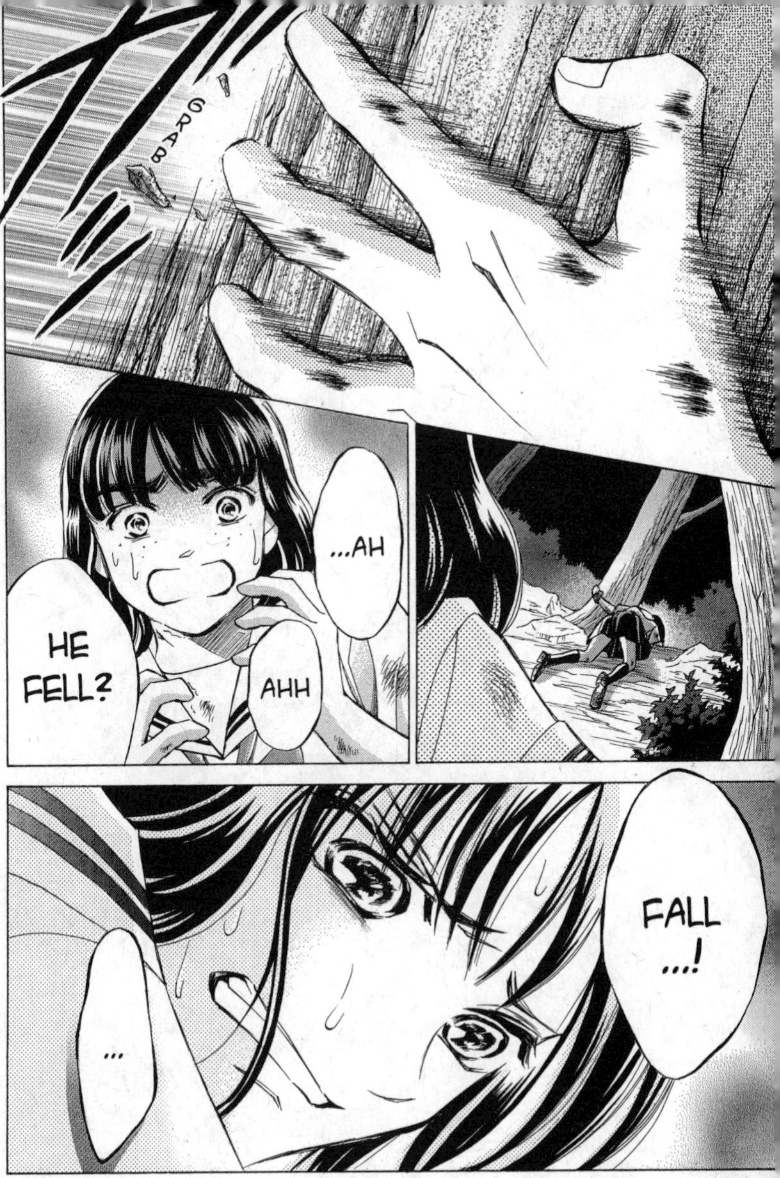
GRAB
...AH
AHH
HE FELL?
FALL ...!
...

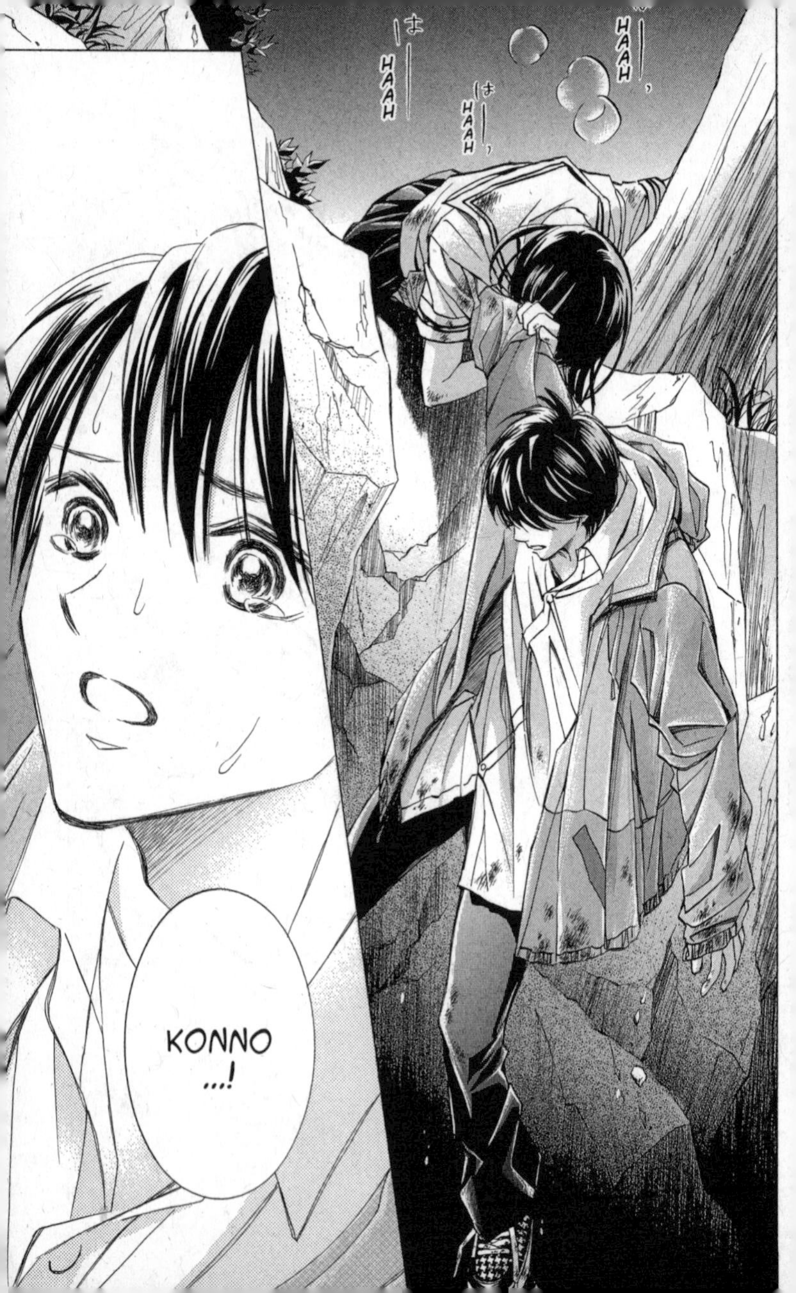

HAAH
は—!, HAAH
は——— HAAH
KONNO ...!

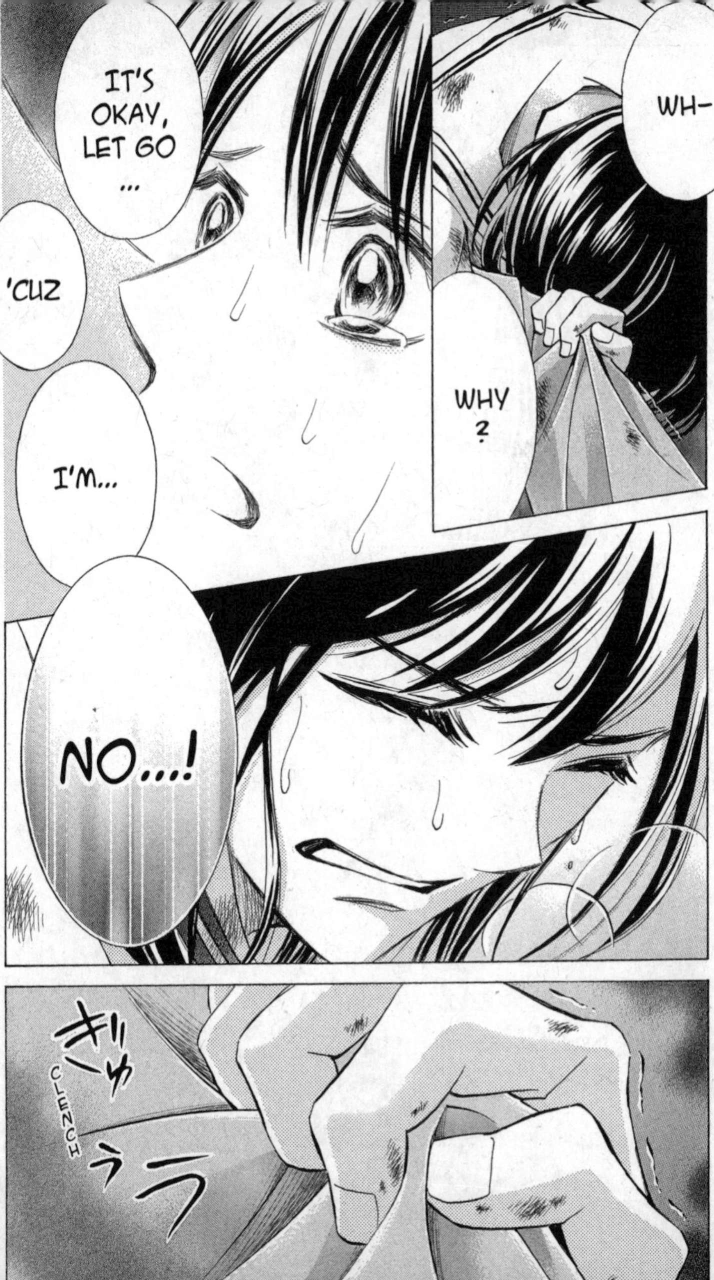
WH-
WHY?
IT'S OKAY, LET GO...
'CUZ
I'M...
NO...!
CLENCH

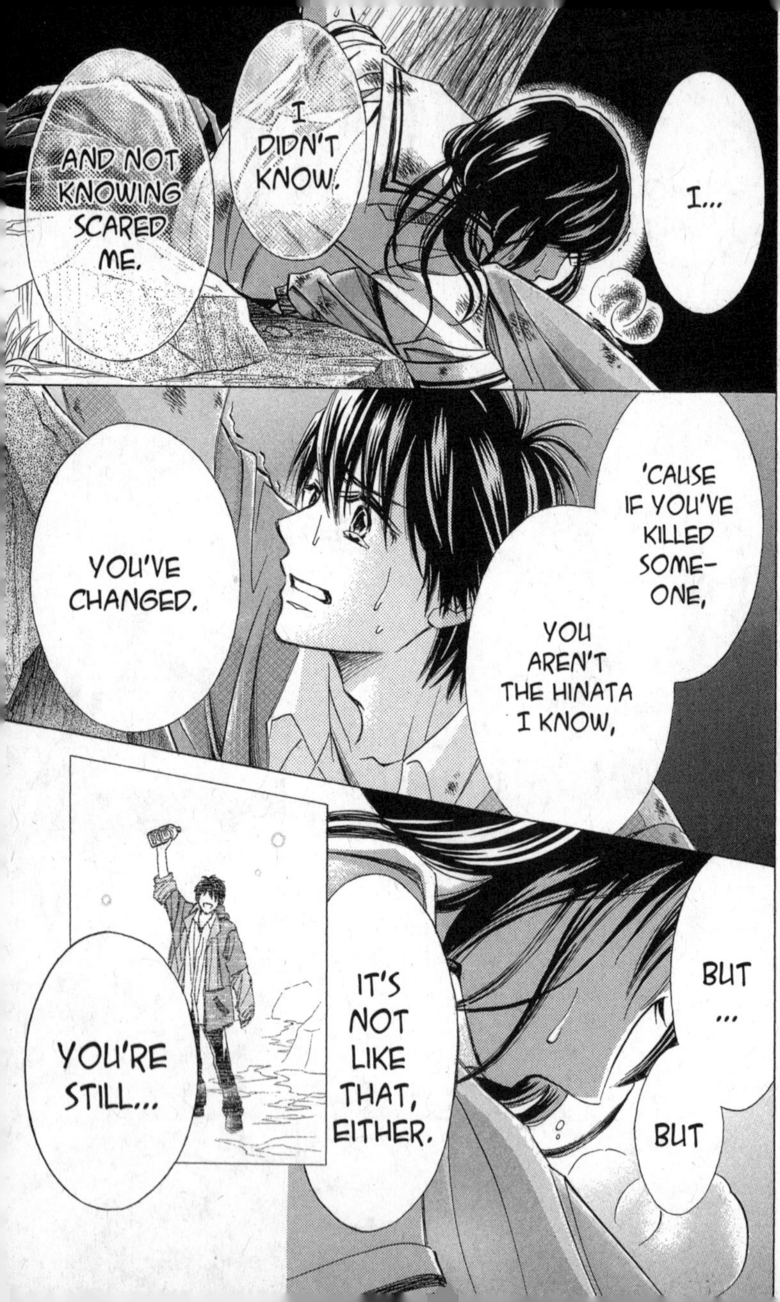
I...
I DIDN'T KNOW.
AND NOT KNOWING SCARED ME.
'CAUSE IF YOU'VE KILLED SOME-ONE,
YOU AREN'T THE HINATA I KNOW,
YOU'VE CHANGED.
BUT ...
BUT
IT'S NOT LIKE THAT, EITHER.
YOU'RE STILL...

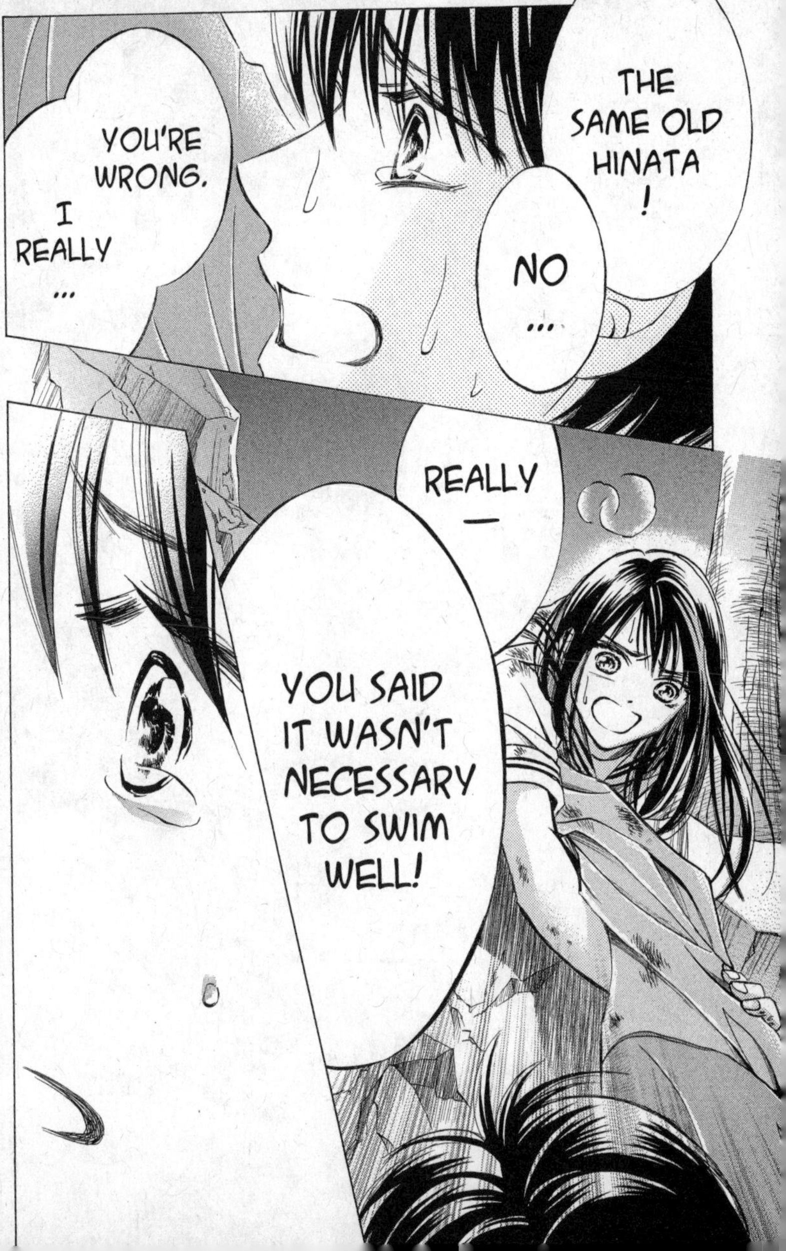
THE SAME OLD HINATA!
NO...
YOU'RE WRONG. I REALLY...
REALLY—
YOU SAID IT WASN'T NECESSARY TO SWIM WELL!

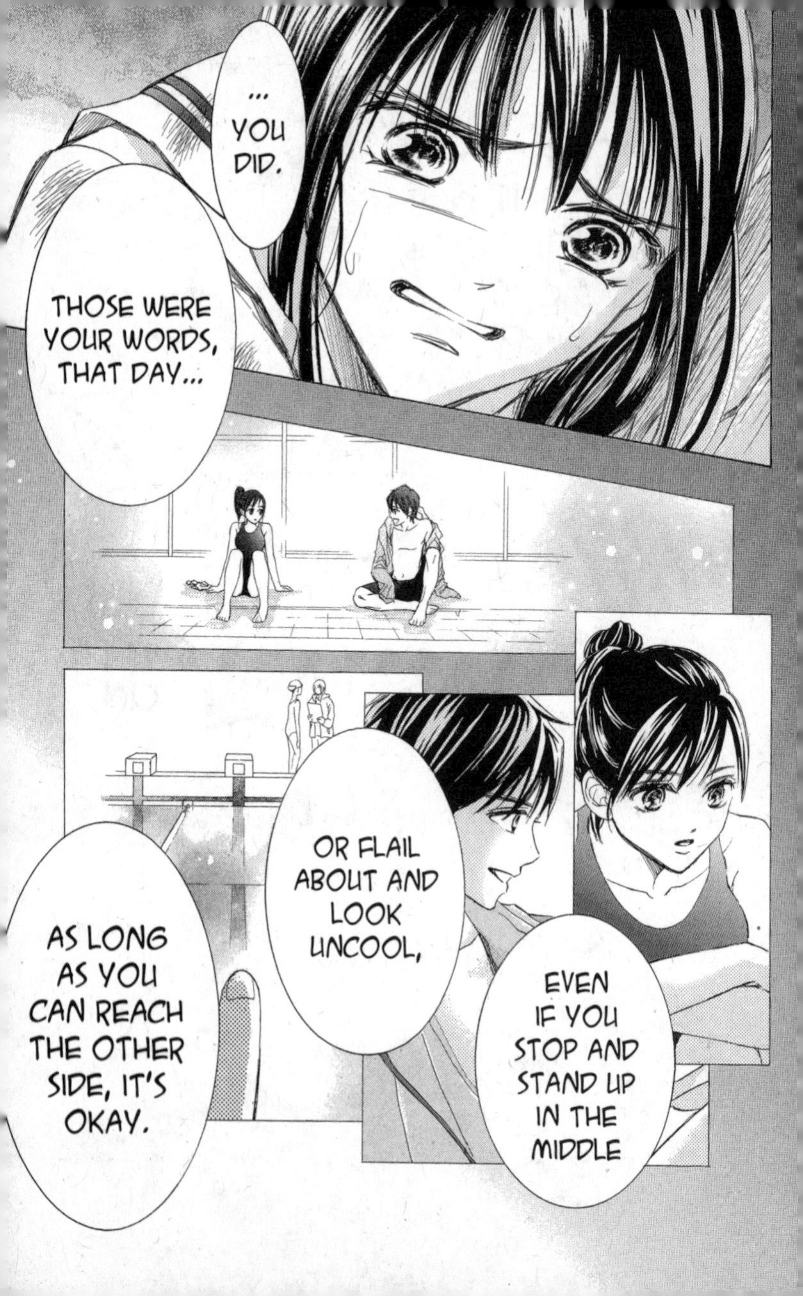
... YOU DID.
THOSE WERE YOUR WORDS, THAT DAY...
EVEN IF YOU STOP AND STAND UP IN THE MIDDLE
OR FLAIL ABOUT AND LOOK UNCOOL,
AS LONG AS YOU CAN REACH THE OTHER SIDE, IT'S OKAY.

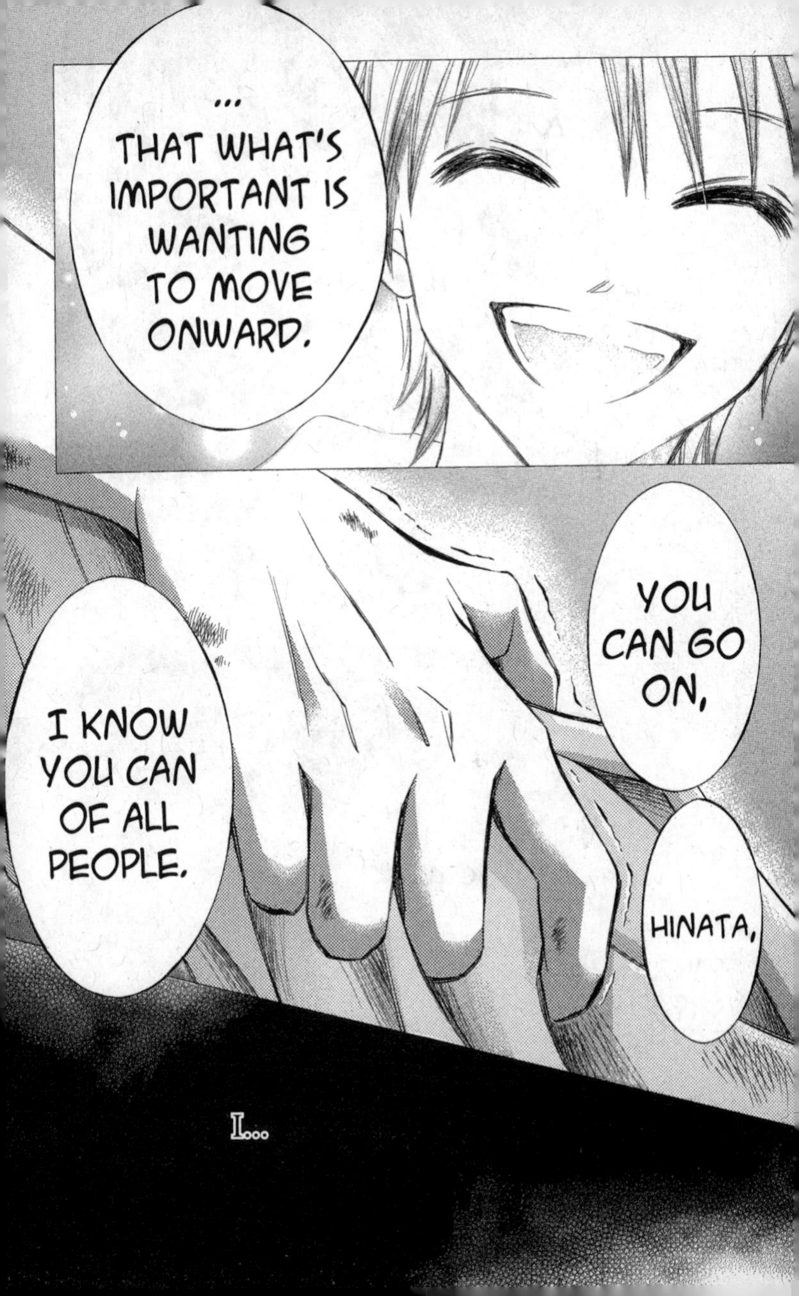
...THAT WHAT'S IMPORTANT IS WANTING TO MOVE ONWARD.
YOU CAN GO ON,
HINATA,
I KNOW YOU CAN OF ALL PEOPLE.
I...

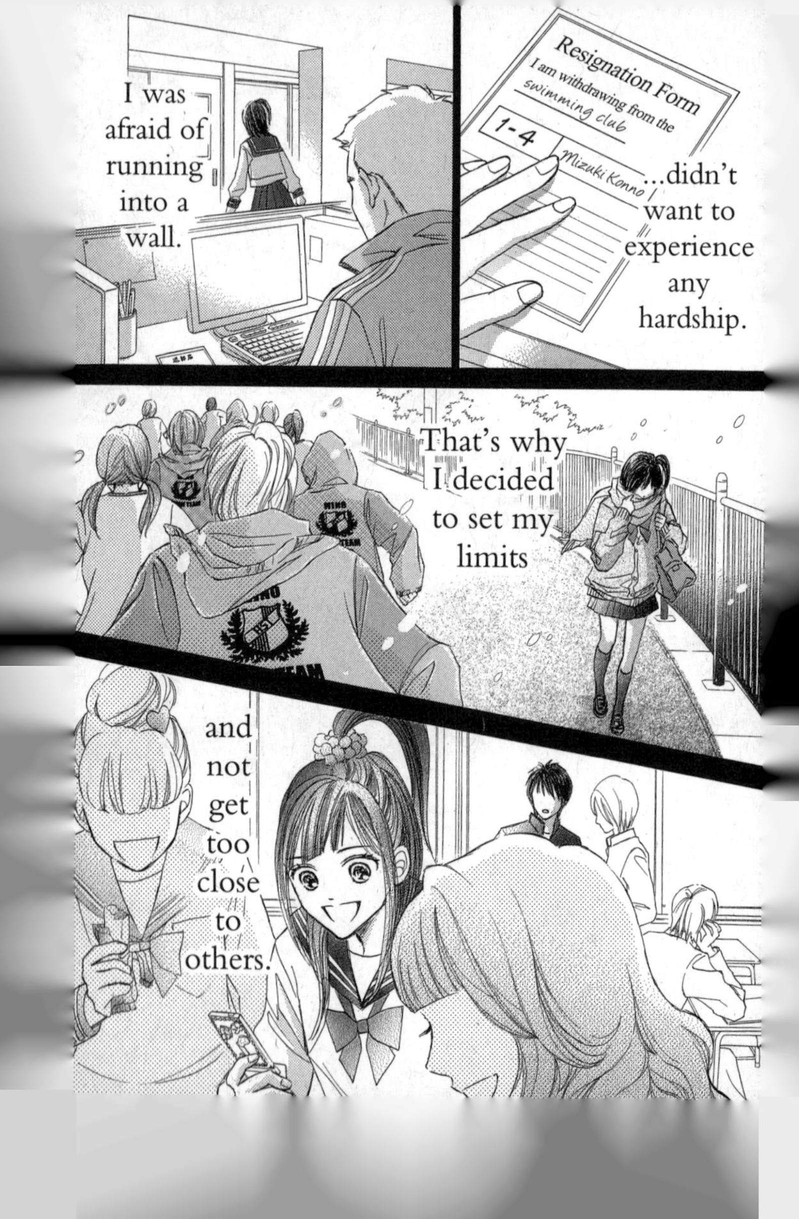
Resignation Form
I am withdrawing from the swimming club
1-4
Mizuki Konno
...didn't want to experience any hardship.
I was afraid of running into a wall.
That's why I decided to set my limits
and not get too close to others.

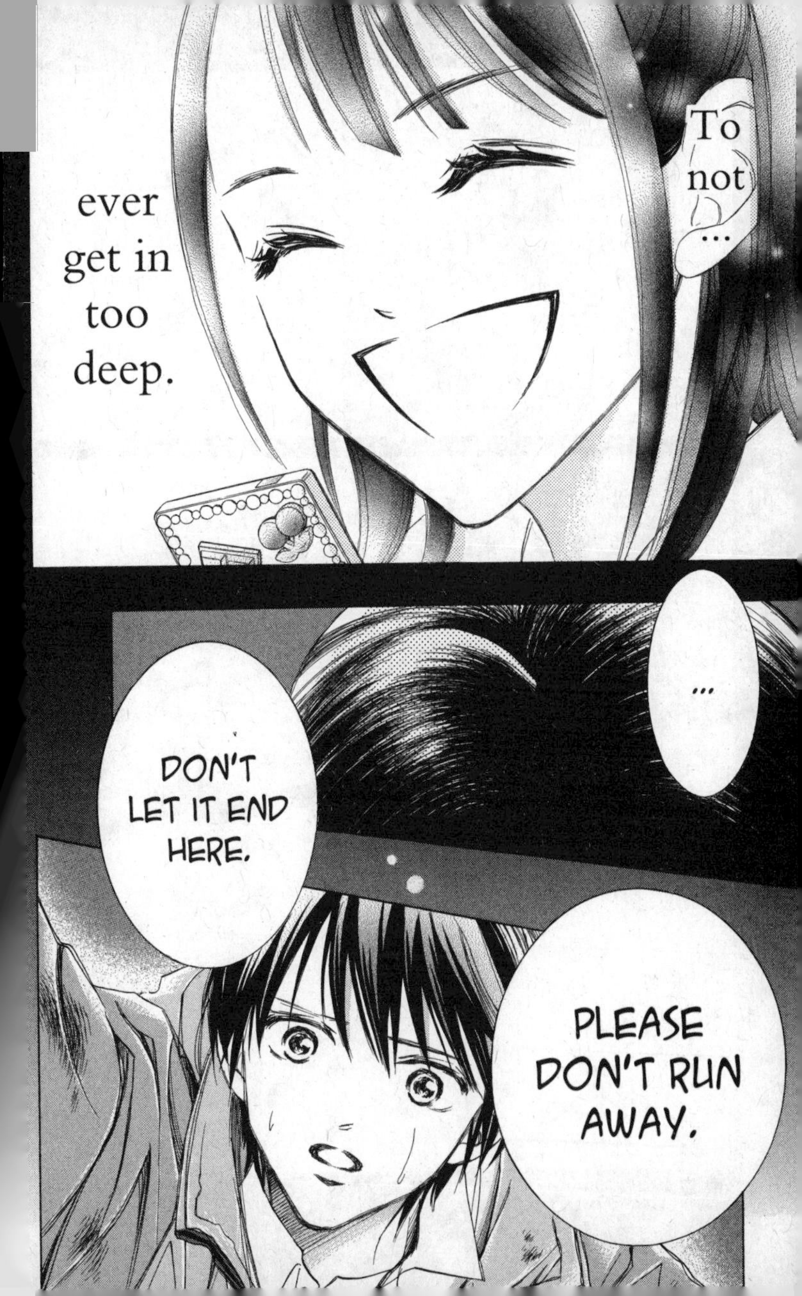
To not ...
ever get in too deep.
...
DON'T LET IT END HERE.
PLEASE DON'T RUN AWAY.

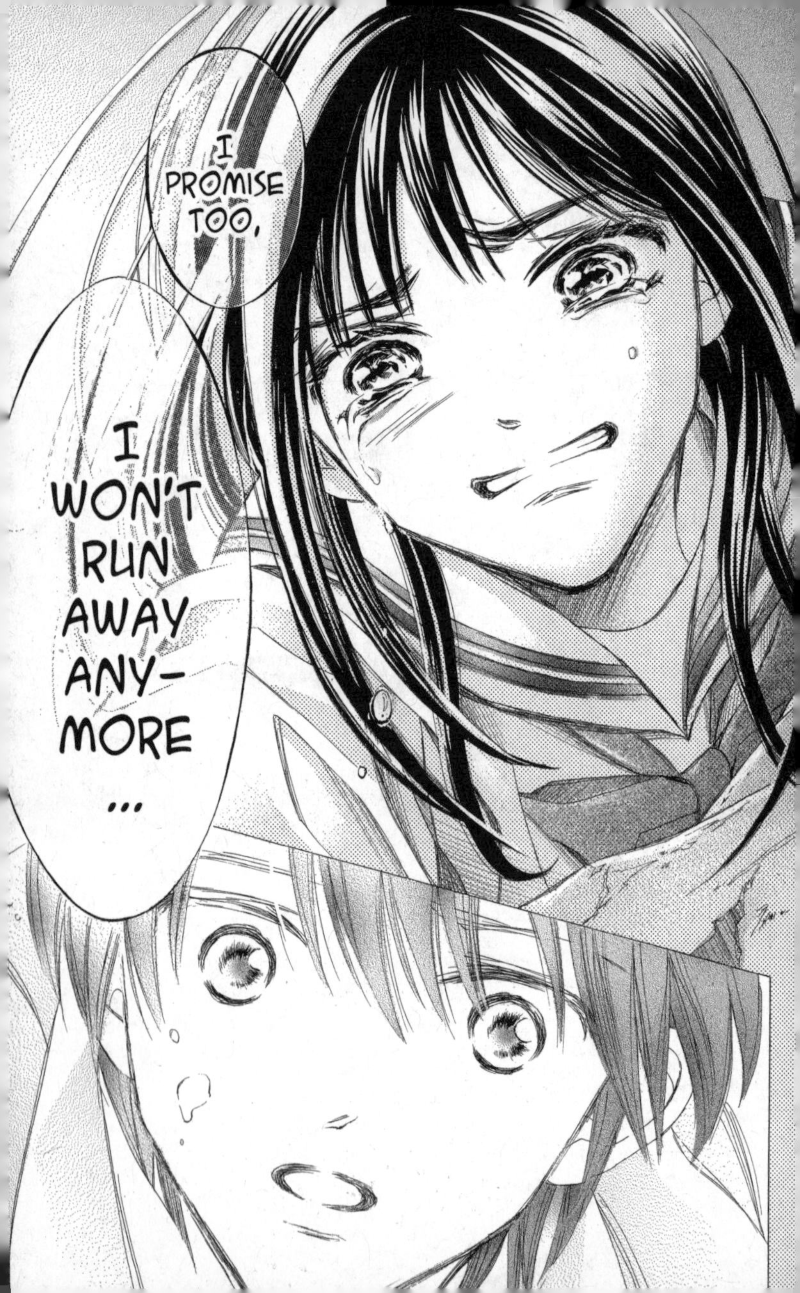
I PROMISE TOO,
I WON'T RUN AWAY ANY-MORE ...

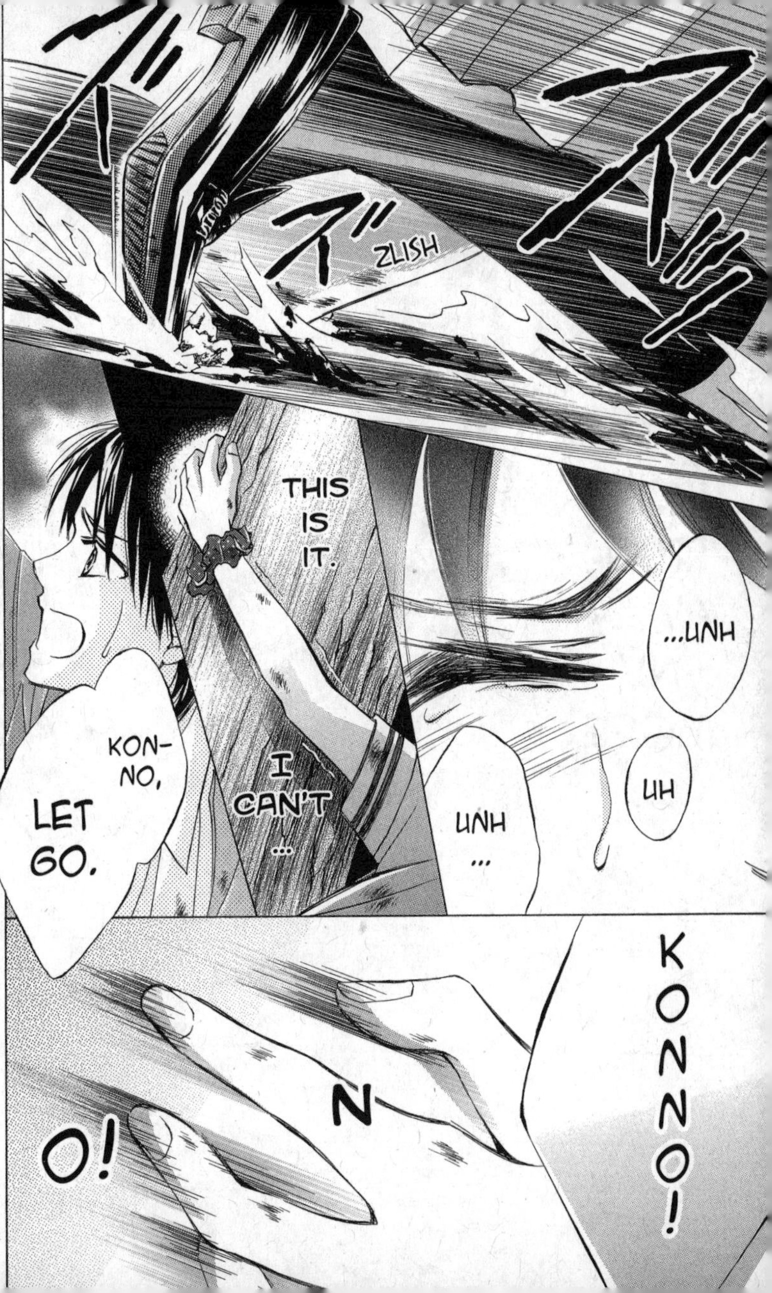
ZLISH
...UNH
UH
UNH ...
THIS IS IT.
I CAN'T ...
KON-NO, LET GO.
KONNO!
N
O!

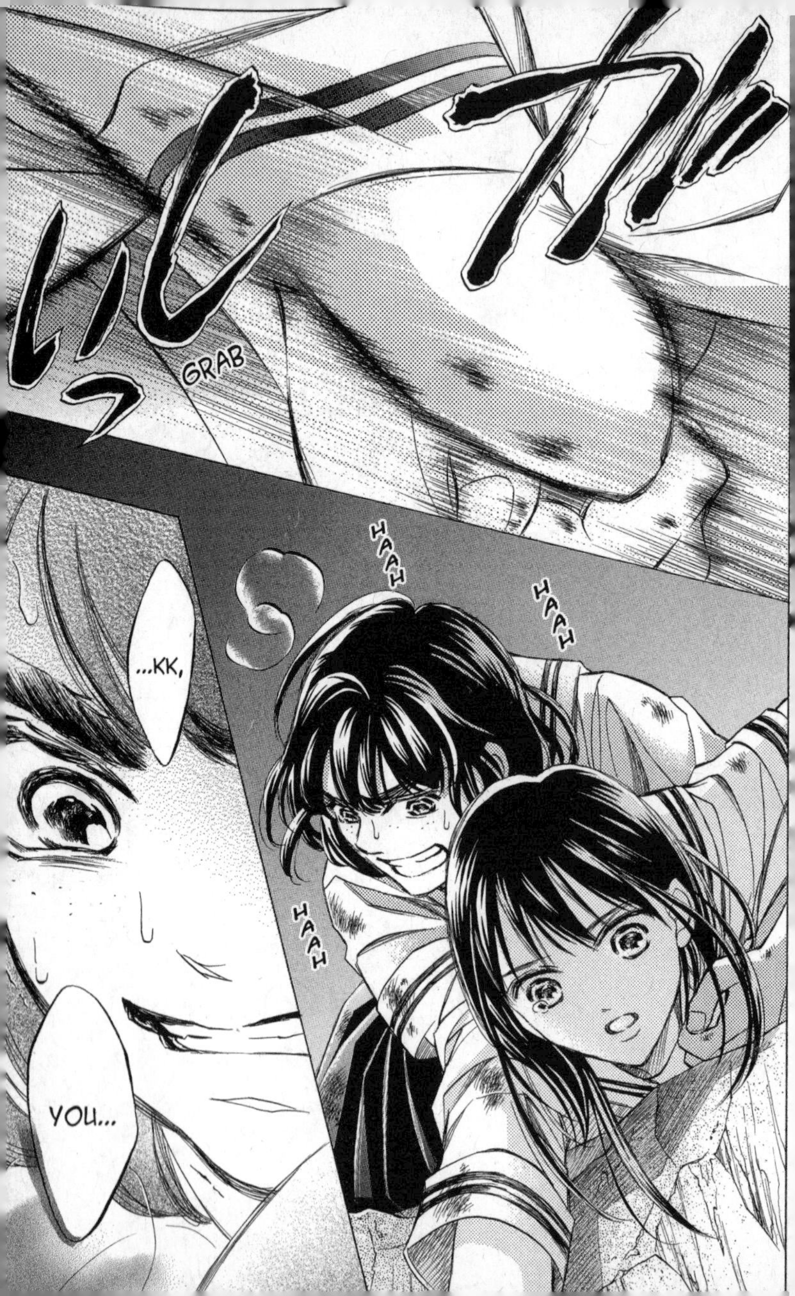
GRAB
HAAAH
HAAAH
HAAAH
...KK,
YOU...

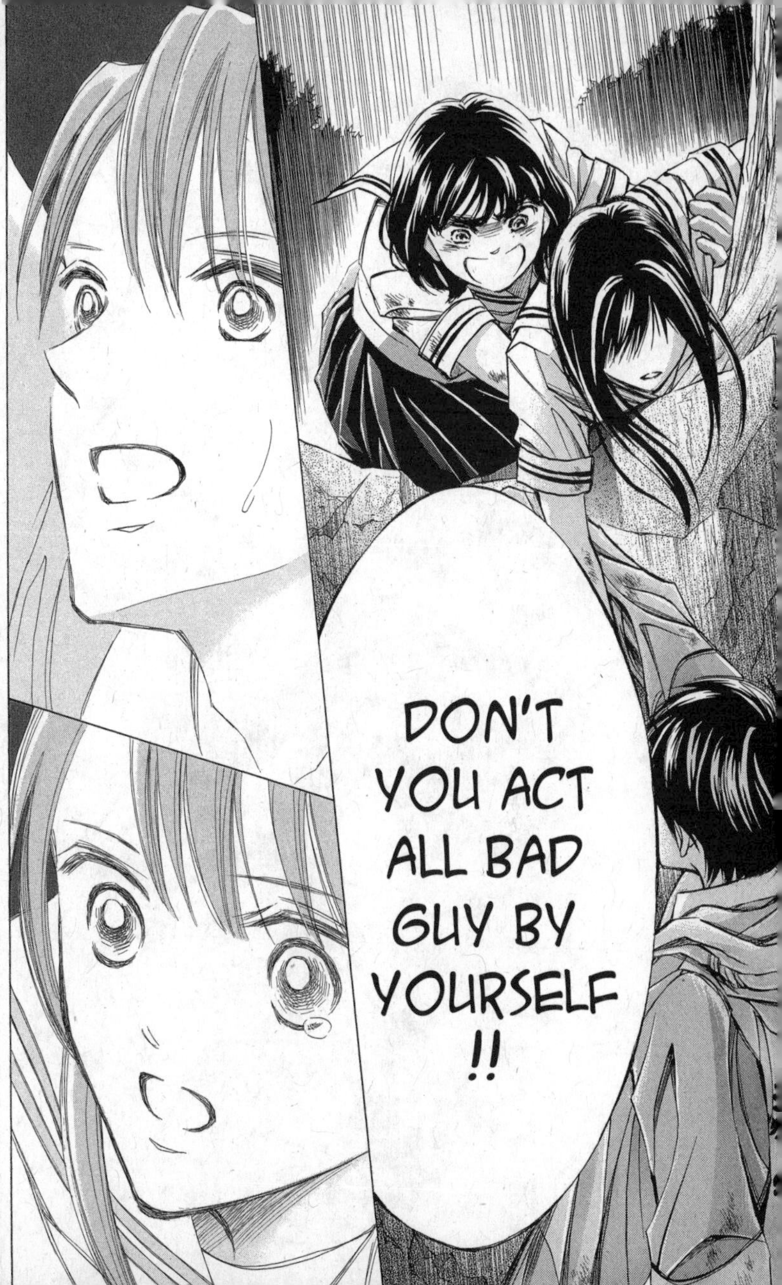
DON'T YOU ACT ALL BAD GUY BY YOURSELF !!

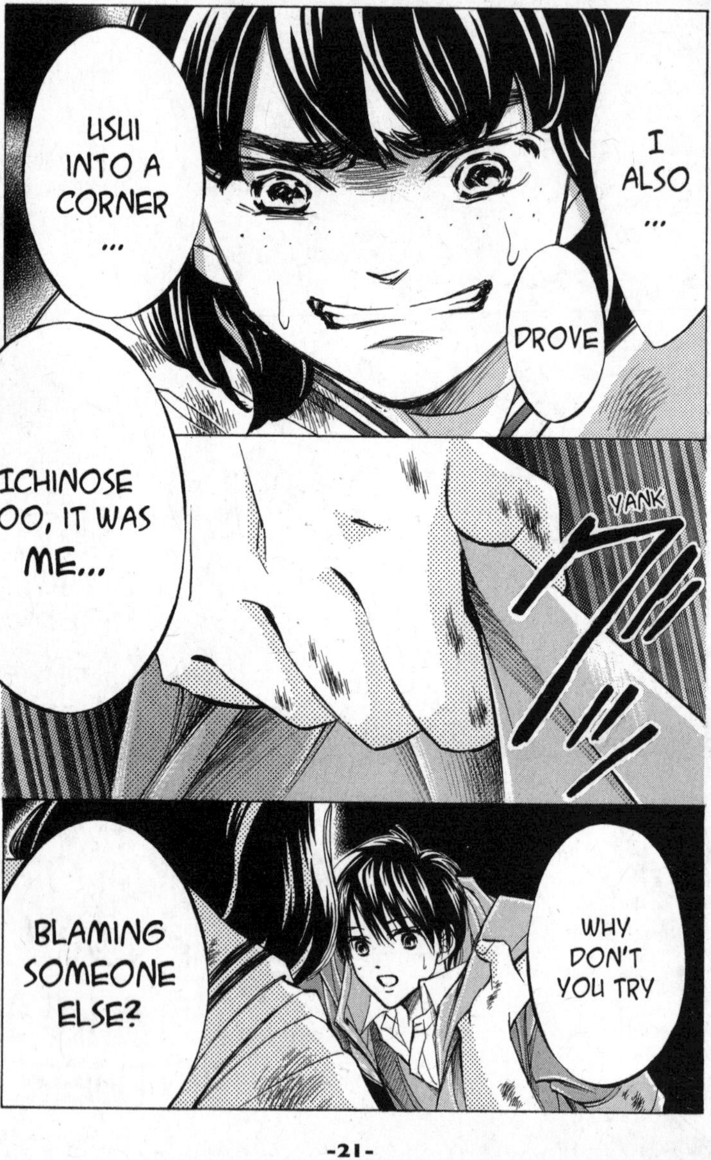
I ALSO ...
DROVE
USUI INTO A CORNER ...
ICHINOSE TOO, IT WAS ME...
YANK
WHY DON'T YOU TRY
BLAMING SOMEONE ELSE?

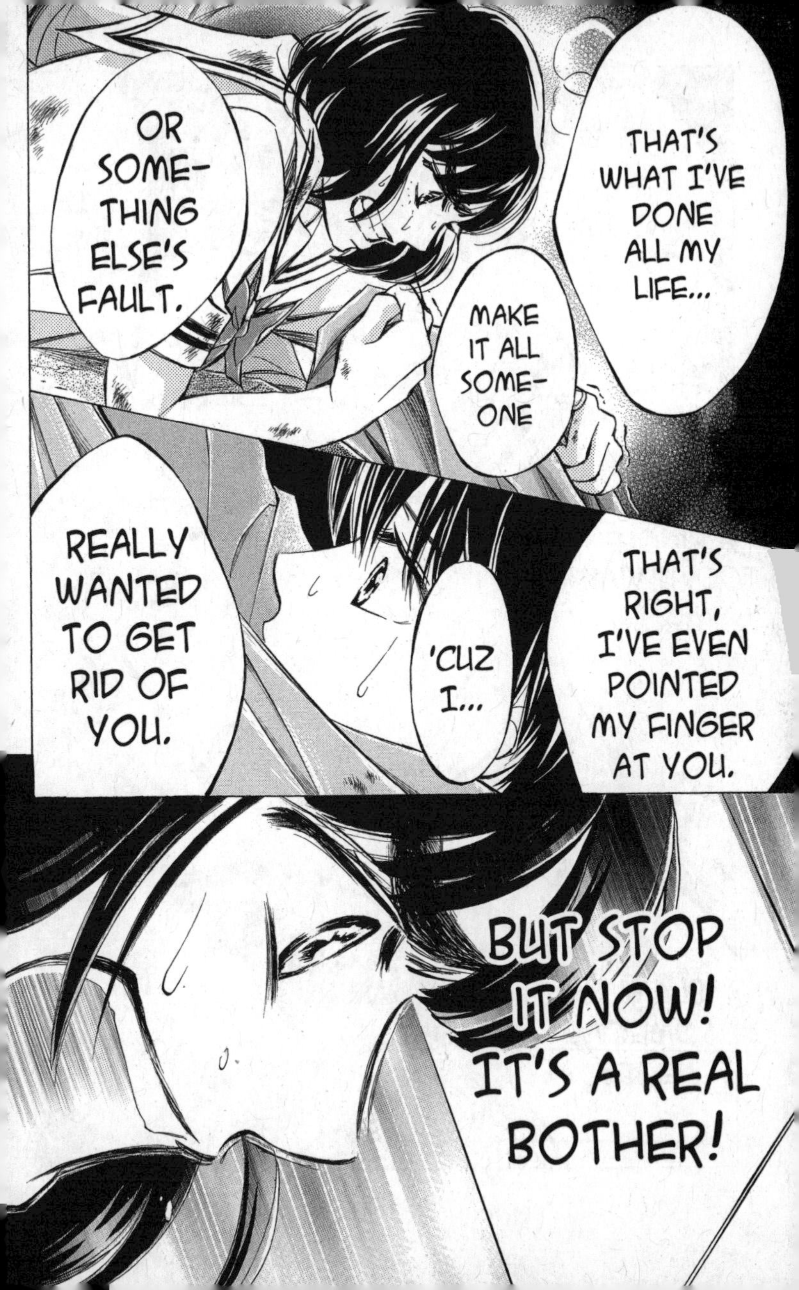
THAT'S WHAT I'VE DONE ALL MY LIFE...
MAKE IT ALL SOMEONE
OR SOMETHING ELSE'S FAULT.
THAT'S RIGHT, I'VE EVEN POINTED MY FINGER AT YOU.
'CUZ I...
REALLY WANTED TO GET RID OF YOU.
BUT STOP IT NOW! IT'S A REAL BOTHER!

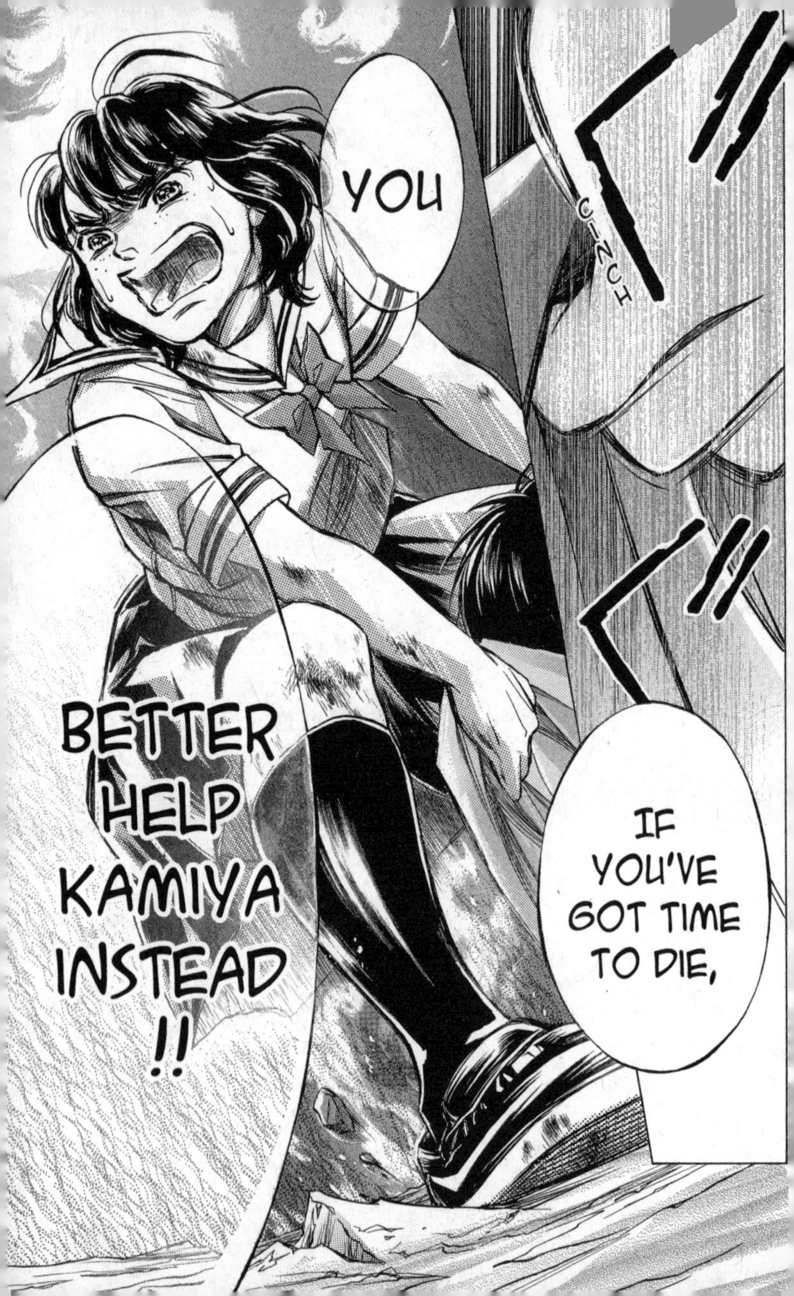
CINCH
YOU
IF YOU'VE GOT TIME TO DIE,
BETTER HELP KAMIYA INSTEAD!!

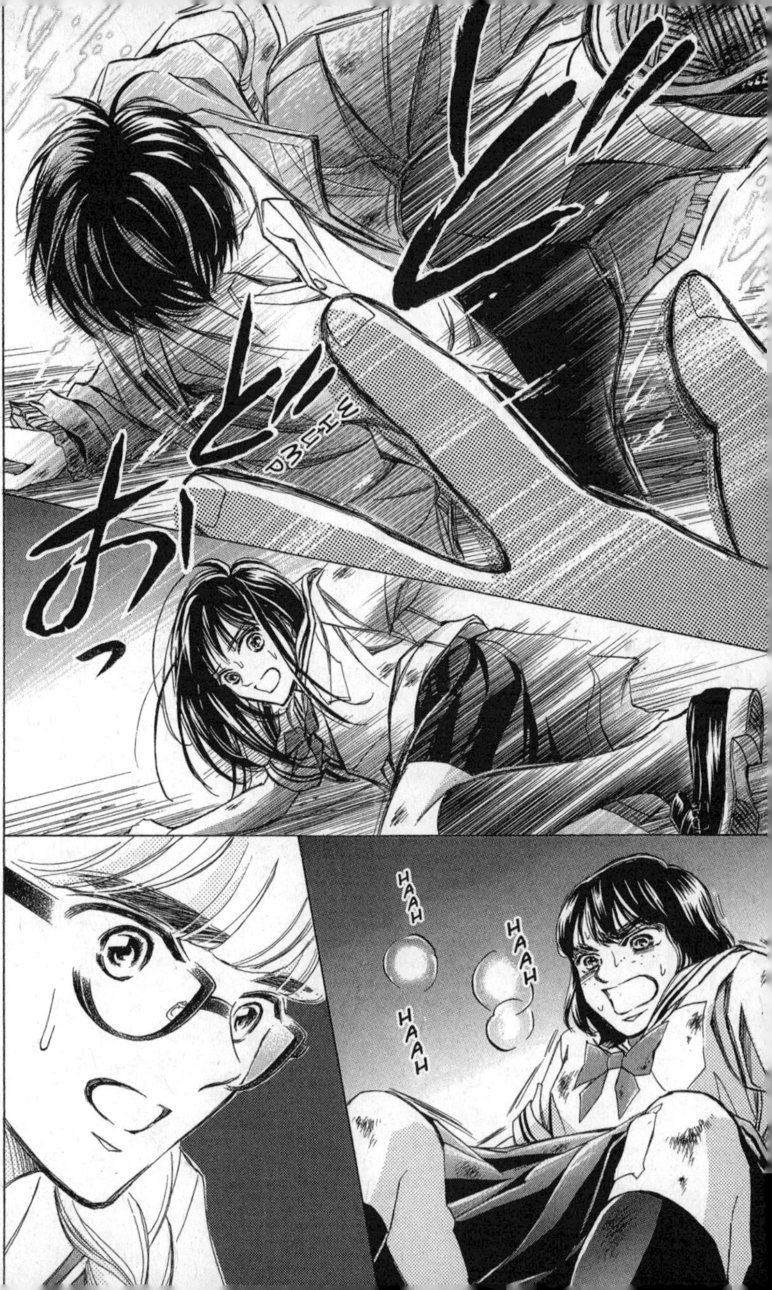
WHIP
あっ
HAAH
HAAH
HAAH

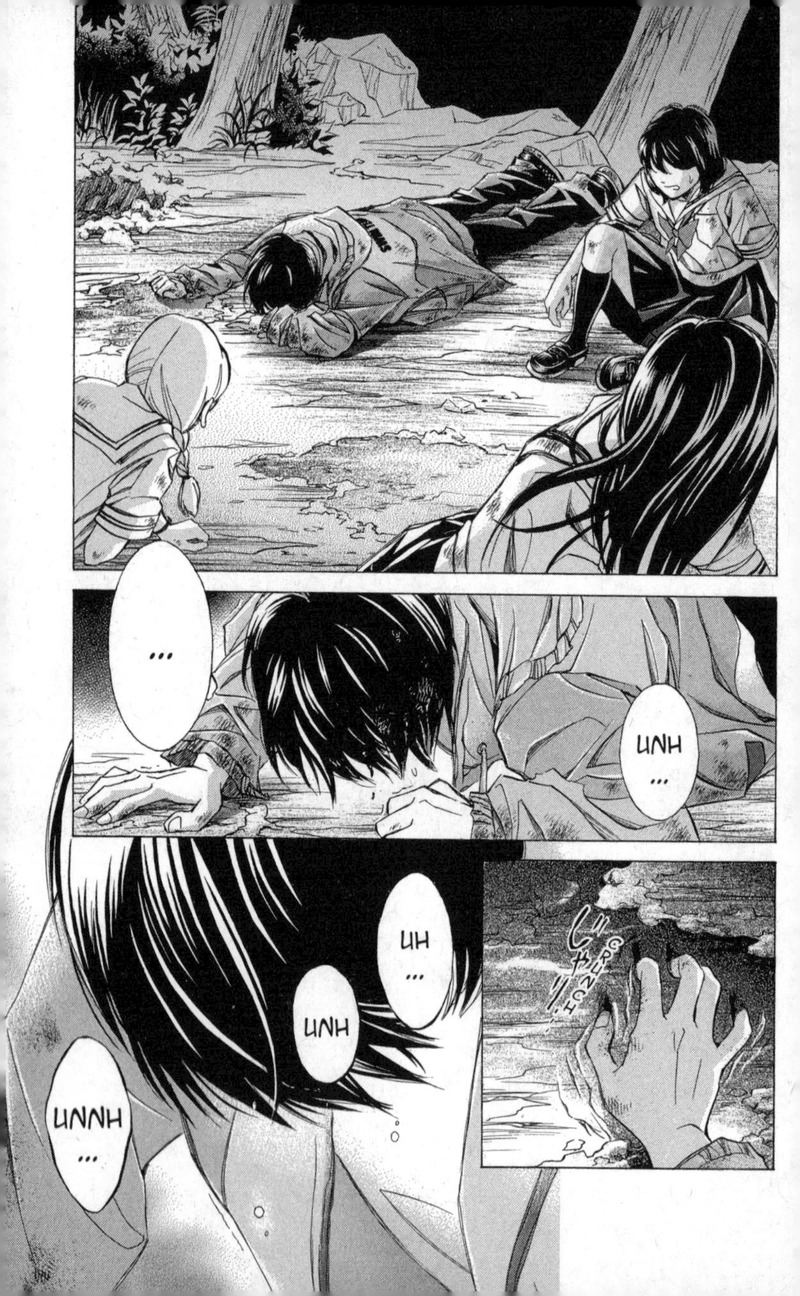
UNH ...
...
CRUNCH
UH ...
UNH
UNNH ...

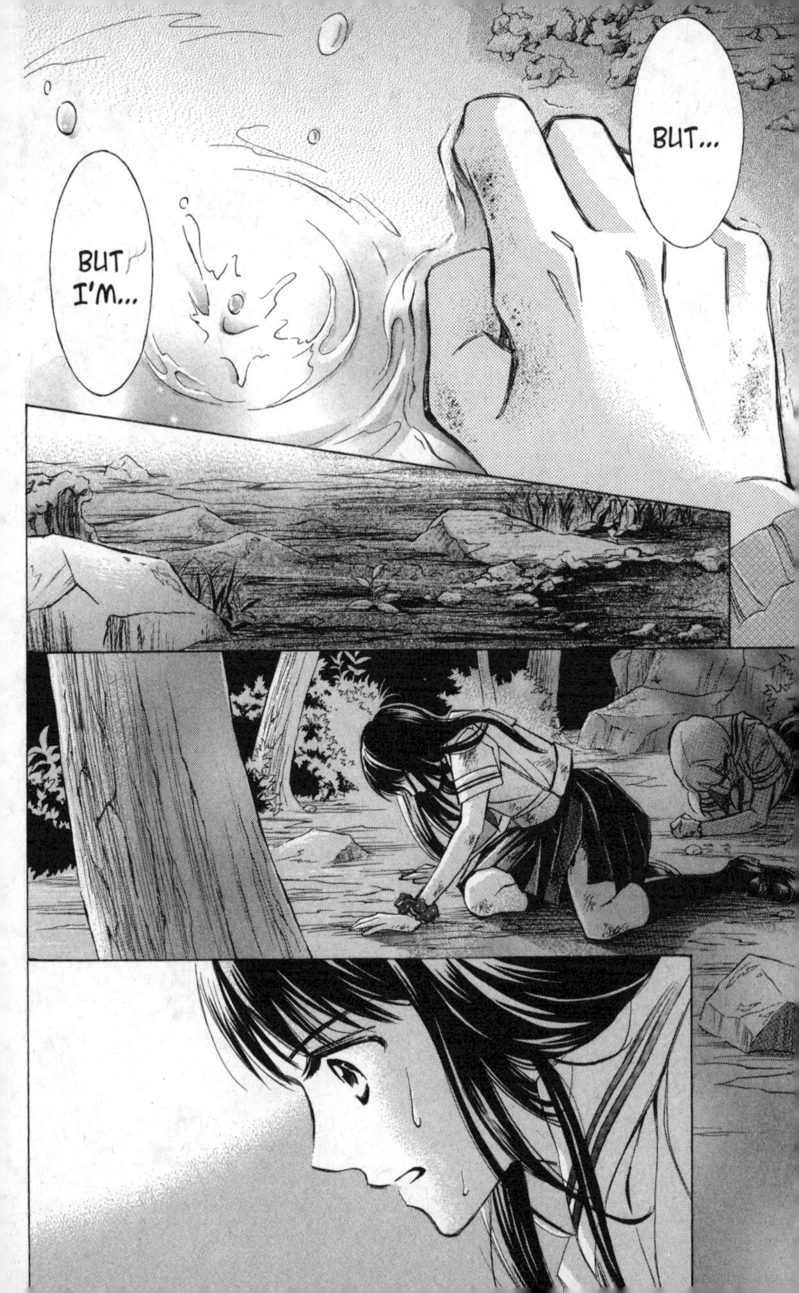
BUT...
BUT I'M...

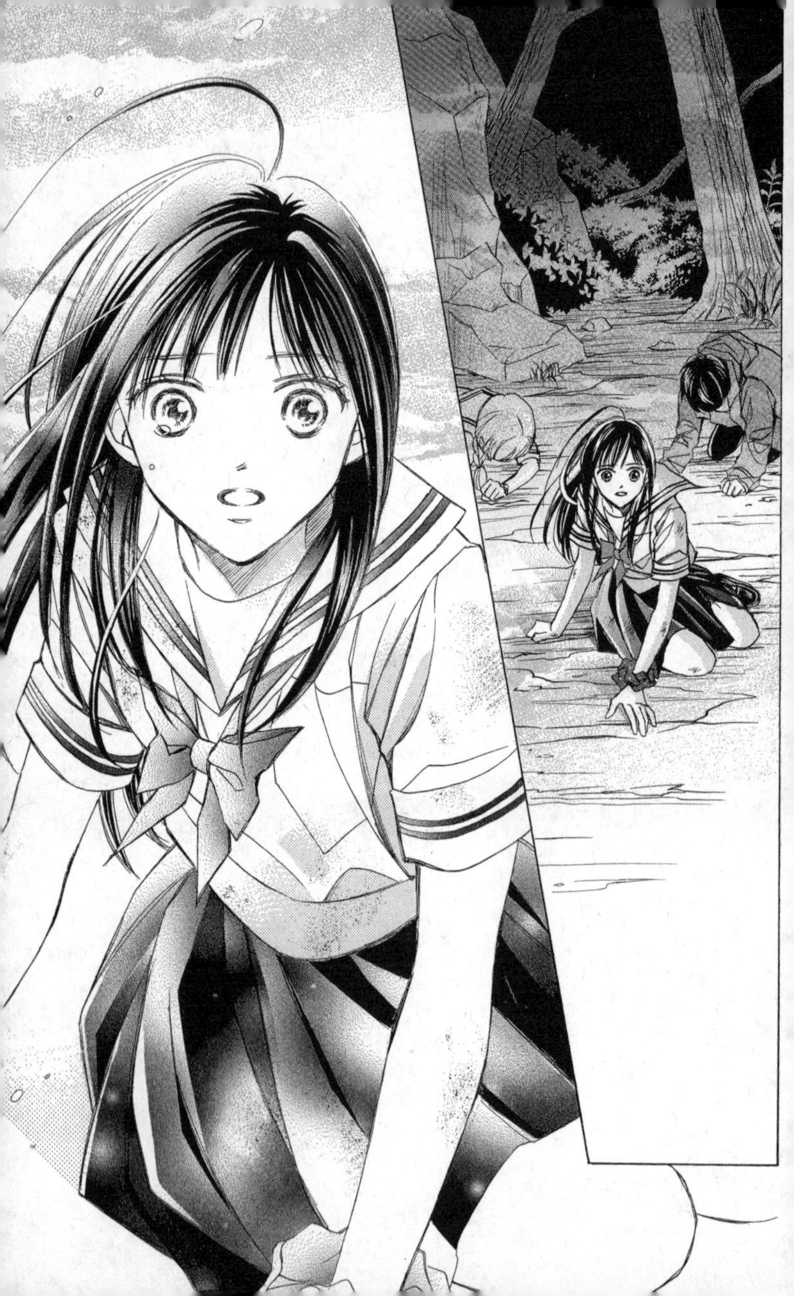

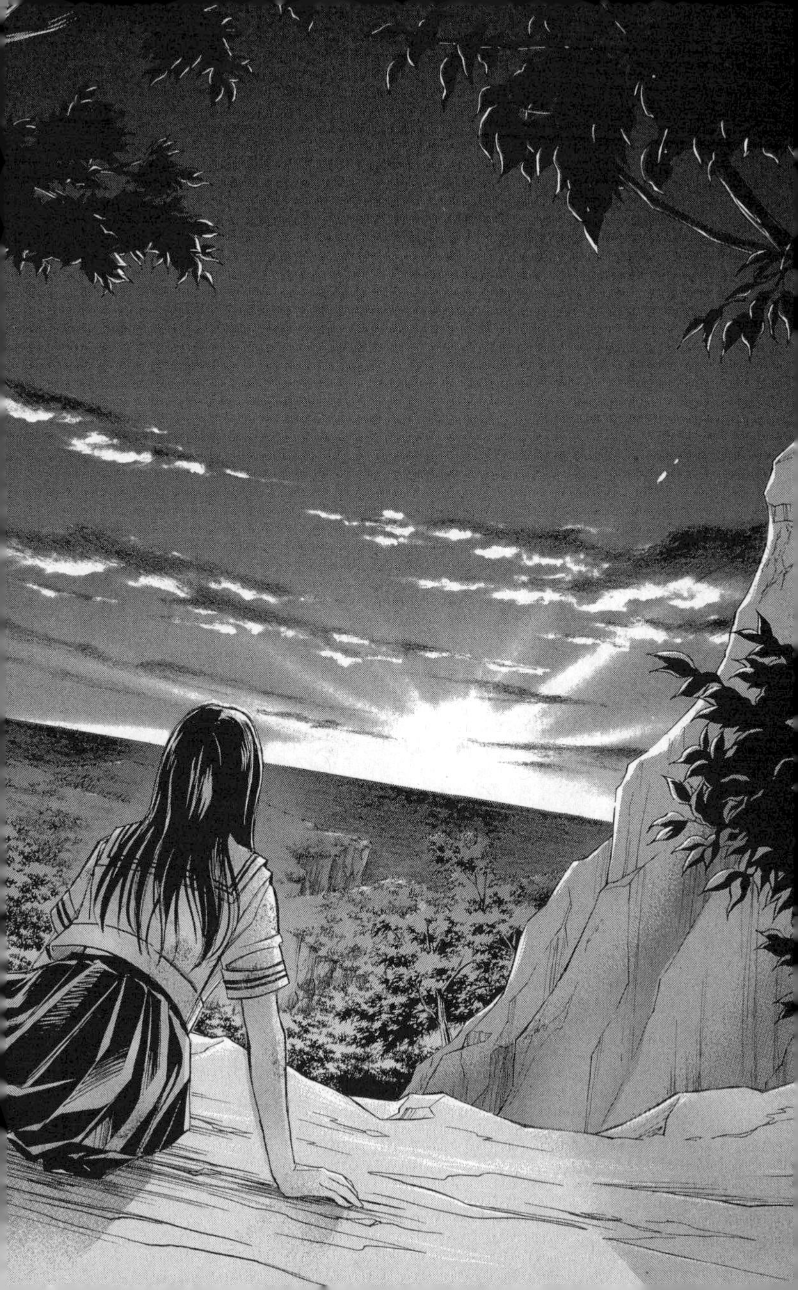

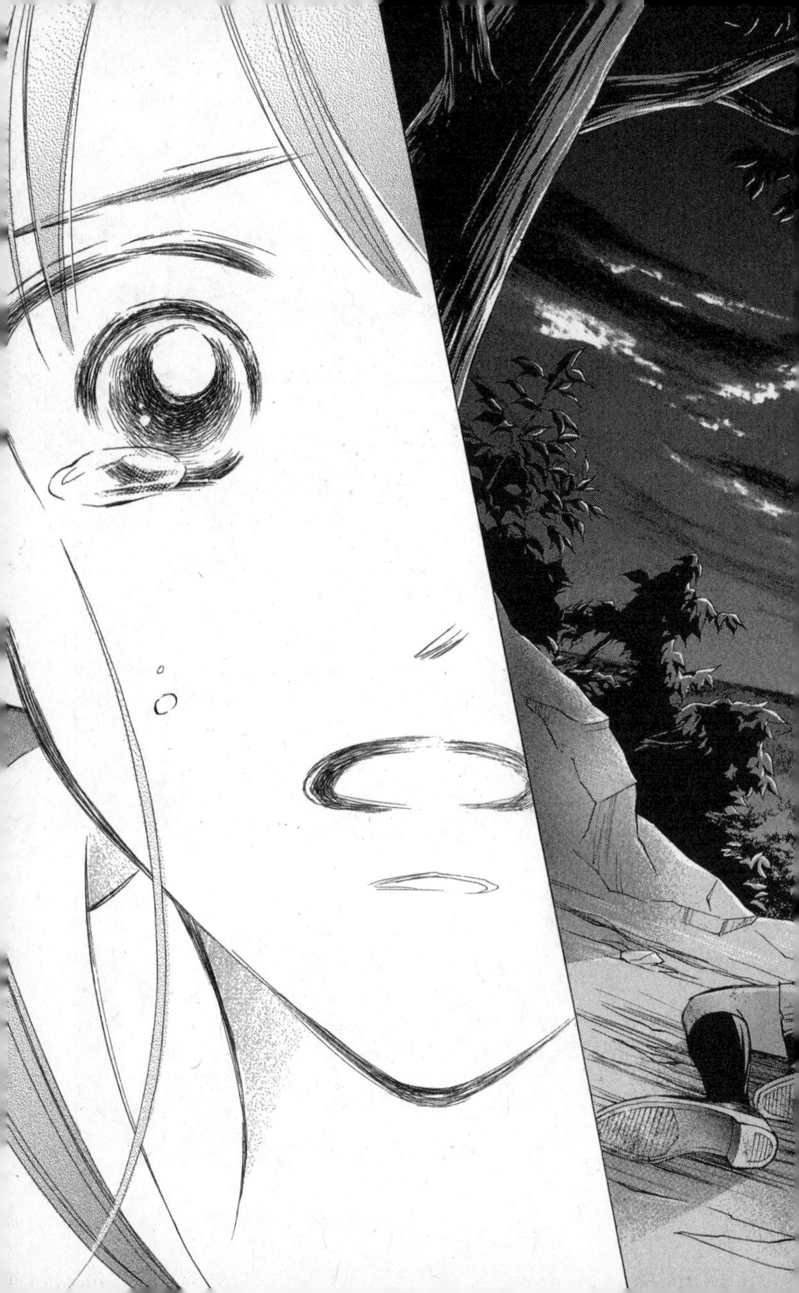

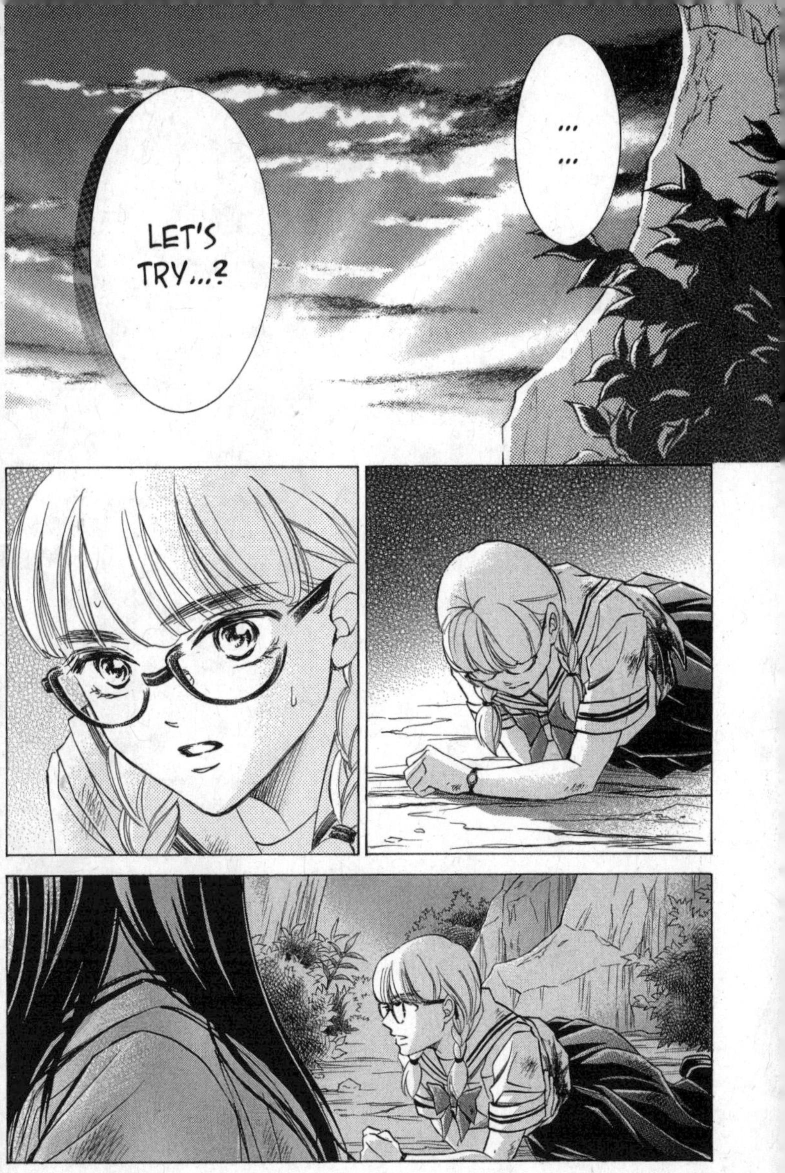
……
LET'S TRY...?

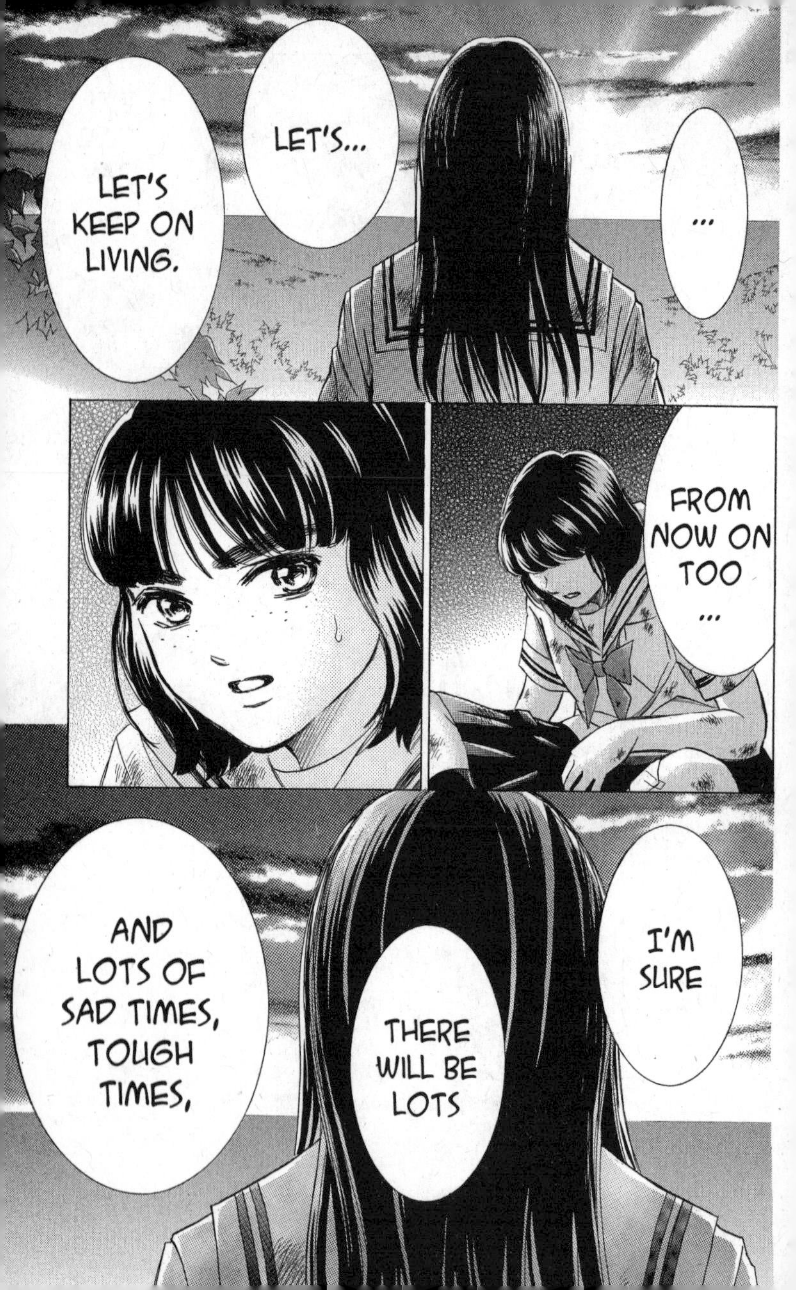
...
LET'S...
LET'S KEEP ON LIVING.
FROM NOW ON TOO ...
I'M SURE
THERE WILL BE LOTS
AND LOTS OF SAD TIMES, TOUGH TIMES,

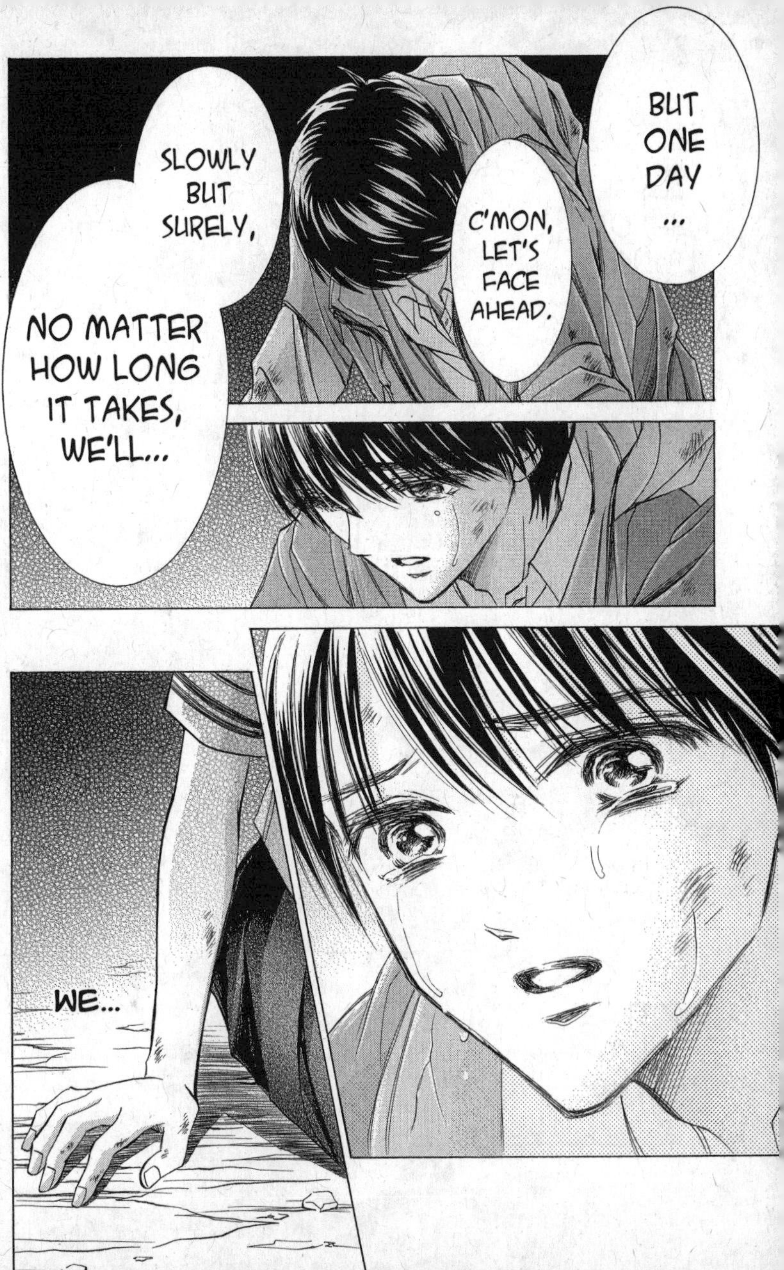
BUT ONE DAY ...
C'MON, LET'S FACE AHEAD.
SLOWLY BUT SURELY,
NO MATTER HOW LONG IT TAKES, WE'LL...
WE...

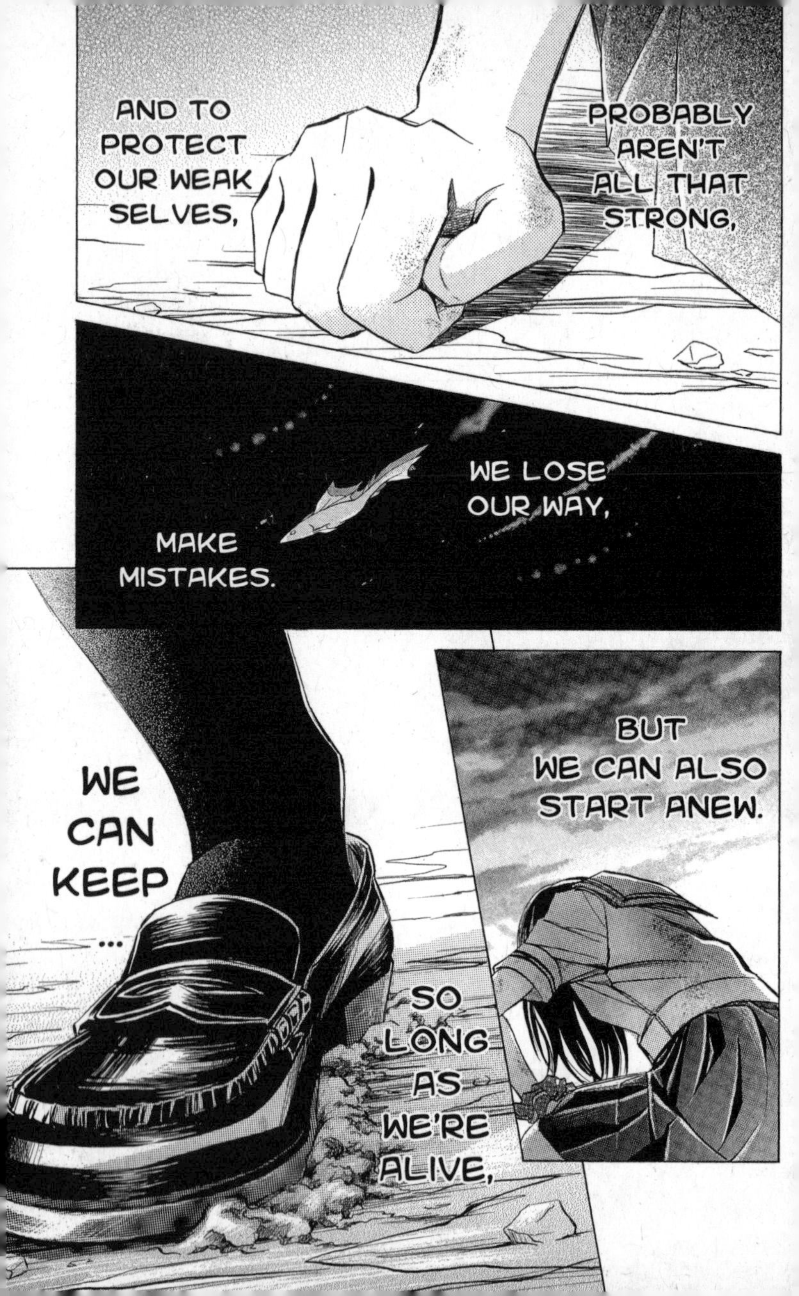
PROBABLY AREN'T ALL THAT STRONG,
AND TO PROTECT OUR WEAK SELVES,
WE LOSE OUR WAY,
MAKE MISTAKES.
BUT WE CAN ALSO START ANEW.
SO LONG AS WE'RE ALIVE,
WE CAN KEEP ...

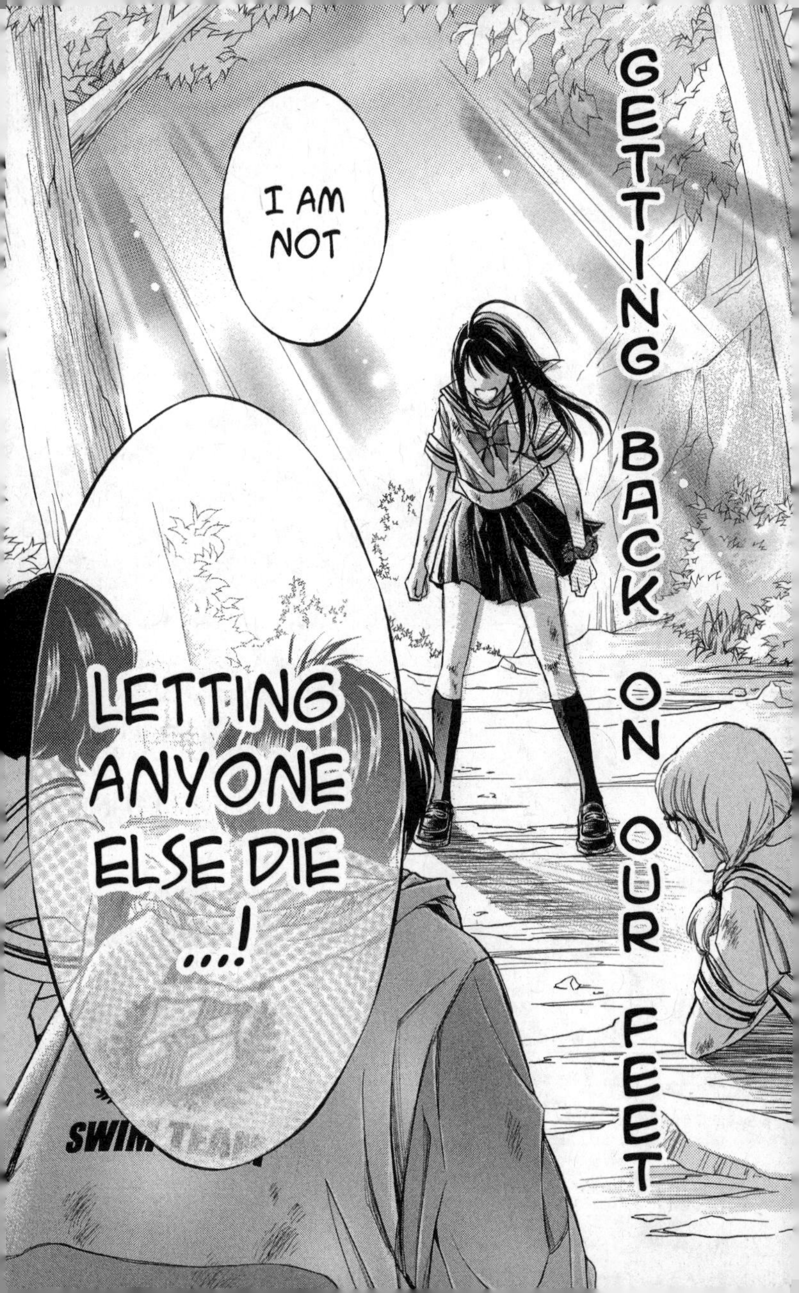
GETTING BACK ON OUR FEET
I AM NOT
LETTING ANYONE ELSE DIE ...!

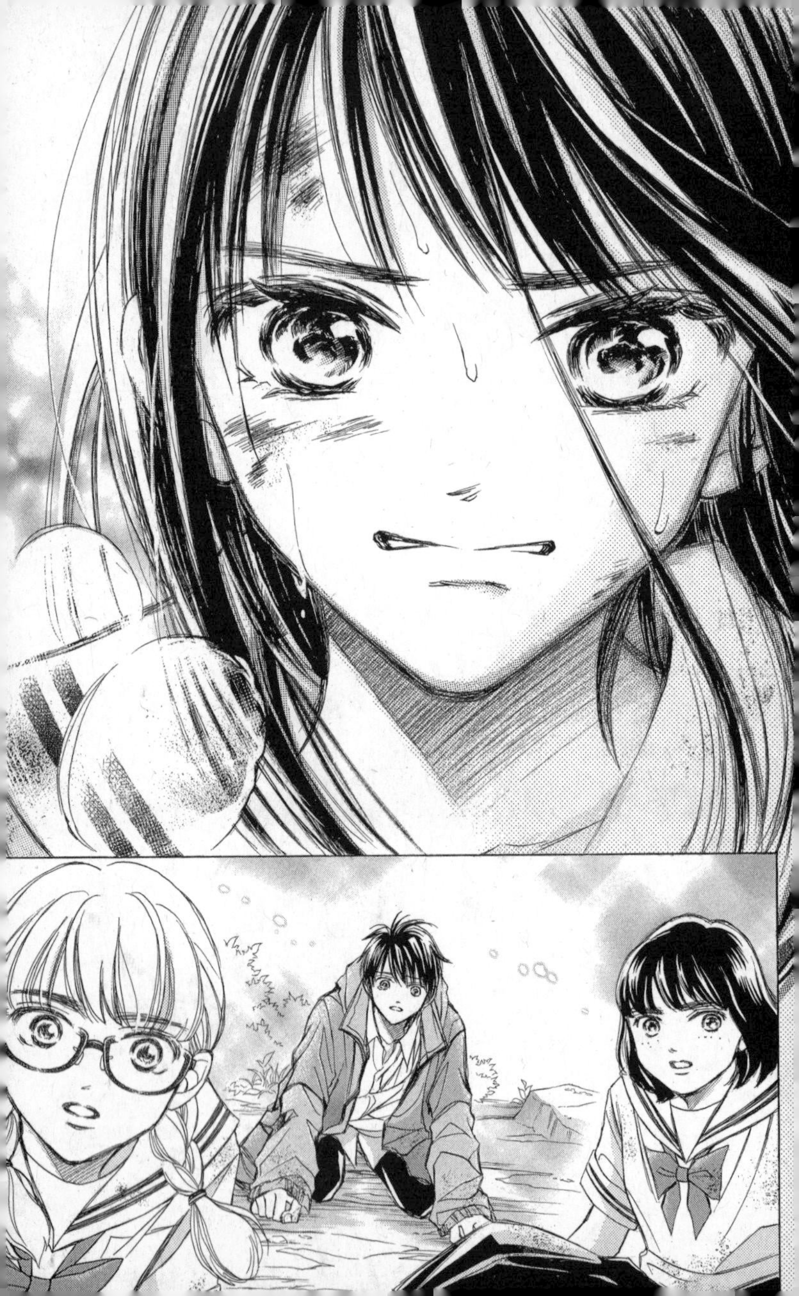

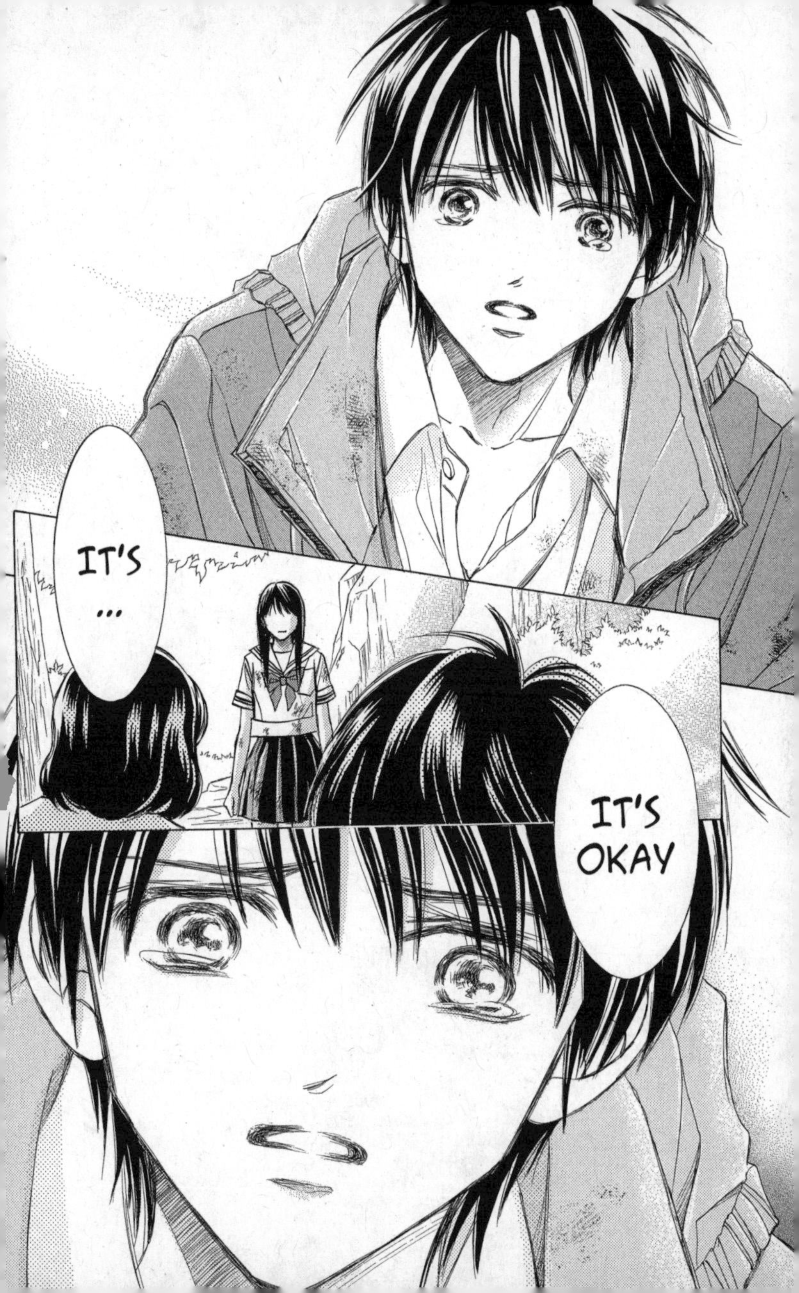
IT'S OKAY
IT'S ...

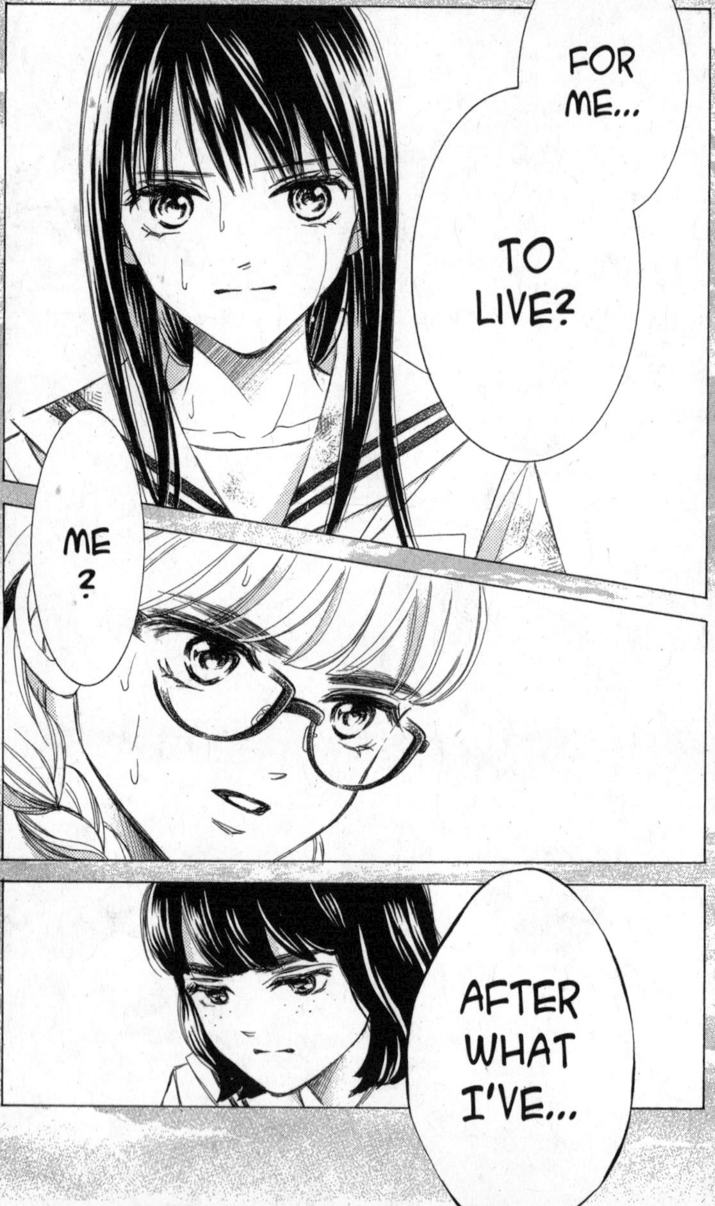
FOR ME...
TO LIVE?
ME ?
AFTER WHAT I'VE...

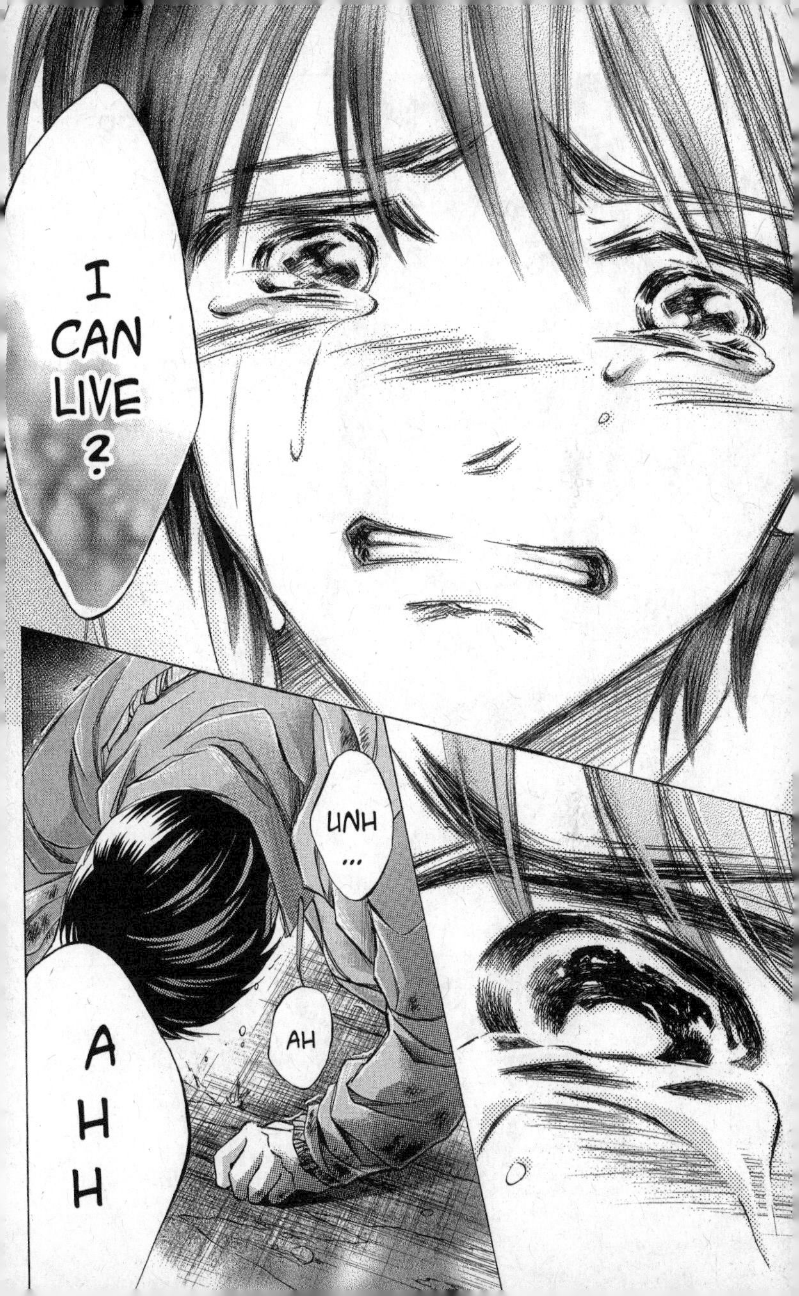
I CAN LIVE?
UNH ...
AH
AHH

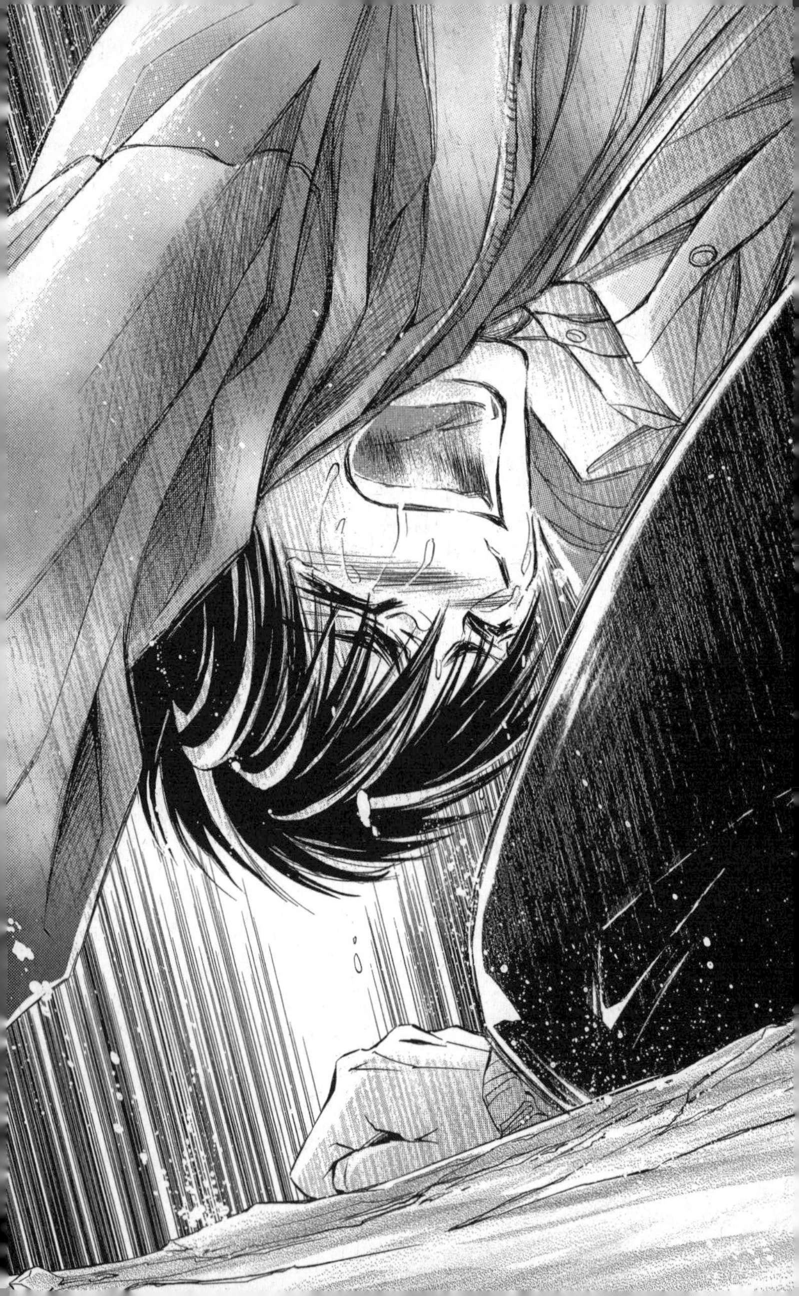

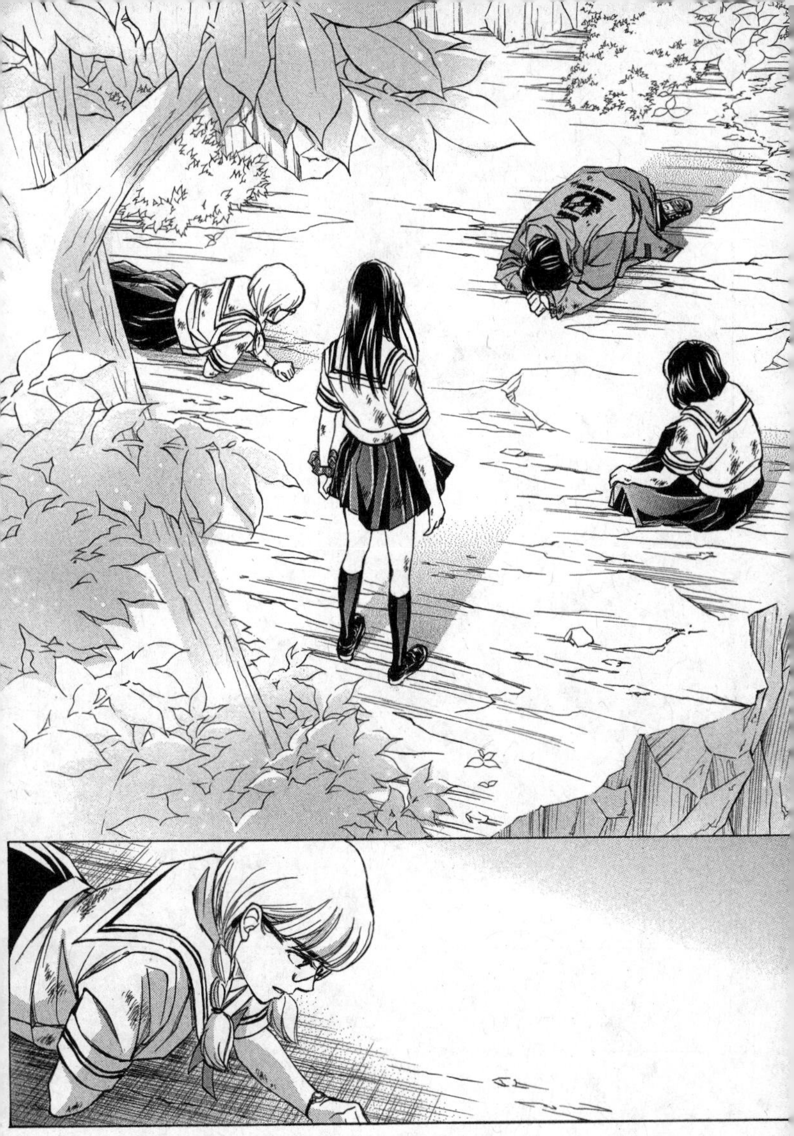

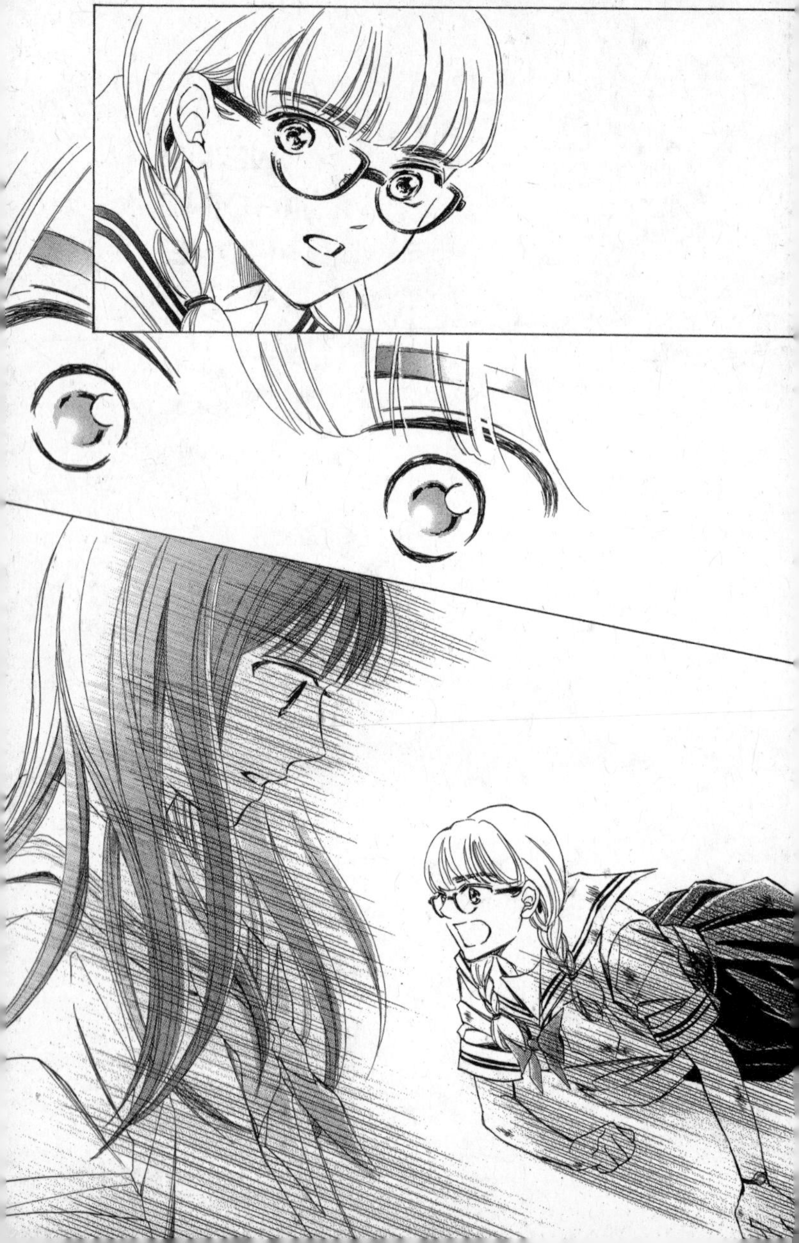

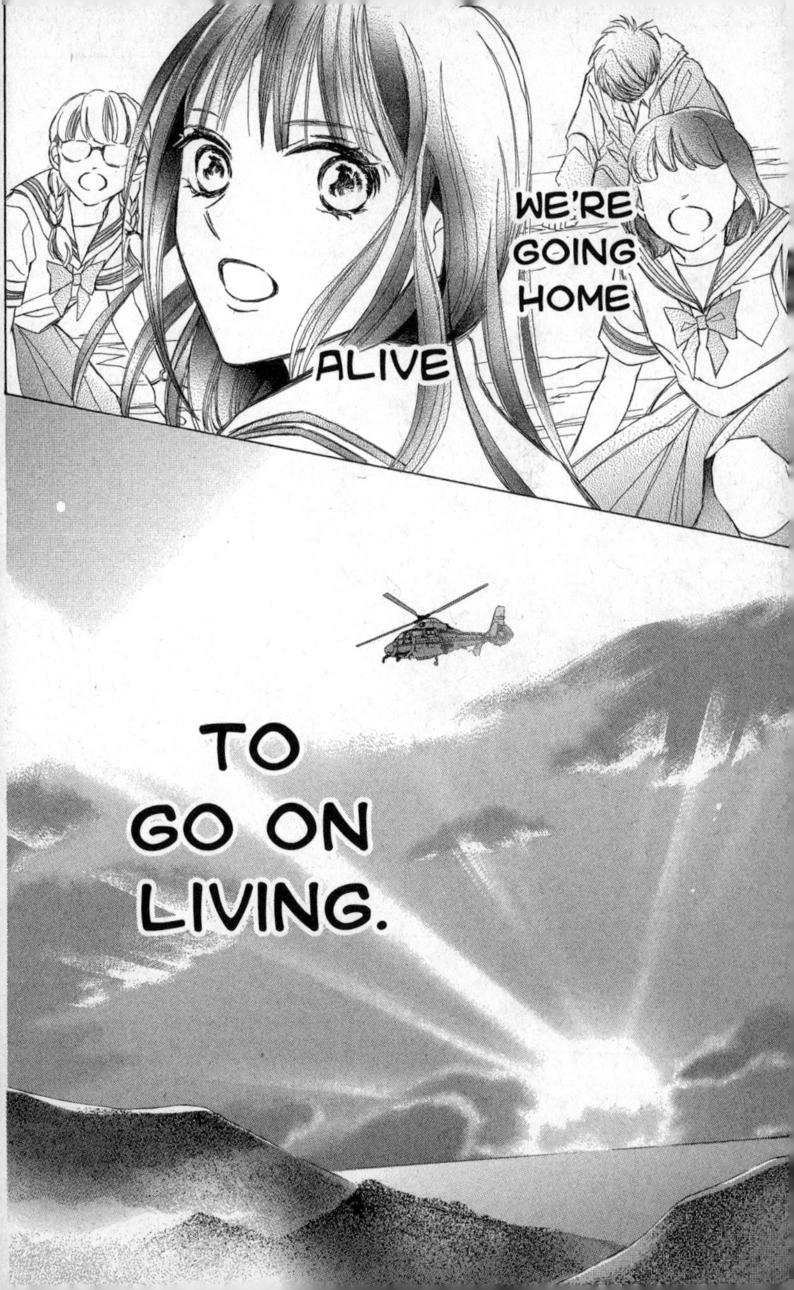
WE'RE GOING HOME
ALIVE
TO GO ON LIVING.

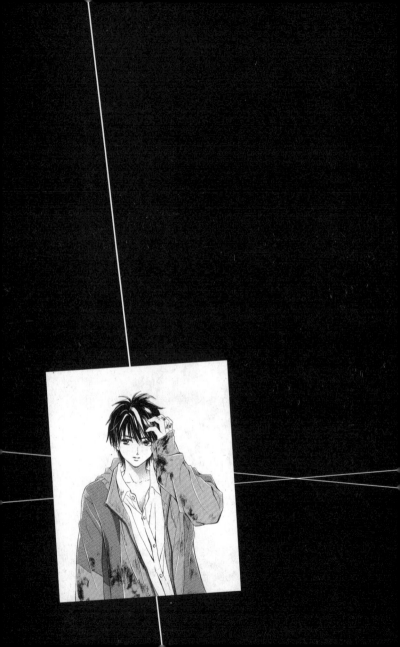

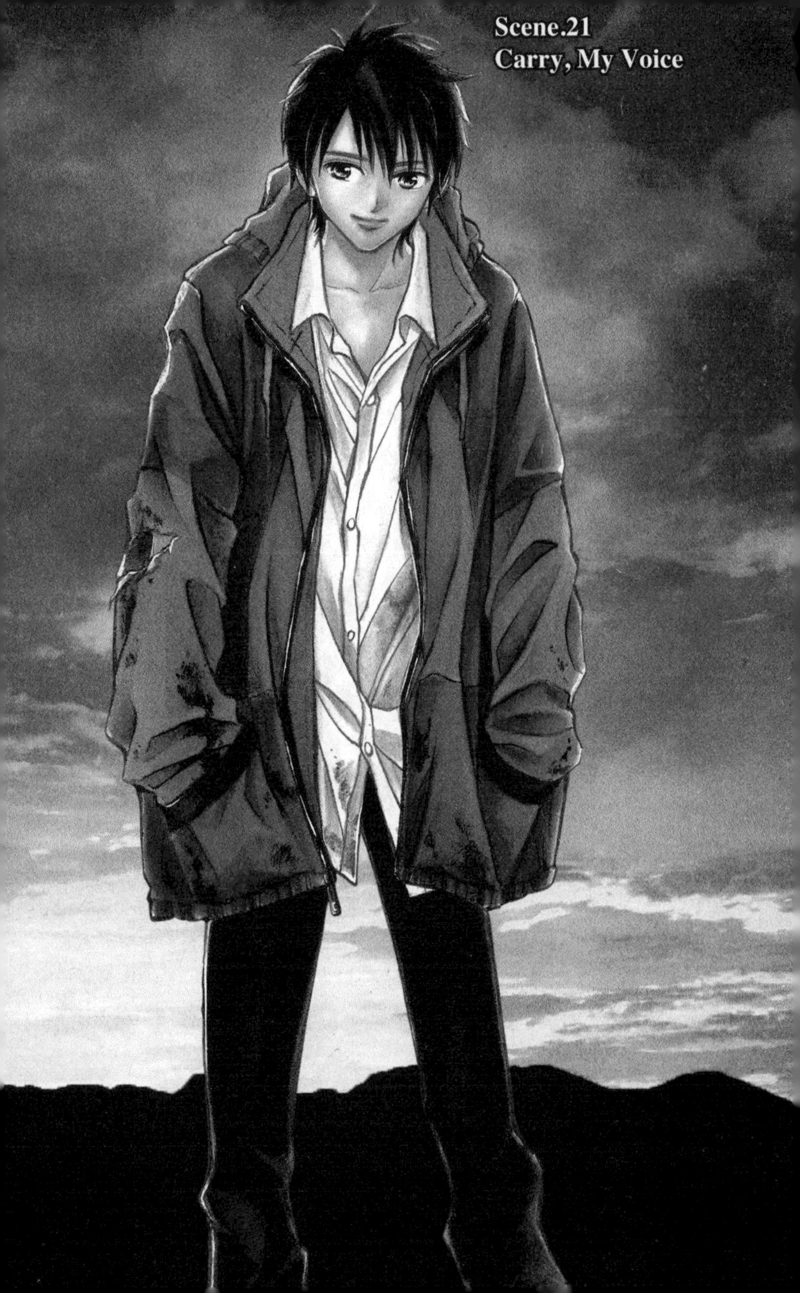
Scene.21
Carry, My Voice

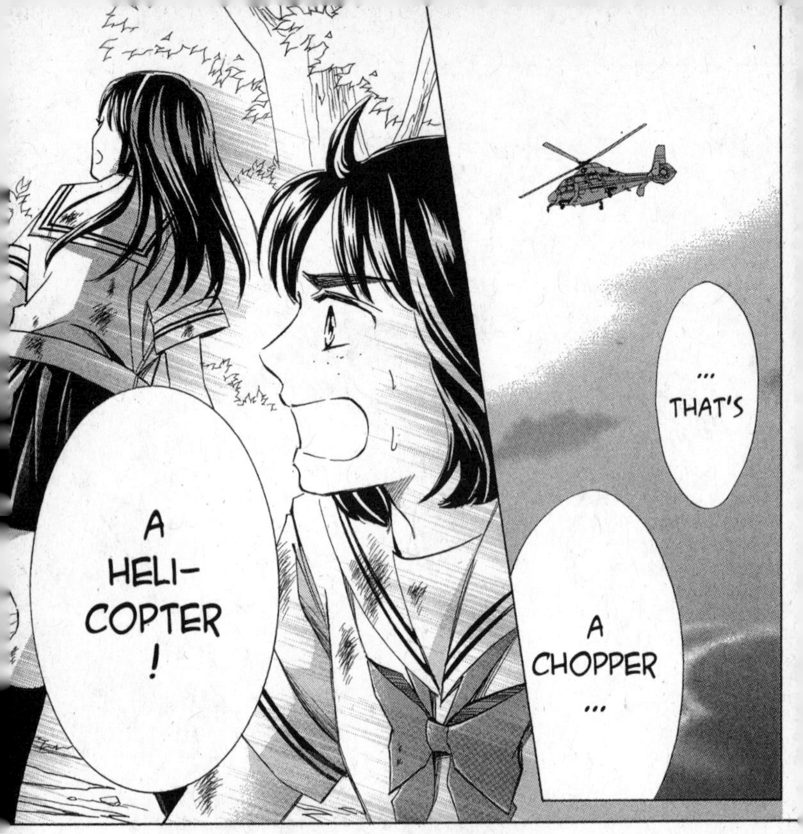
... THAT'S
A CHOPPER ...
A HELI-COPTER !

LIMIT

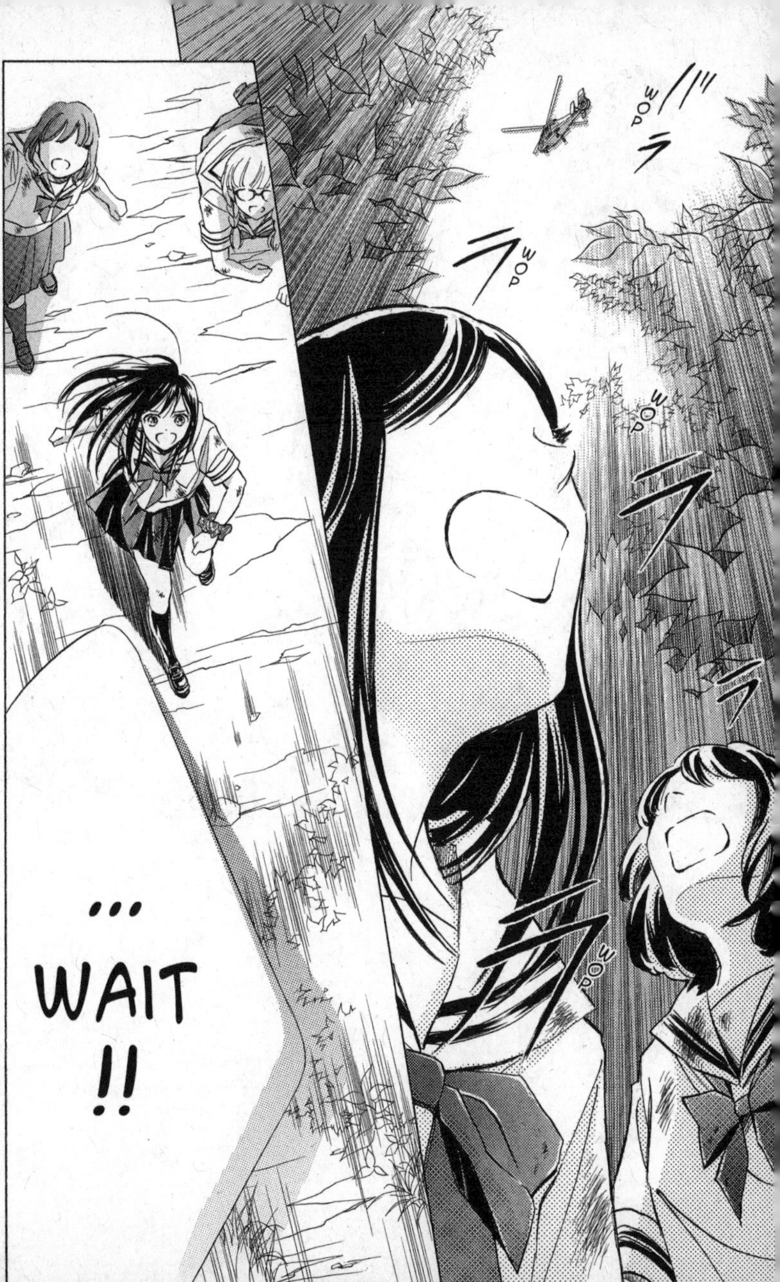
WOP
WOP
WOP
WOP
... WAIT !!

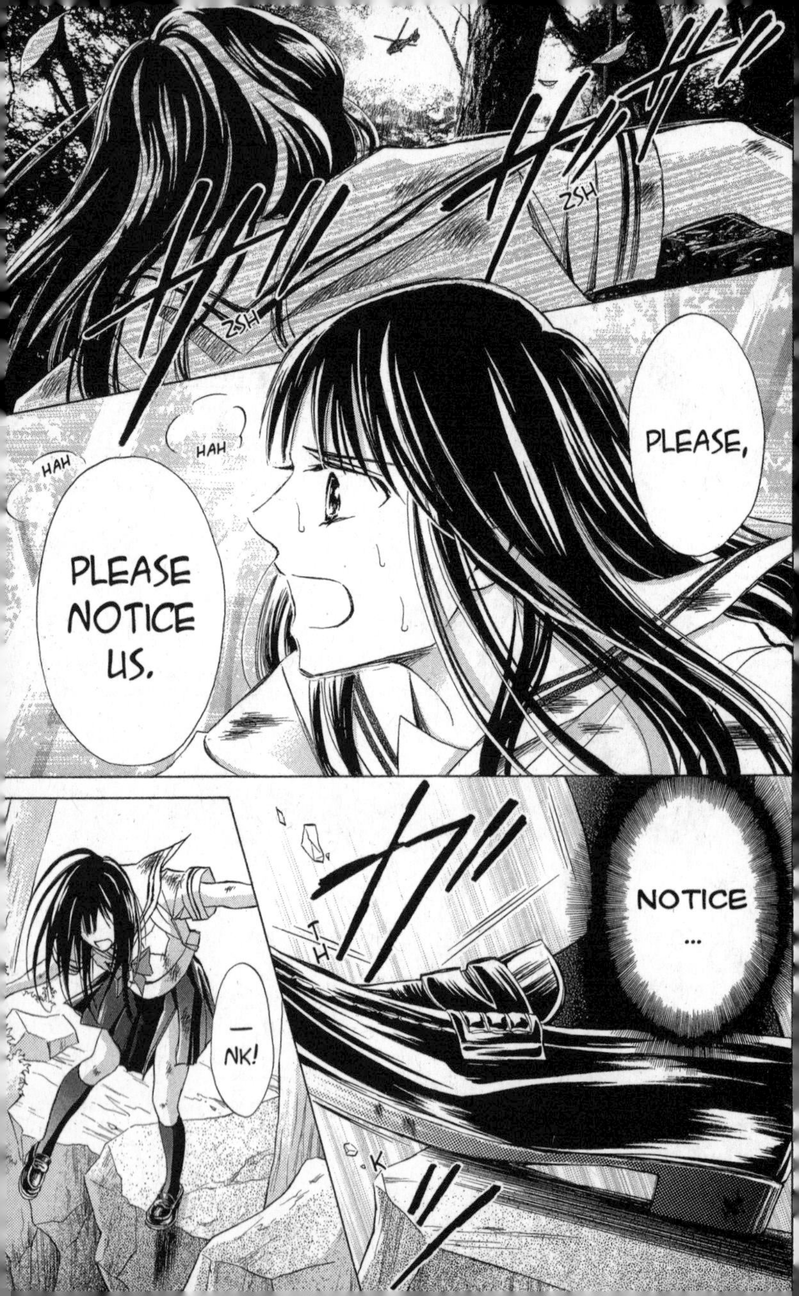
ZSH
ZSH
PLEASE,
HAH
HAH
PLEASE NOTICE US.
NOTICE ...
TH
—NK!
K

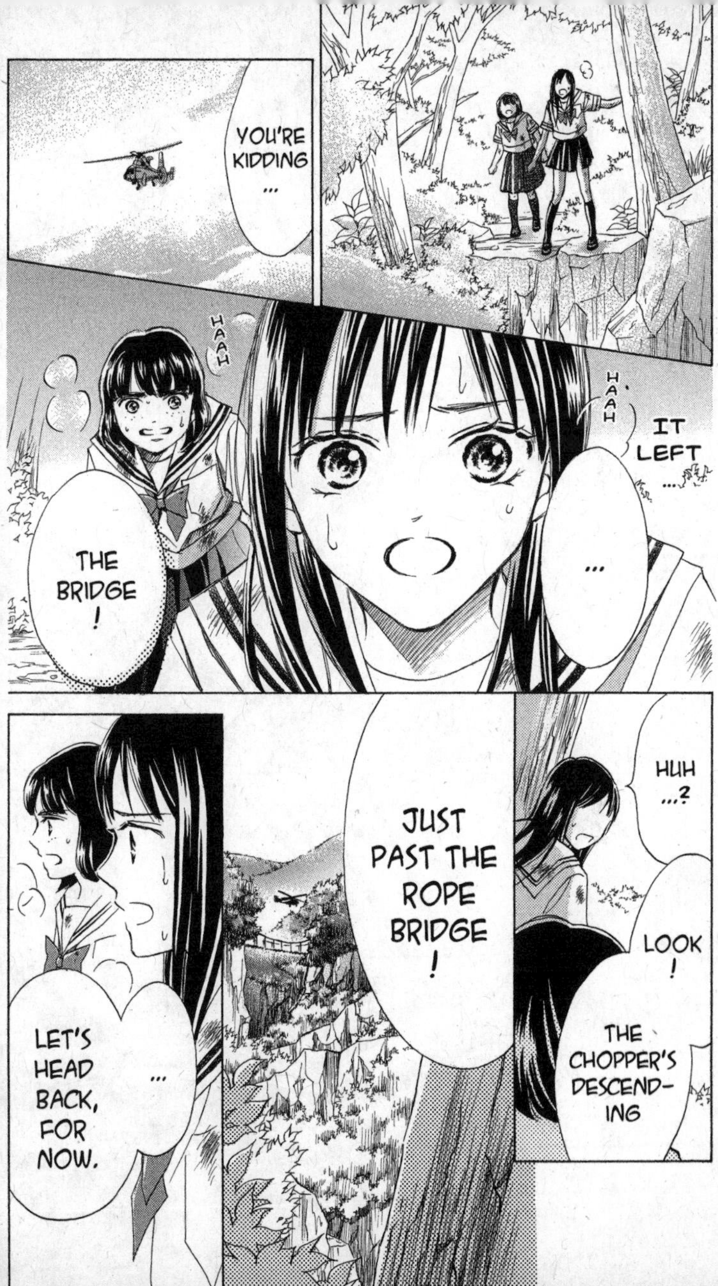
YOU'RE KIDDING ...
HAAH
IT LEFT ...
...
HAAH
THE BRIDGE!
HUH ...?
LOOK!
THE CHOPPER'S DESCEND-ING
JUST PAST THE ROPE BRIDGE!
... LET'S HEAD BACK, FOR NOW.

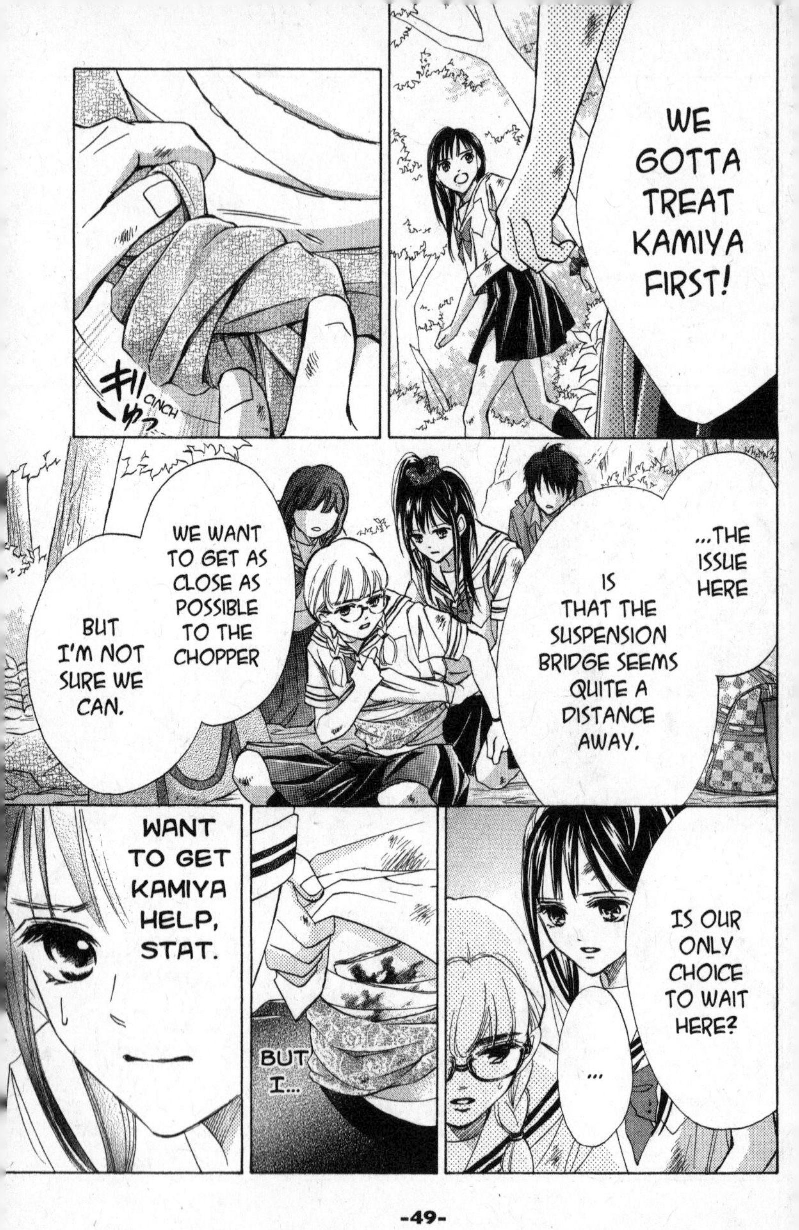
WE GOTTA TREAT KAMIYA FIRST!
キリゅっ
CINCH
...THE ISSUE HERE IS THAT THE SUSPENSION BRIDGE SEEMS QUITE A DISTANCE AWAY.
WE WANT TO GET AS CLOSE AS POSSIBLE TO THE CHOPPER
BUT I'M NOT SURE WE CAN.
IS OUR ONLY CHOICE TO WAIT HERE?
...
BUT I...
WANT TO GET KAMIYA HELP, STAT.

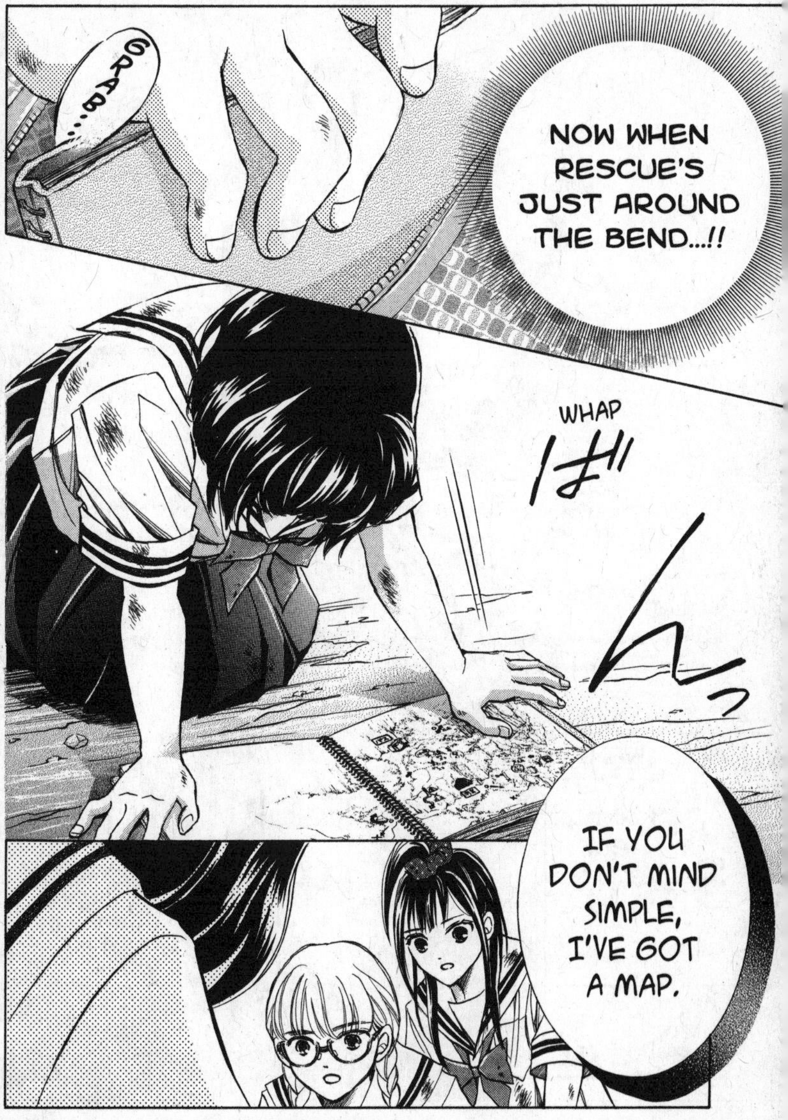
NOW WHEN RESCUE'S JUST AROUND THE BEND...!!
GRAB...
WHAP
ばんっ
IF YOU DON'T MIND SIMPLE, I'VE GOT A MAP.

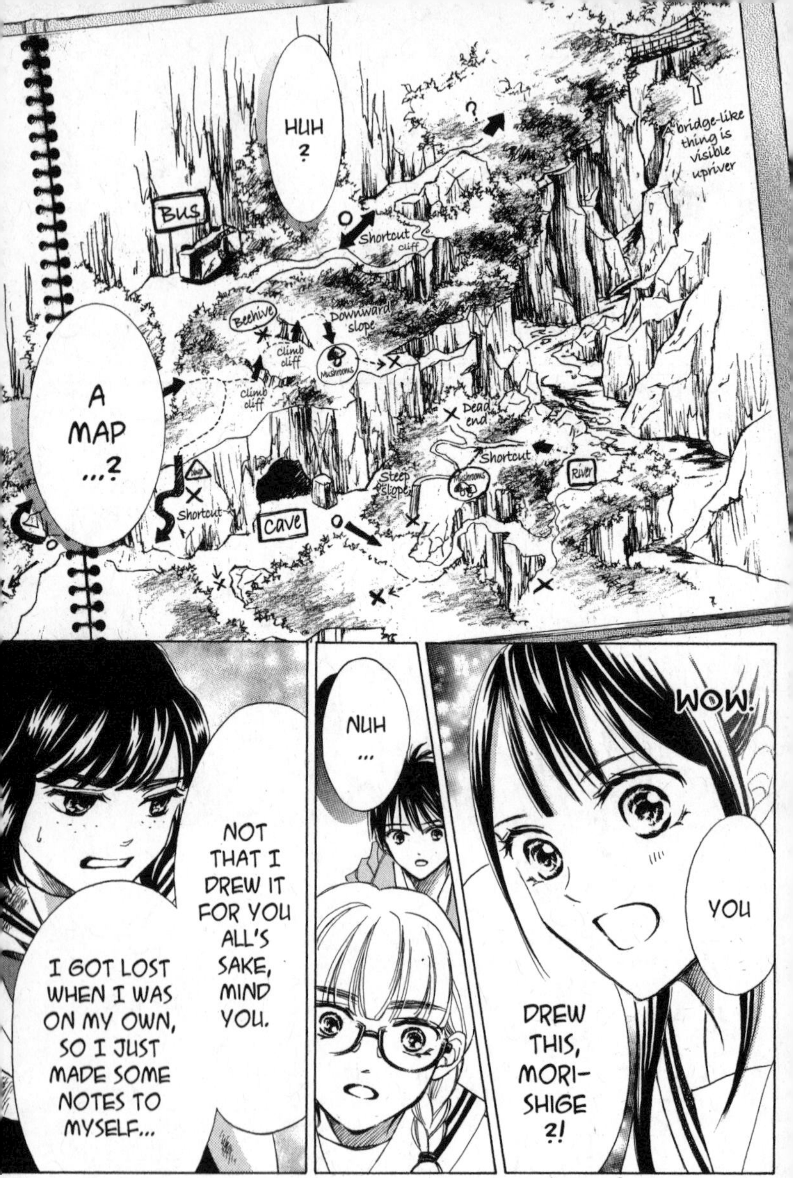
HUH?
A bridge-like thing is visible upriver
BUS
Shortcut cliff
A MAP...?
Beehive
Downward slope
Climb cliff
Mushrooms
Climb cliff
Dead end
Shortcut
River
Steep slope
Mushrooms
Shortcut
Cave
WOW!
YOU
DREW THIS, MORISHIGE?!
NUH...
NOT THAT I DREW IT FOR YOU ALL'S SAKE, MIND YOU.
I GOT LOST WHEN I WAS ON MY OWN, SO I JUST MADE SOME NOTES TO MYSELF...

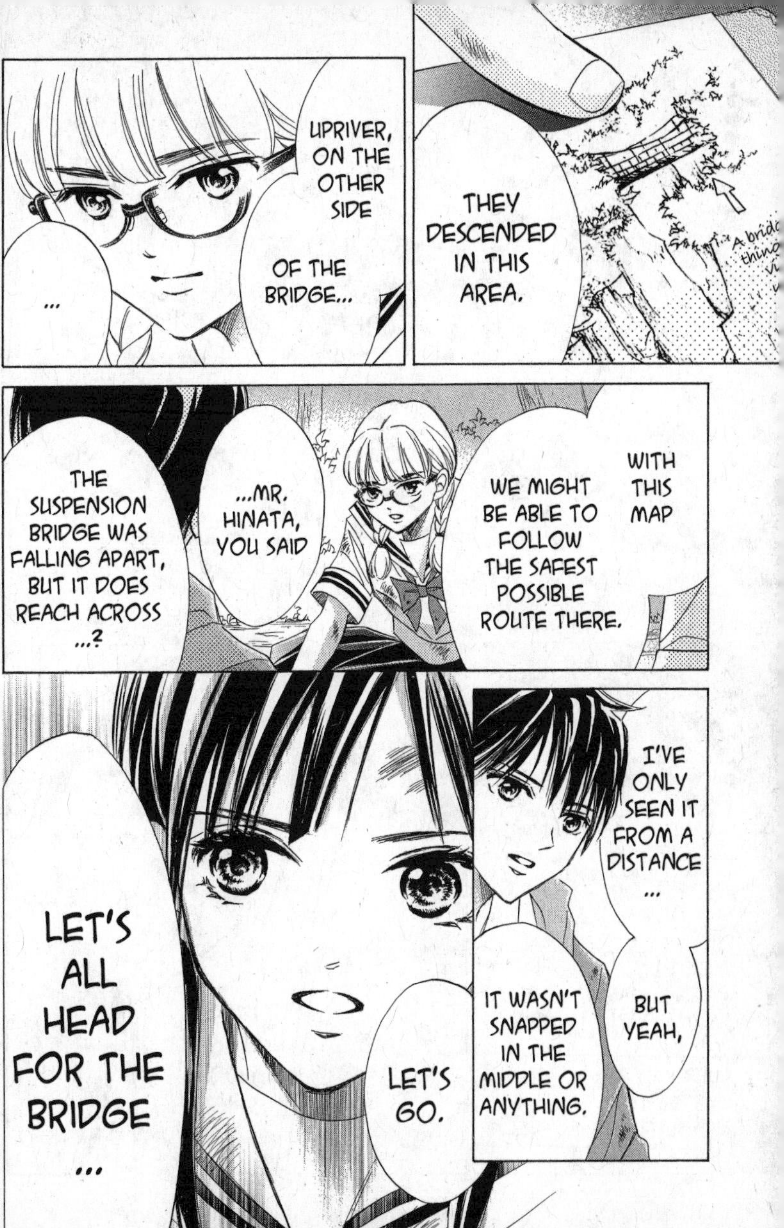
THEY DESCENDED IN THIS AREA.
UPRIVER, ON THE OTHER SIDE
OF THE BRIDGE...
...
WITH THIS MAP
WE MIGHT BE ABLE TO FOLLOW THE SAFEST POSSIBLE ROUTE THERE.
...MR. HINATA, YOU SAID
THE SUSPENSION BRIDGE WAS FALLING APART, BUT IT DOES REACH ACROSS ...?
I'VE ONLY SEEN IT FROM A DISTANCE ...
BUT YEAH,
IT WASN'T SNAPPED IN THE MIDDLE OR ANYTHING.
LET'S GO.
LET'S ALL HEAD FOR THE BRIDGE ...

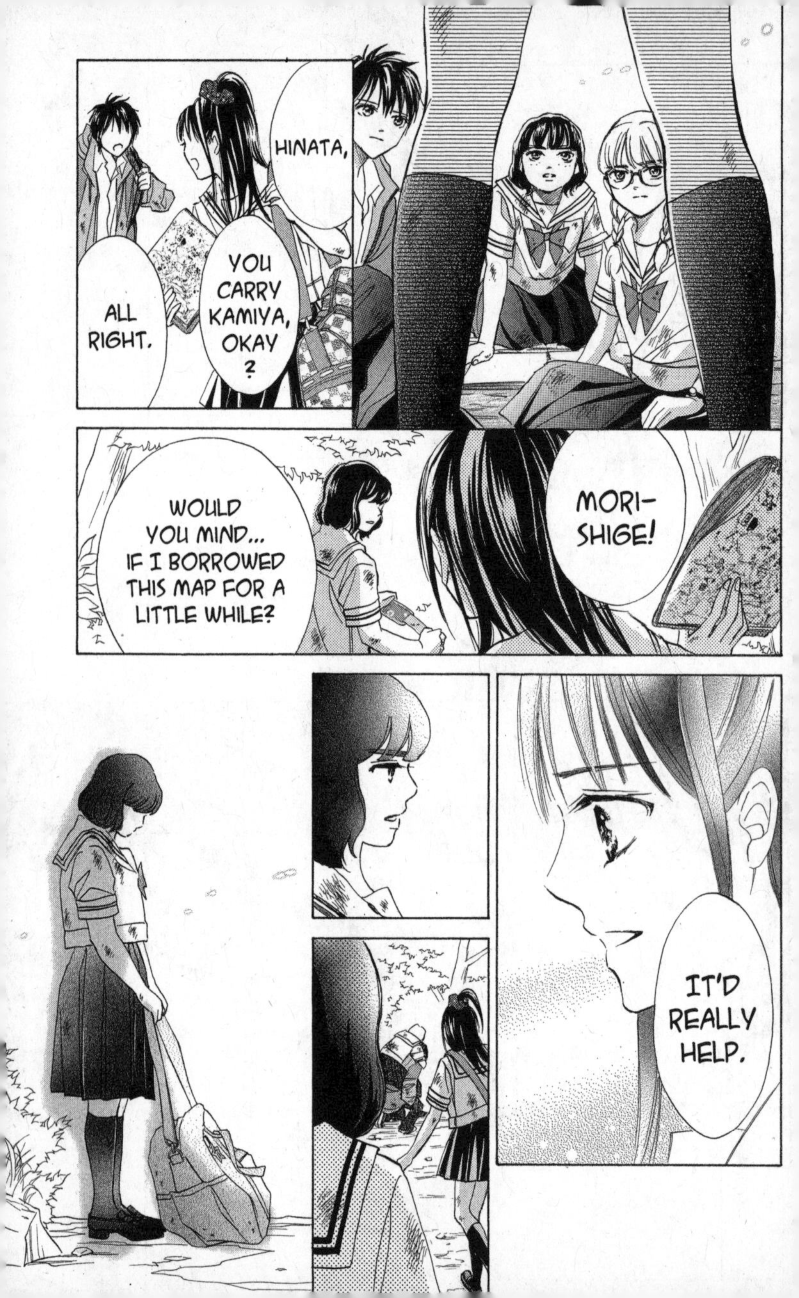
HINATA,
YOU CARRY KAMIYA, OKAY?
ALL RIGHT.
MORI-SHIGE!
WOULD YOU MIND... IF I BORROWED THIS MAP FOR A LITTLE WHILE?
IT'D REALLY HELP.

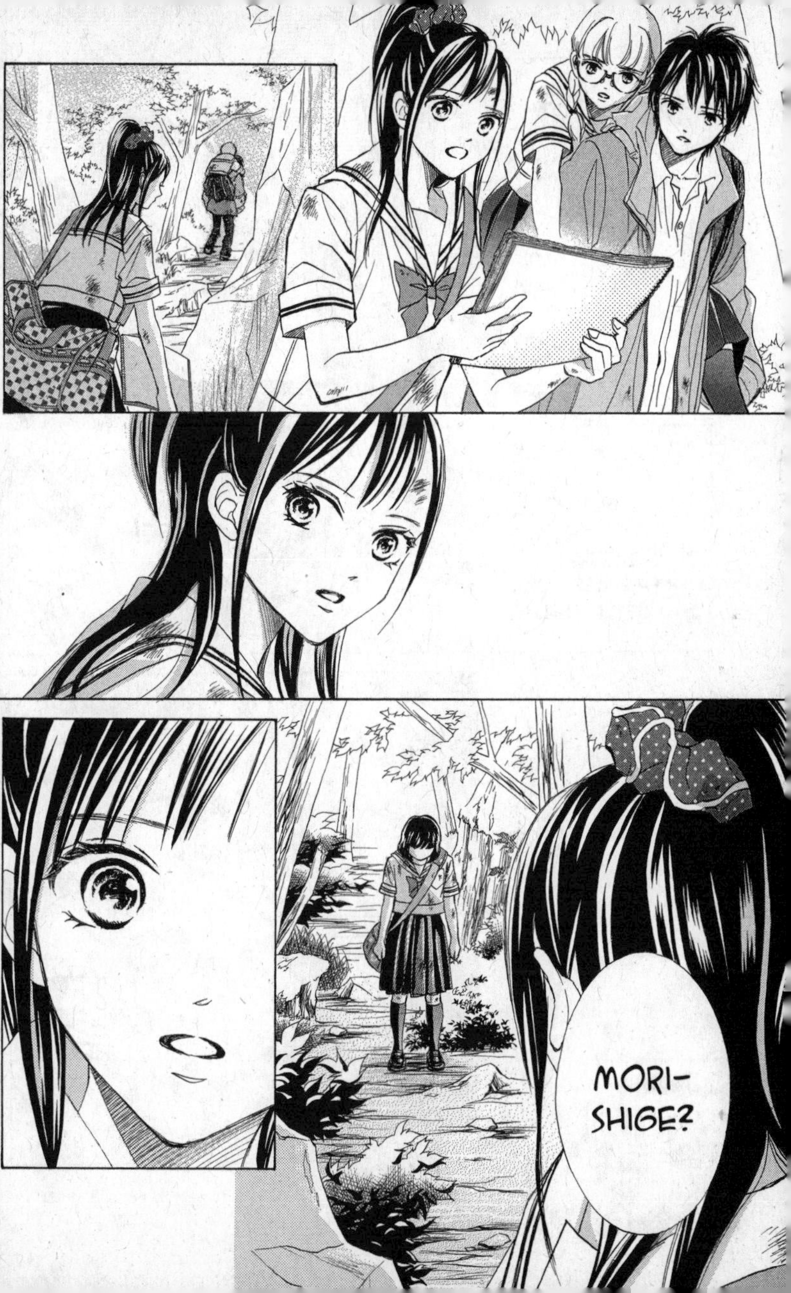
MORI-SHIGE?

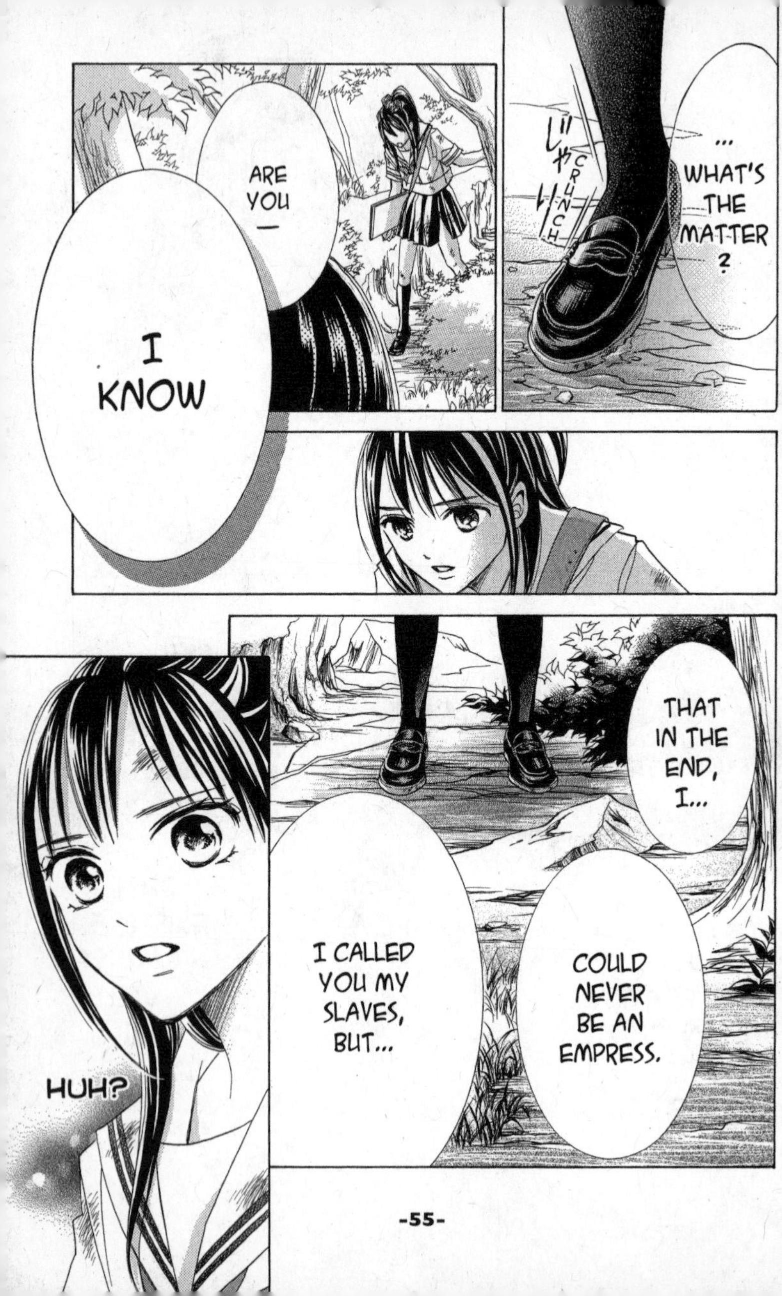
じゃり
CRUNCH
...WHAT'S THE MATTER?
ARE YOU —
I KNOW
THAT IN THE END, I...
COULD NEVER BE AN EMPRESS.
I CALLED YOU MY SLAVES, BUT...
HUH?

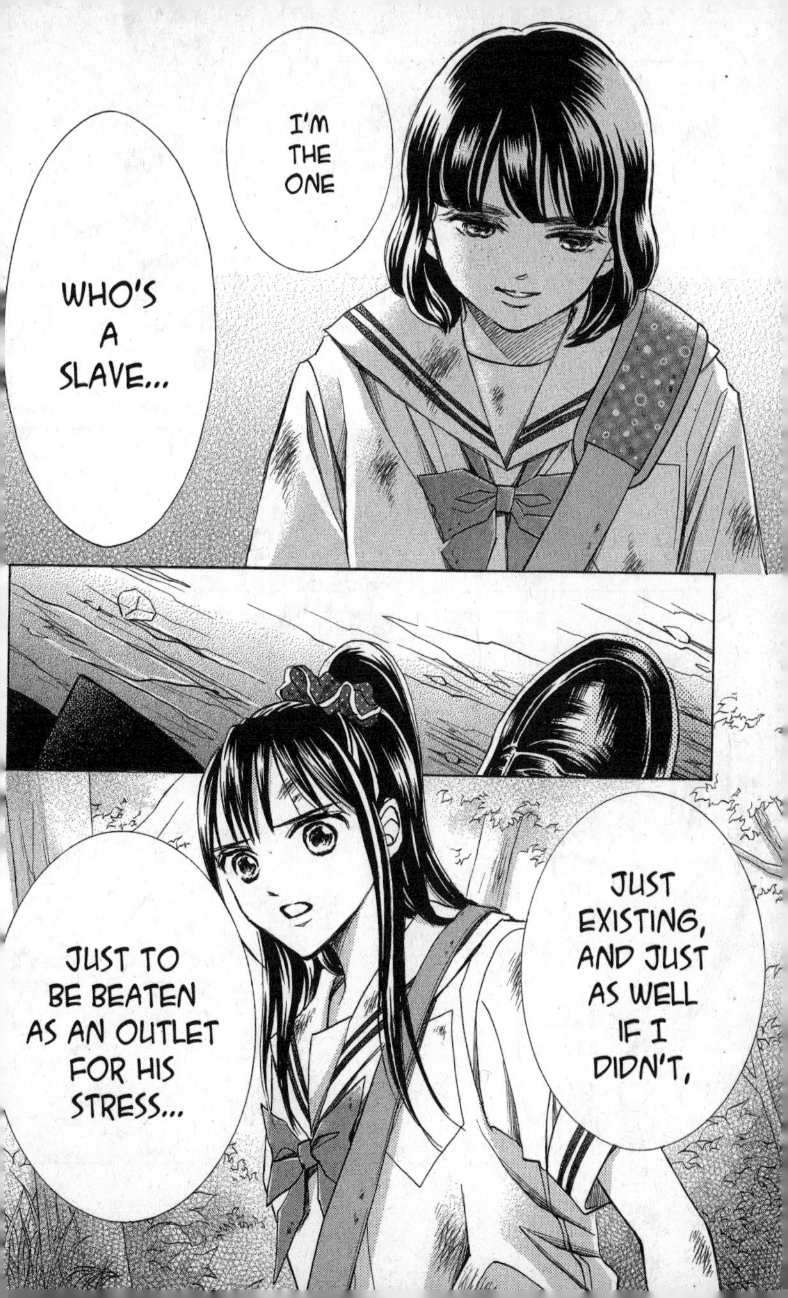
I'M THE ONE
WHO'S A SLAVE...
JUST EXISTING, AND JUST AS WELL IF I DIDN'T,
JUST TO BE BEATEN AS AN OUTLET FOR HIS STRESS...

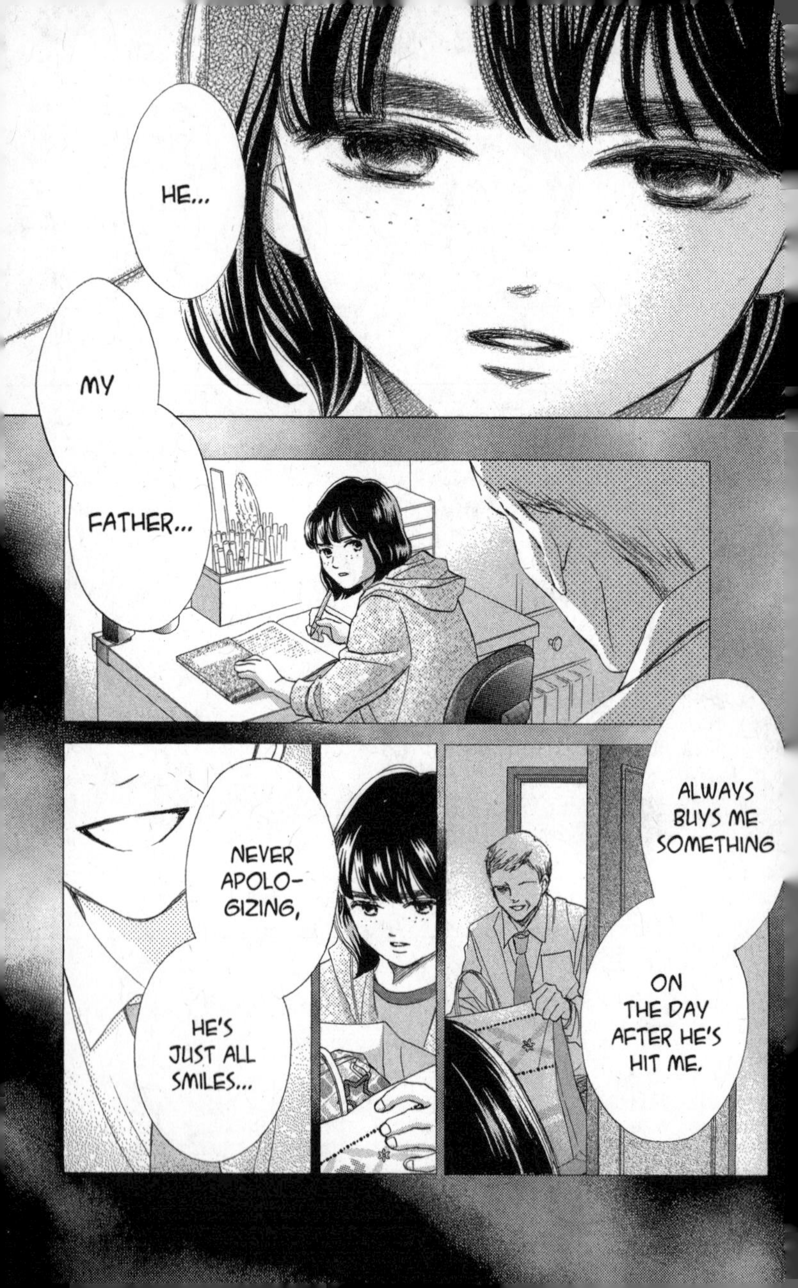
HE...
MY
FATHER...
ALWAYS BUYS ME SOMETHING
ON THE DAY AFTER HE'S HIT ME.
NEVER APOLO-GIZING,
HE'S JUST ALL SMILES...

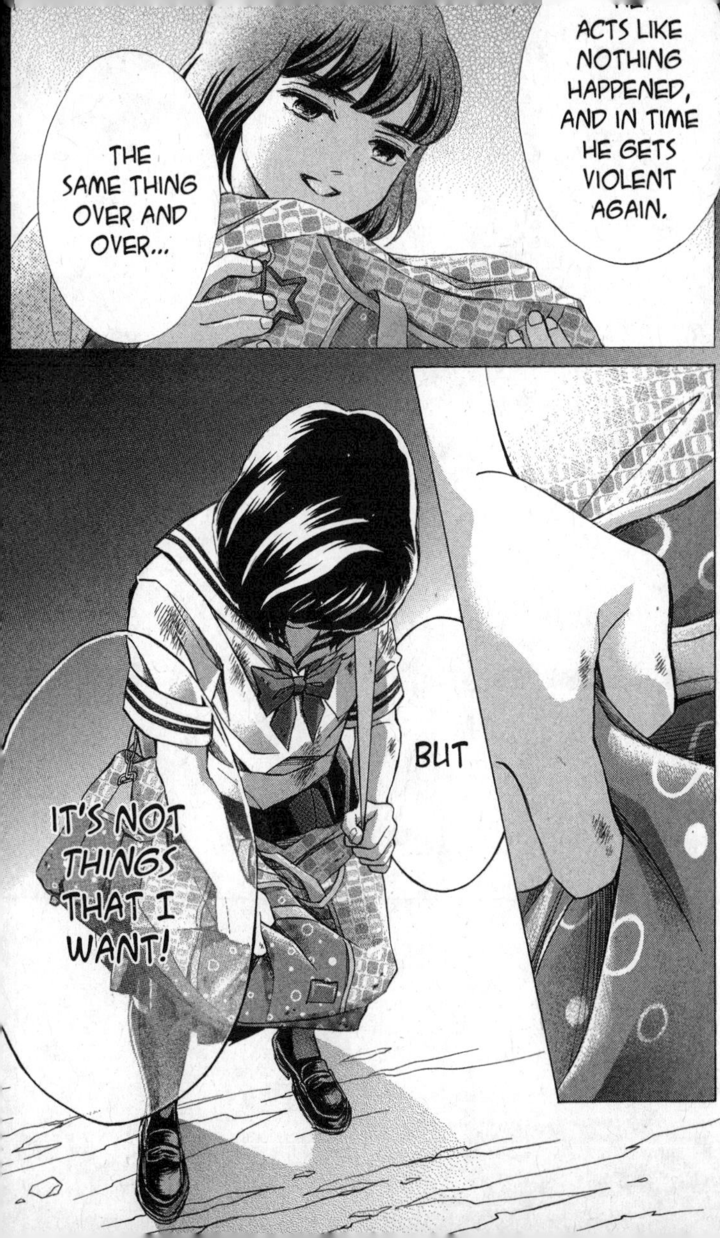
ACTS LIKE NOTHING HAPPENED, AND IN TIME HE GETS VIOLENT AGAIN.
THE SAME THING OVER AND OVER...
BUT
IT'S NOT THINGS THAT I WANT!

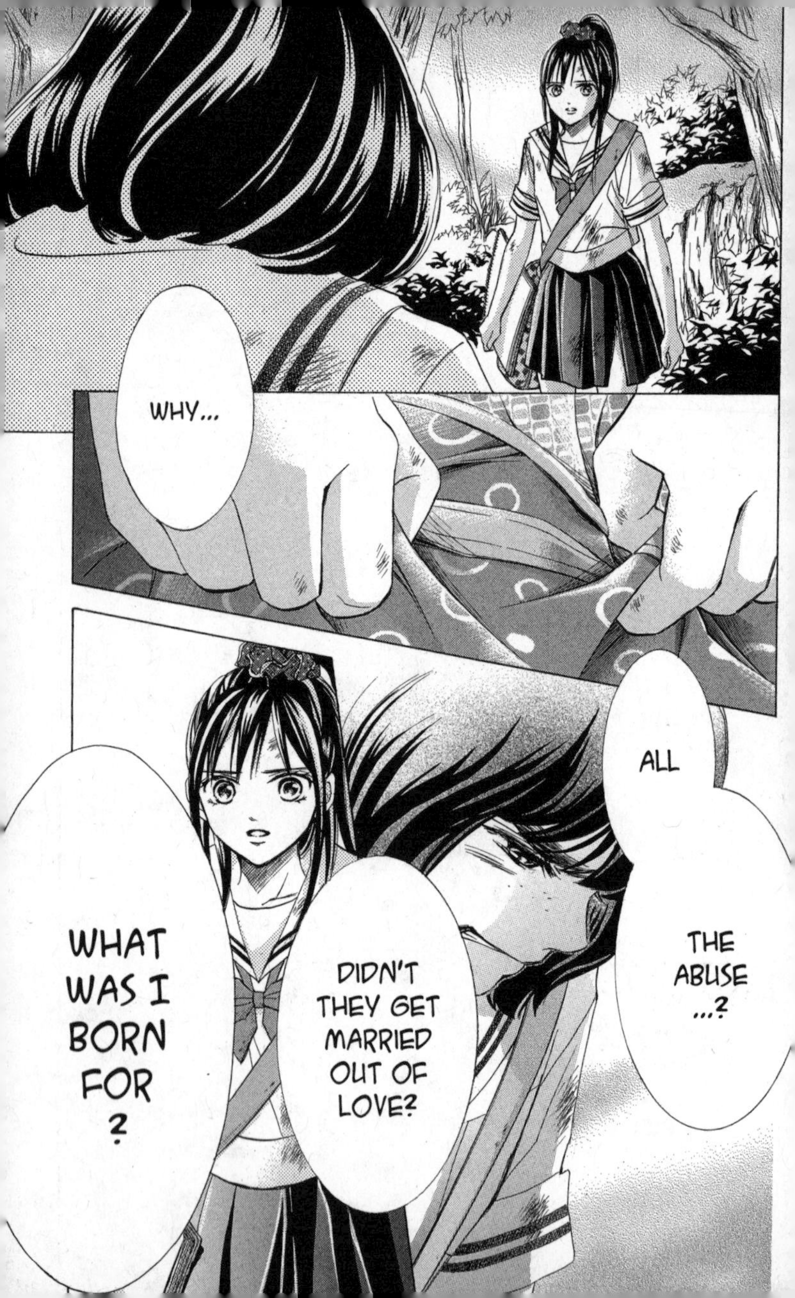
WHY...
ALL THE ABUSE ...?
DIDN'T THEY GET MARRIED OUT OF LOVE?
WHAT WAS I BORN FOR ?

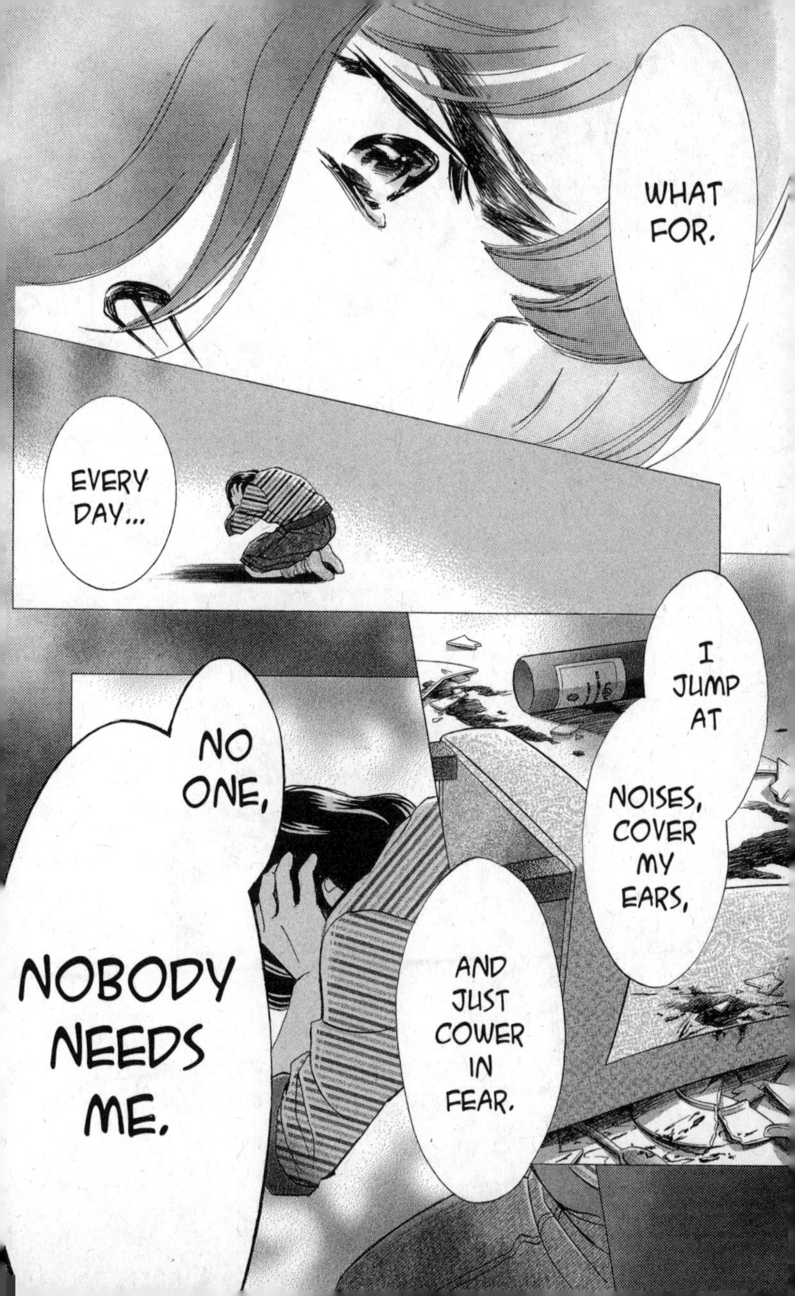
WHAT FOR.
EVERY DAY...
I JUMP AT
NOISES, COVER MY EARS,
AND JUST COWER IN FEAR.
NO ONE,
NOBODY NEEDS ME.

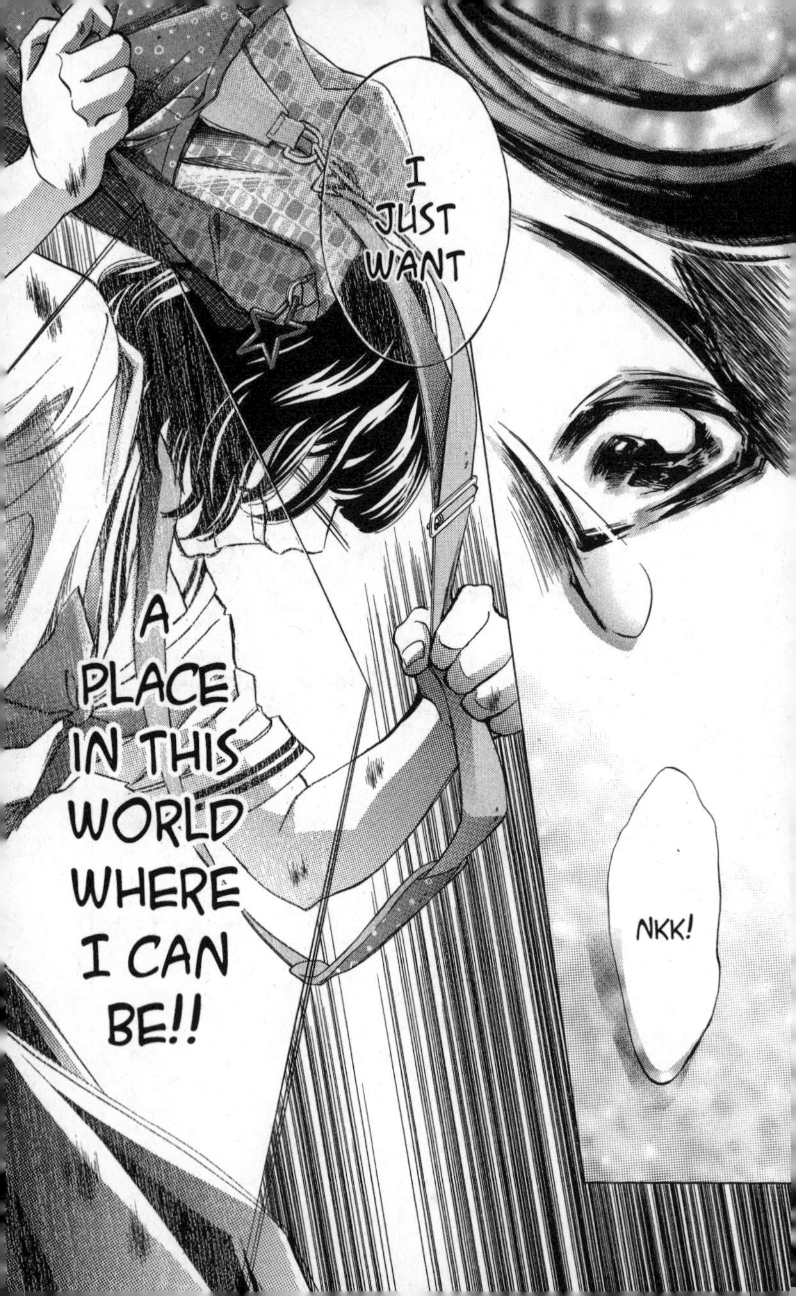
I JUST WANT
A PLACE IN THIS WORLD WHERE I CAN BE!!
NKK!

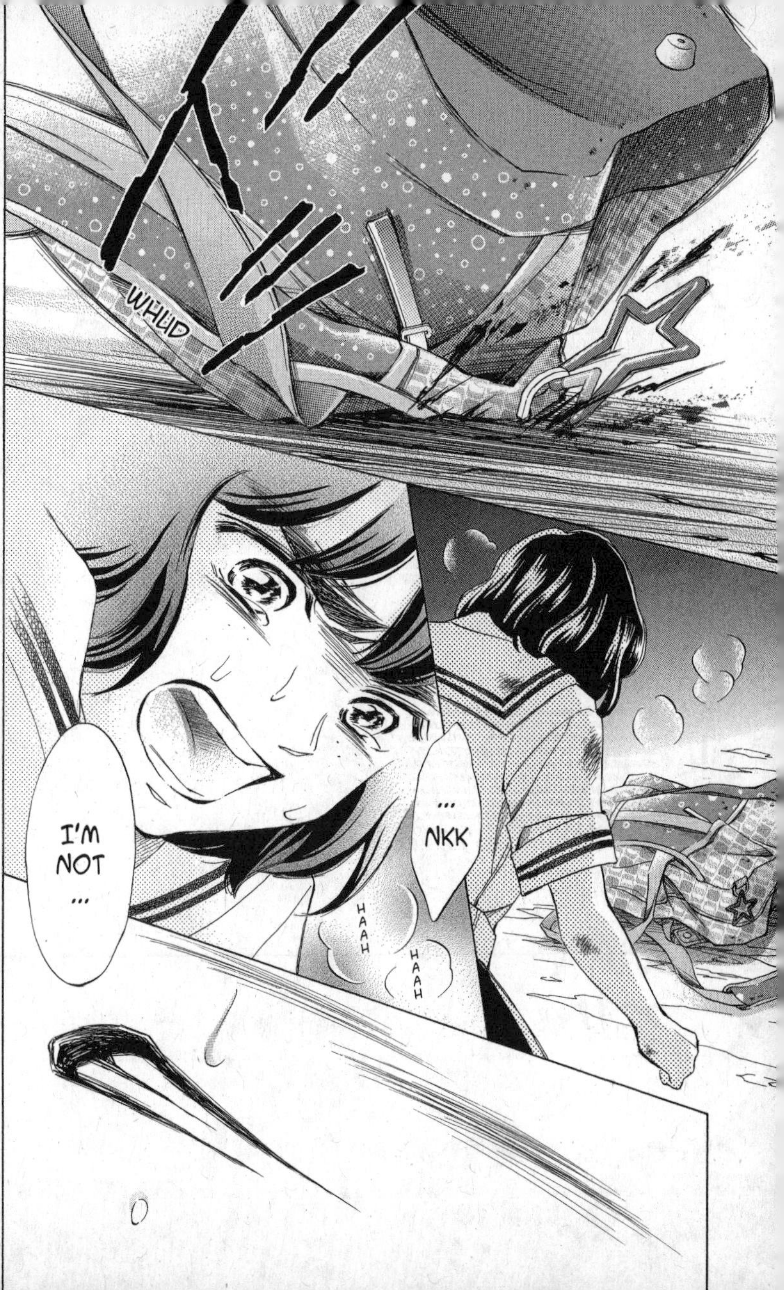
WHUD
... NKK
HAAH
HAAH
I'M NOT ...

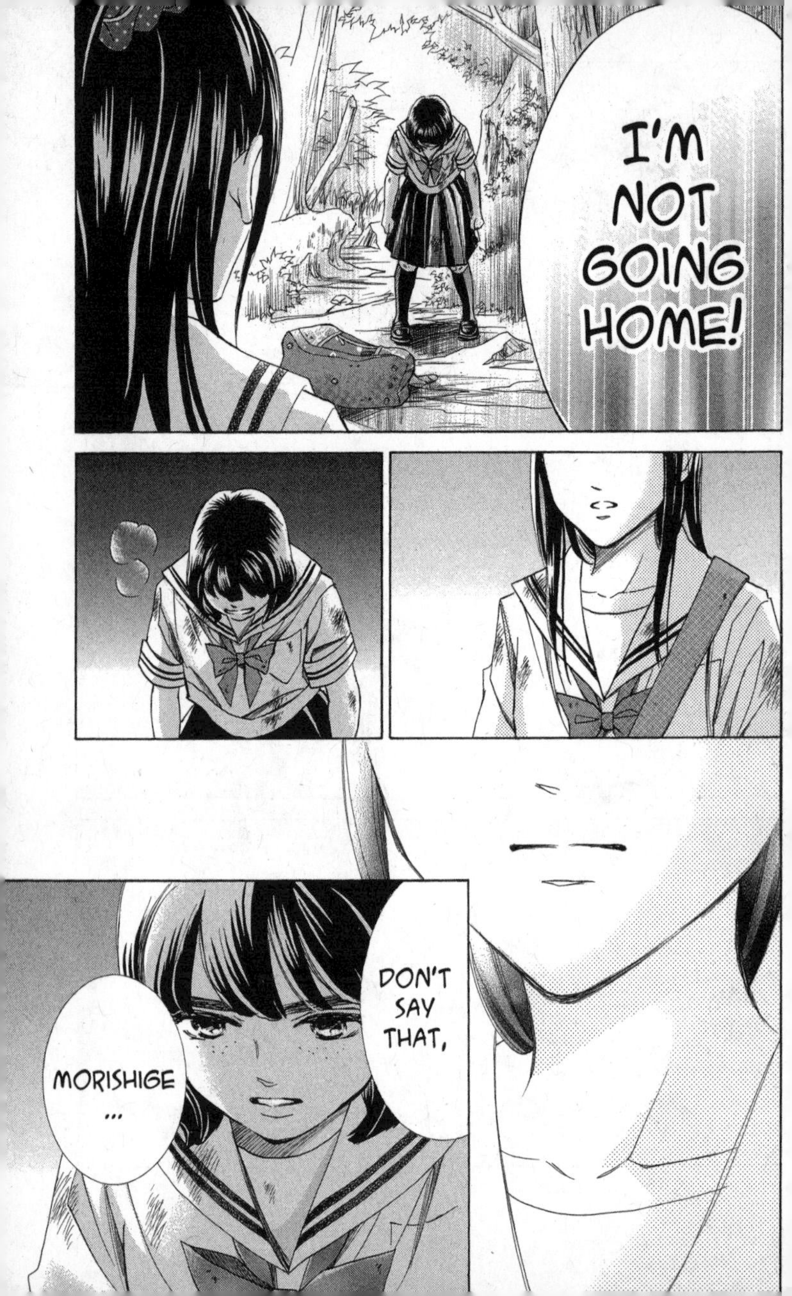
I'M NOT GOING HOME!
DON'T SAY THAT,
MORISHIGE ...

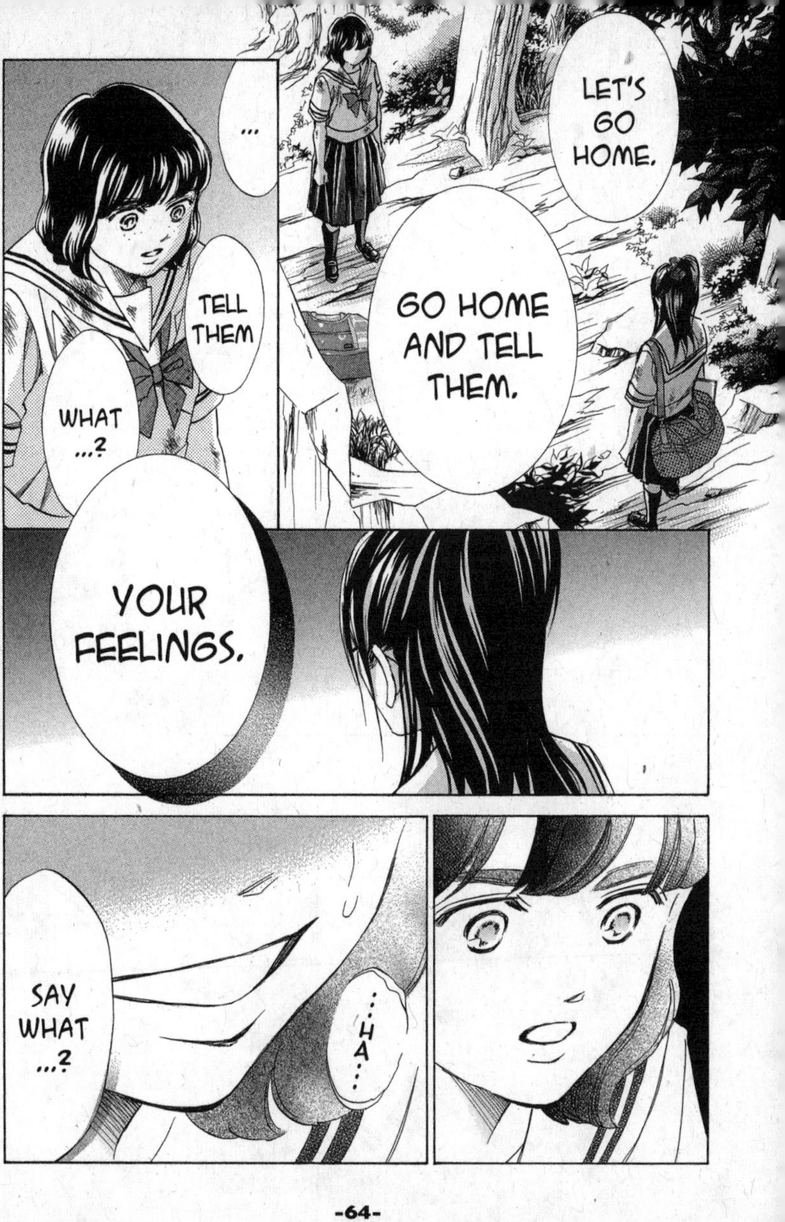
LET'S GO HOME.
GO HOME AND TELL THEM.
...
TELL THEM
WHAT ...?
YOUR FEELINGS.
...HA...
SAY WHAT ...?

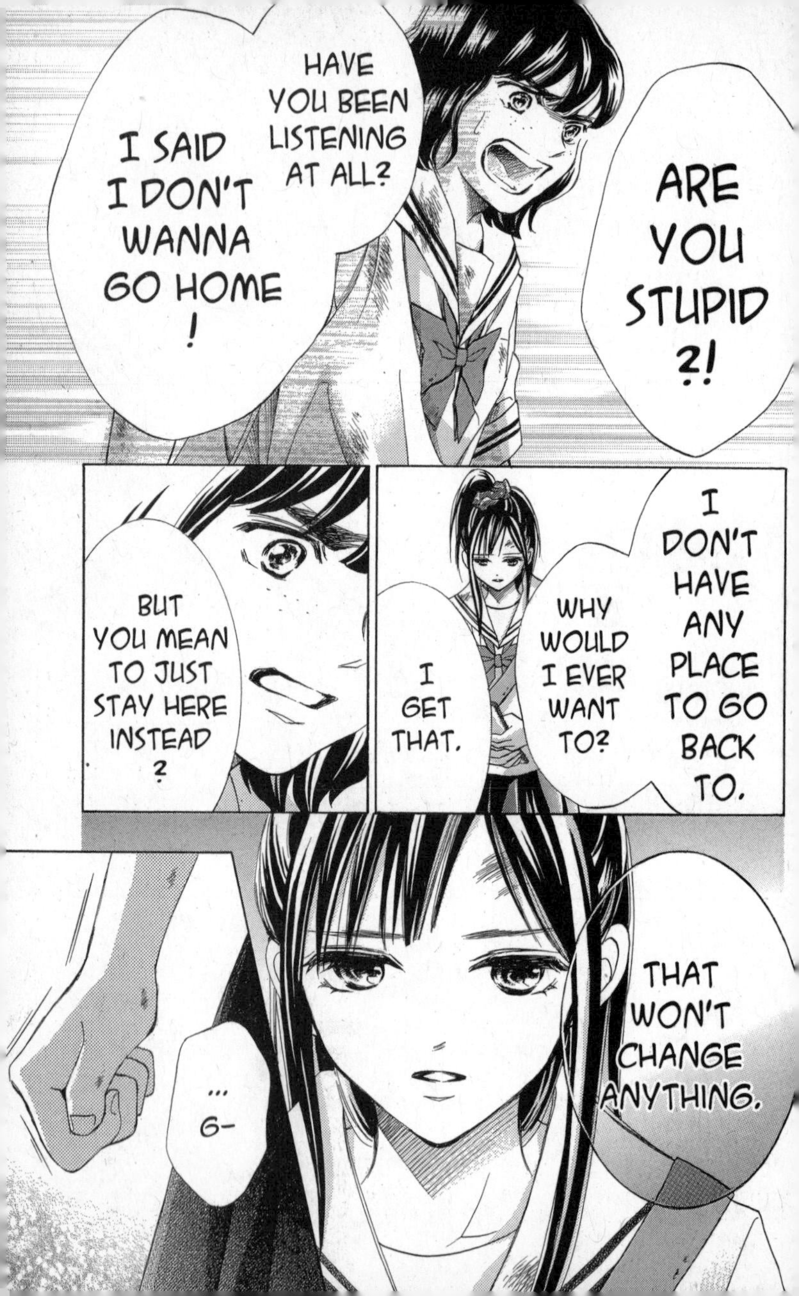
ARE YOU STUPID ?!
HAVE YOU BEEN LISTENING AT ALL?
I SAID I DON'T WANNA GO HOME !
I DON'T HAVE ANY PLACE TO GO BACK TO.
WHY WOULD I EVER WANT TO?
I GET THAT.
BUT YOU MEAN TO JUST STAY HERE INSTEAD ?
THAT WON'T CHANGE ANYTHING.
... G-

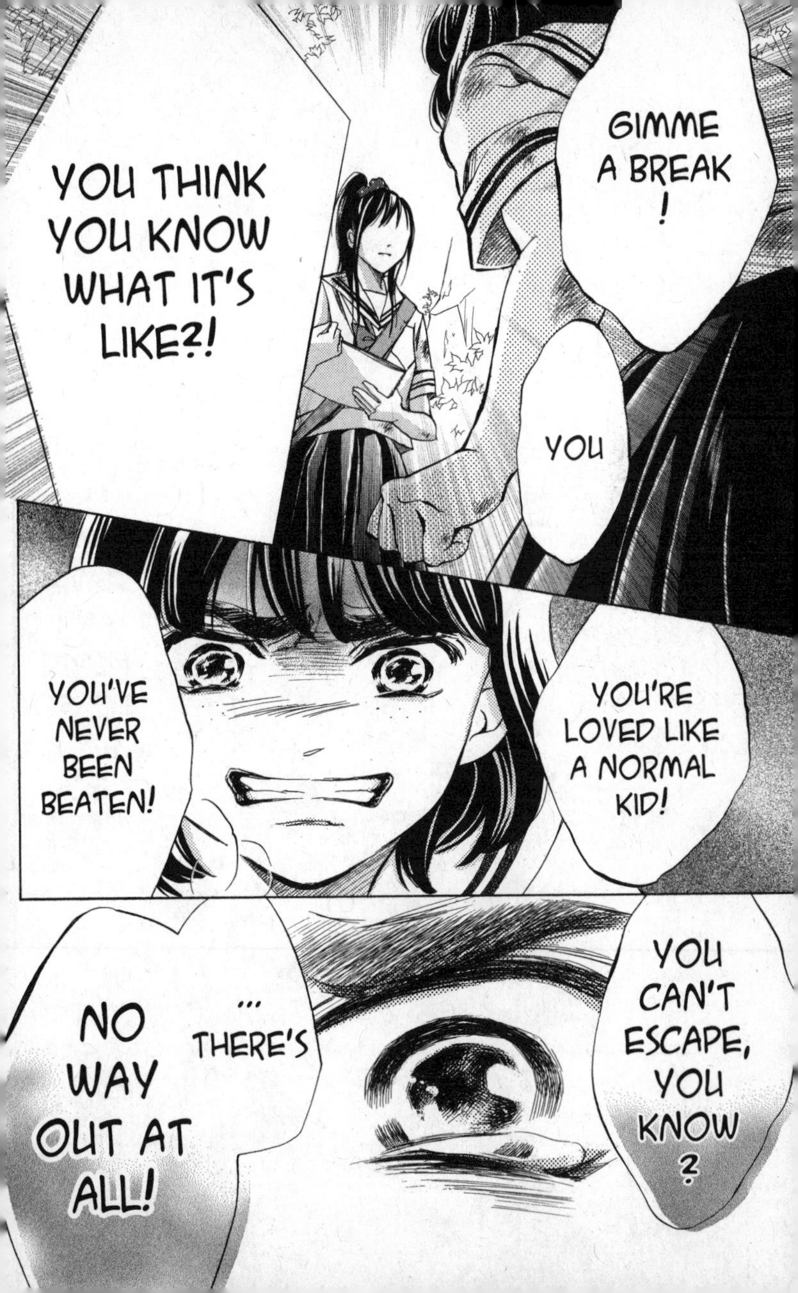

GIMME A BREAK!
YOU THINK YOU KNOW WHAT IT'S LIKE?!
YOU
YOU'RE LOVED LIKE A NORMAL KID!
YOU'VE NEVER BEEN BEATEN!
YOU CAN'T ESCAPE, YOU KNOW?
...THERE'S
NO WAY OUT AT ALL!

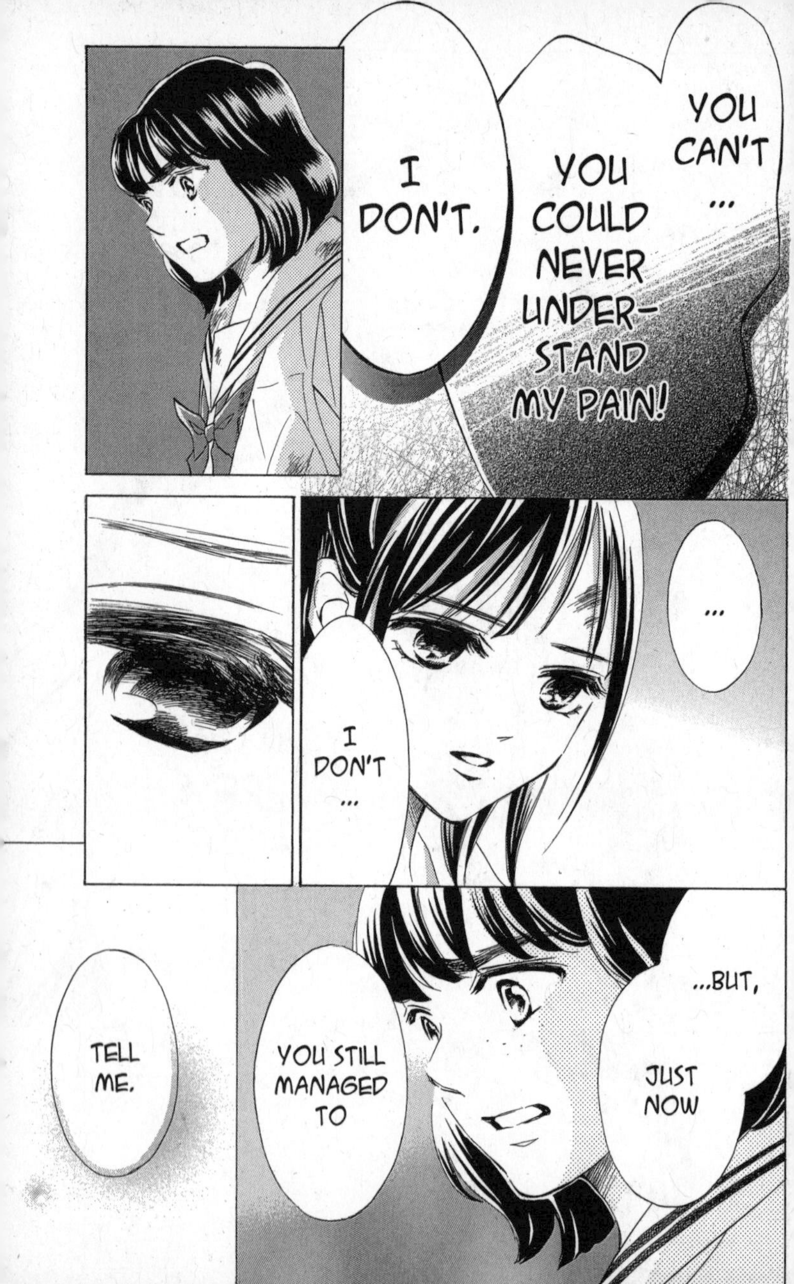
YOU CAN'T ...
YOU COULD NEVER UNDER-STAND MY PAIN!
I DON'T.
...
I DON'T ...
...BUT, JUST NOW
YOU STILL MANAGED TO
TELL ME.

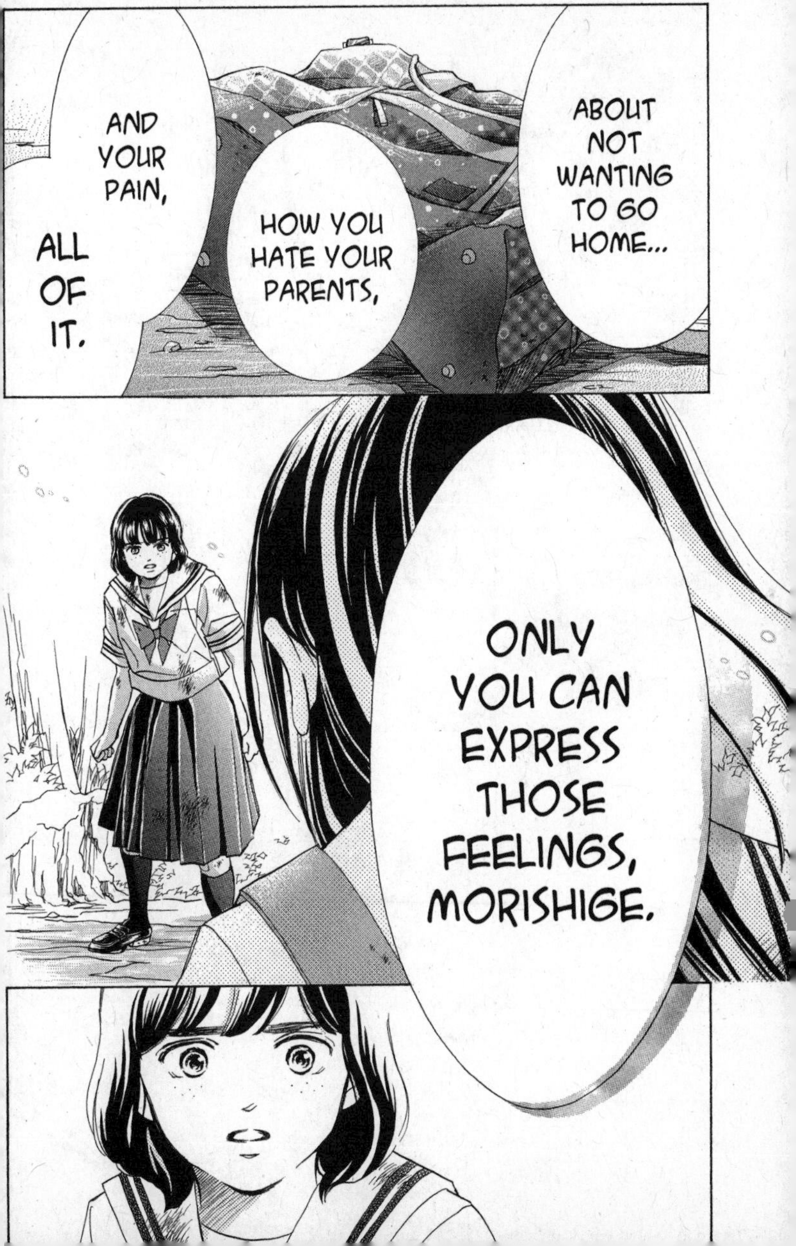
ABOUT NOT WANTING TO GO HOME...
HOW YOU HATE YOUR PARENTS,
AND YOUR PAIN,
ALL OF IT.
ONLY YOU CAN EXPRESS THOSE FEELINGS, MORISHIGE.

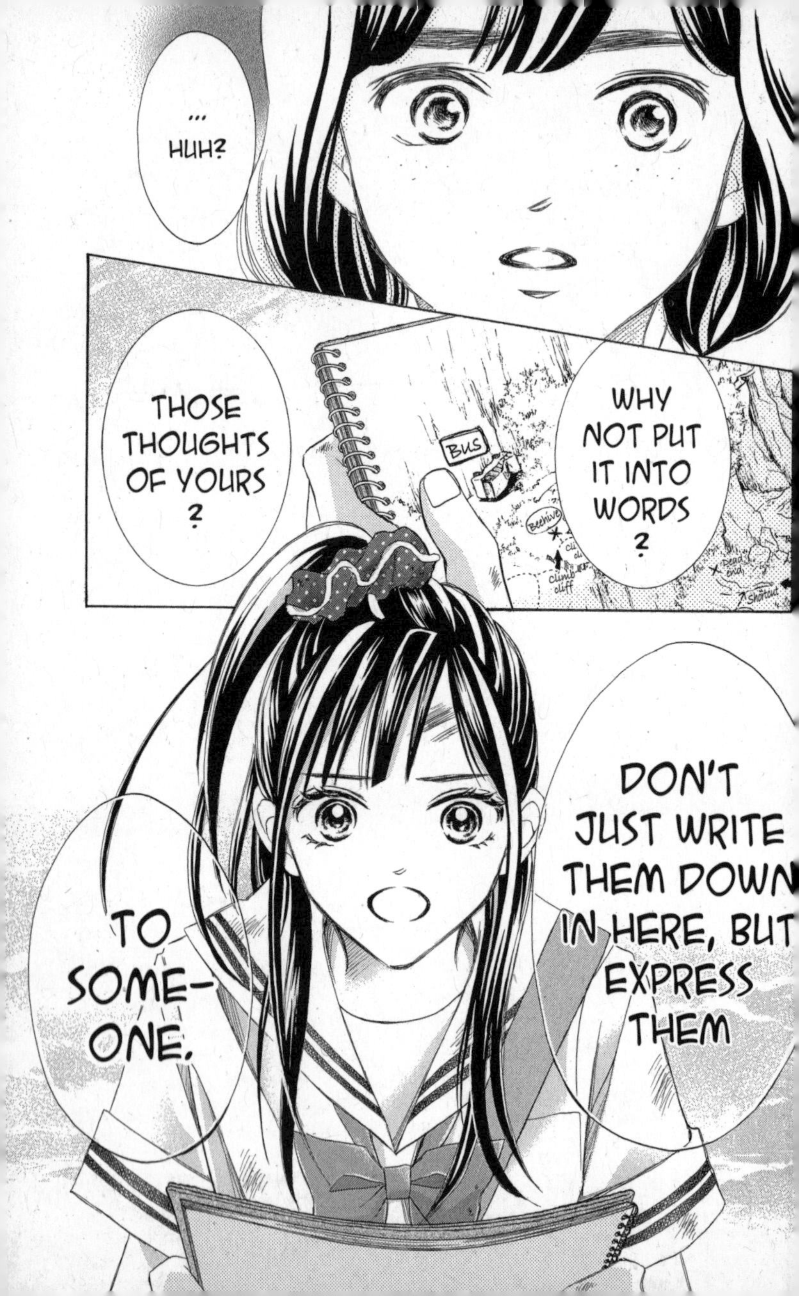
...
HUH?
WHY NOT PUT IT INTO WORDS?
THOSE THOUGHTS OF YOURS?
Bus
Beehive
climb cliff
Dead end
Shortcut
DON'T JUST WRITE THEM DOWN IN HERE, BUT EXPRESS THEM
TO SOME-ONE.

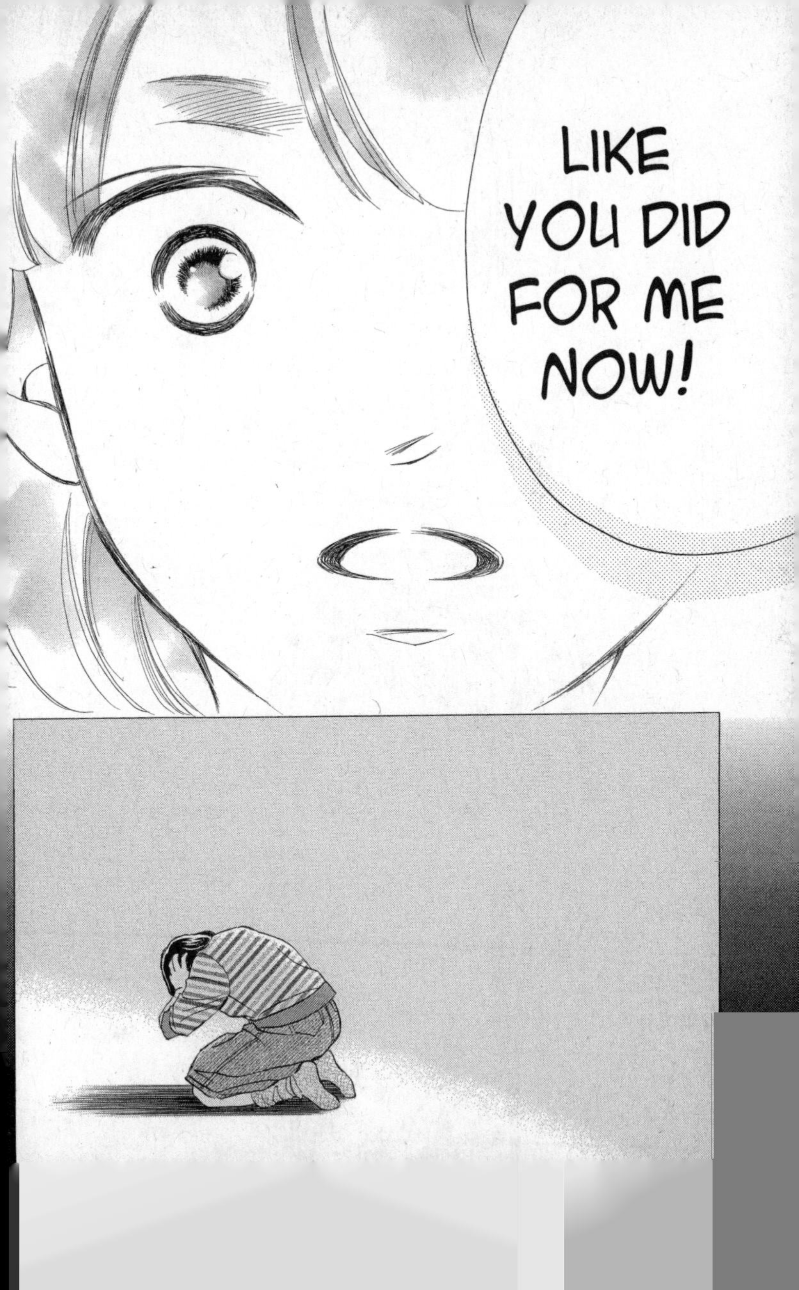
LIKE YOU DID FOR ME NOW!

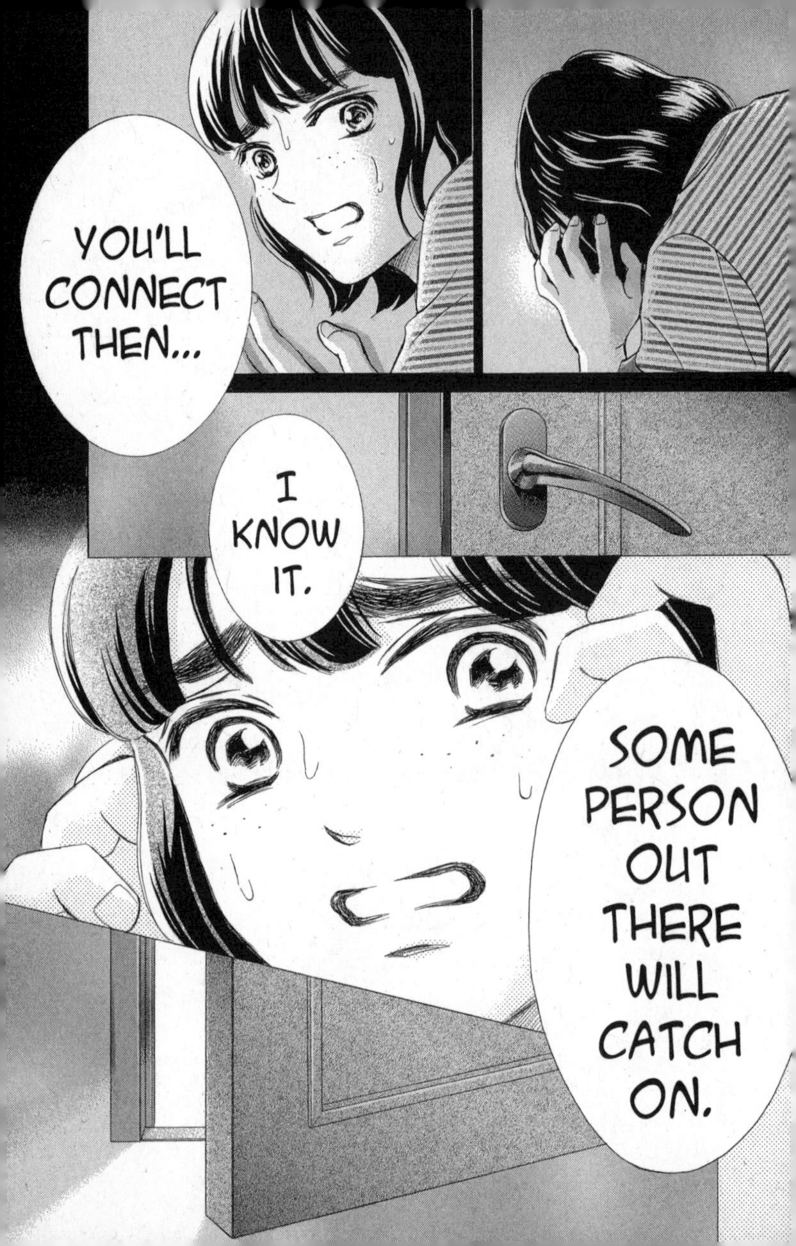
YOU'LL CONNECT THEN...
I KNOW IT.
SOME PERSON OUT THERE WILL CATCH ON.

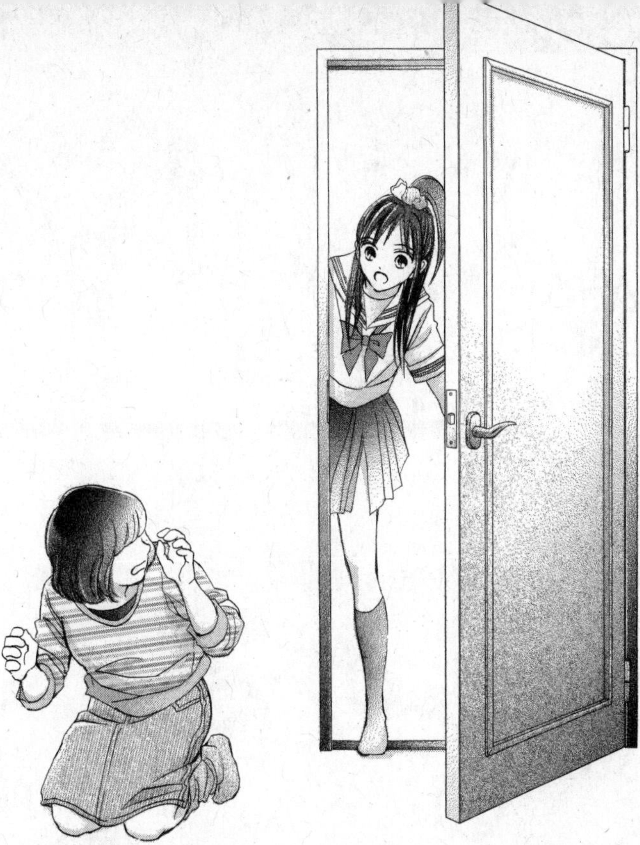
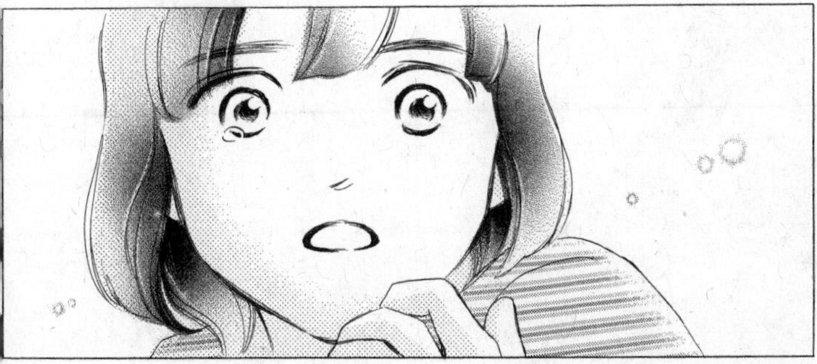

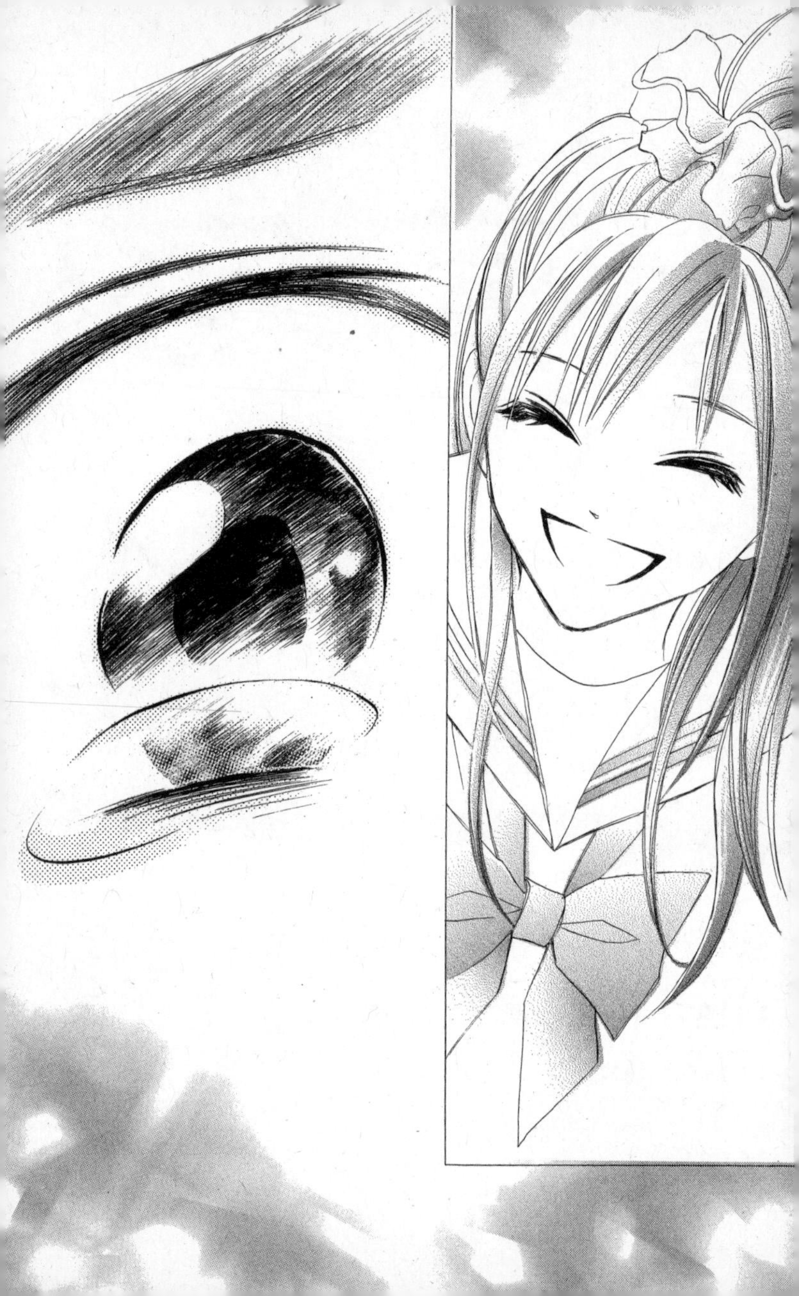

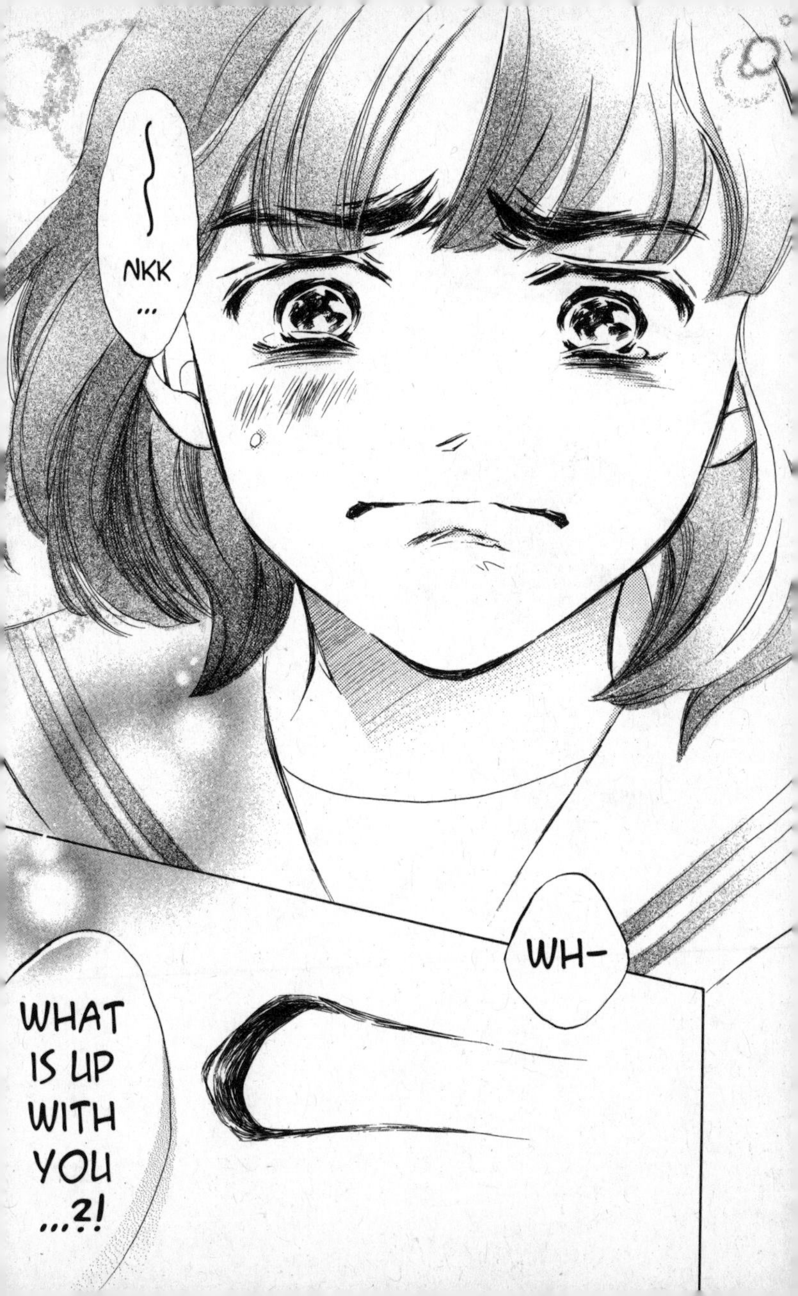
NKK...
WH-
WHAT IS UP WITH YOU...?!

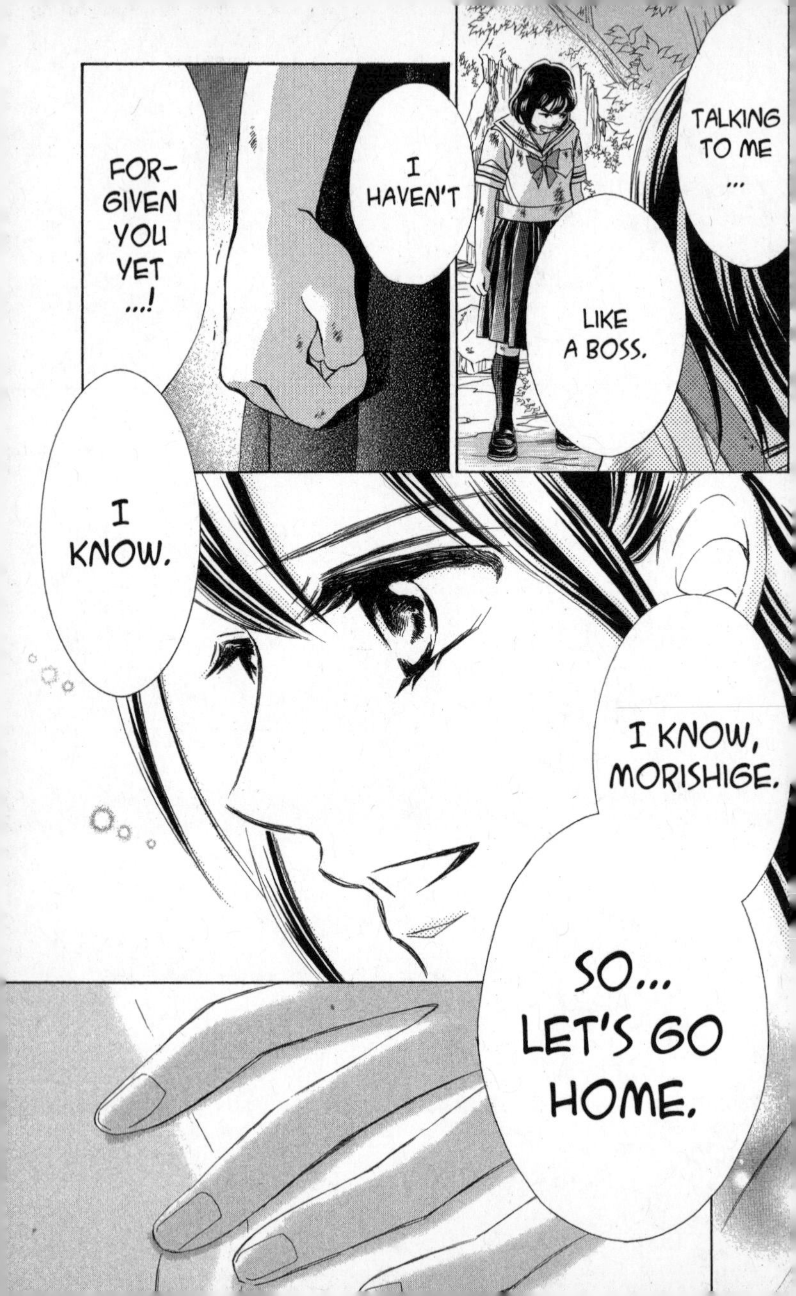
TALKING TO ME ...
LIKE A BOSS.
I HAVEN'T
FOR-GIVEN YOU YET ...!
I KNOW.
I KNOW, MORISHIGE.
SO... LET'S GO HOME.

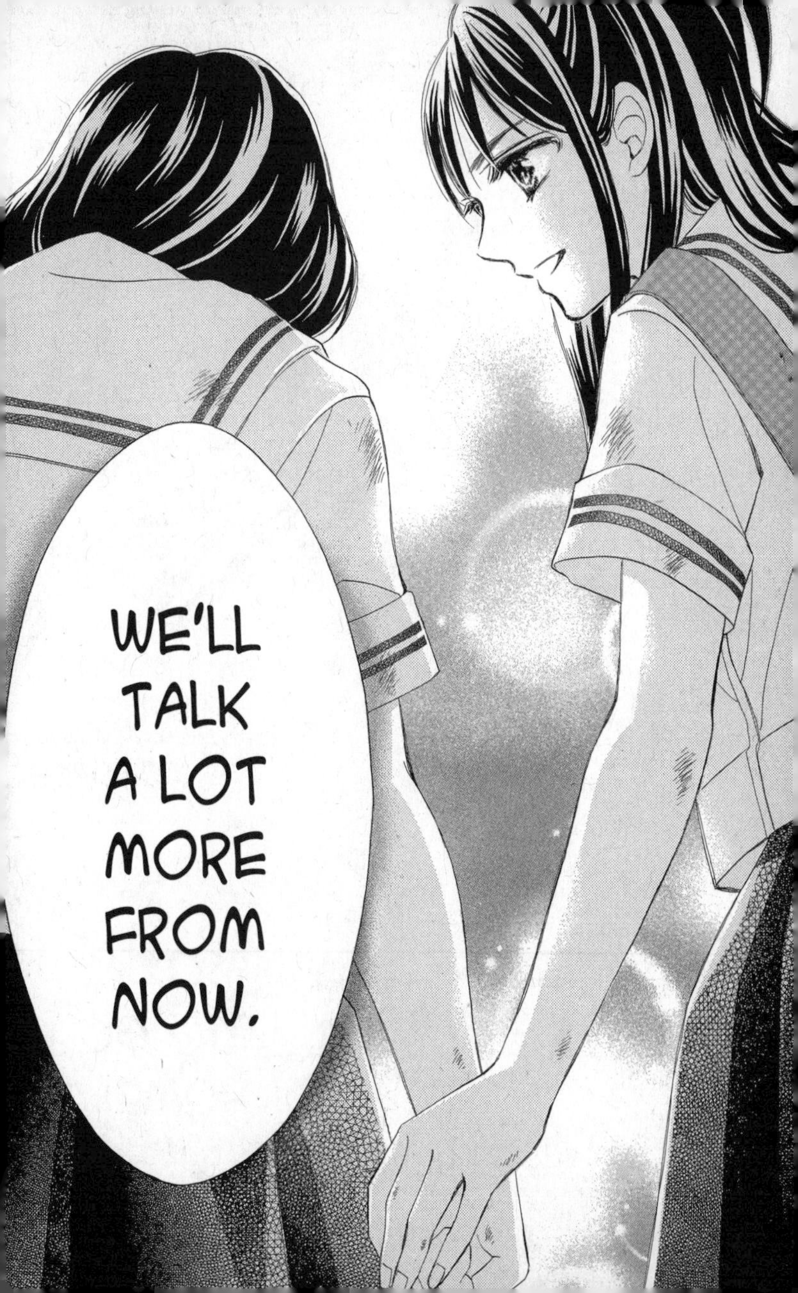
WE'LL TALK A LOT MORE FROM NOW.

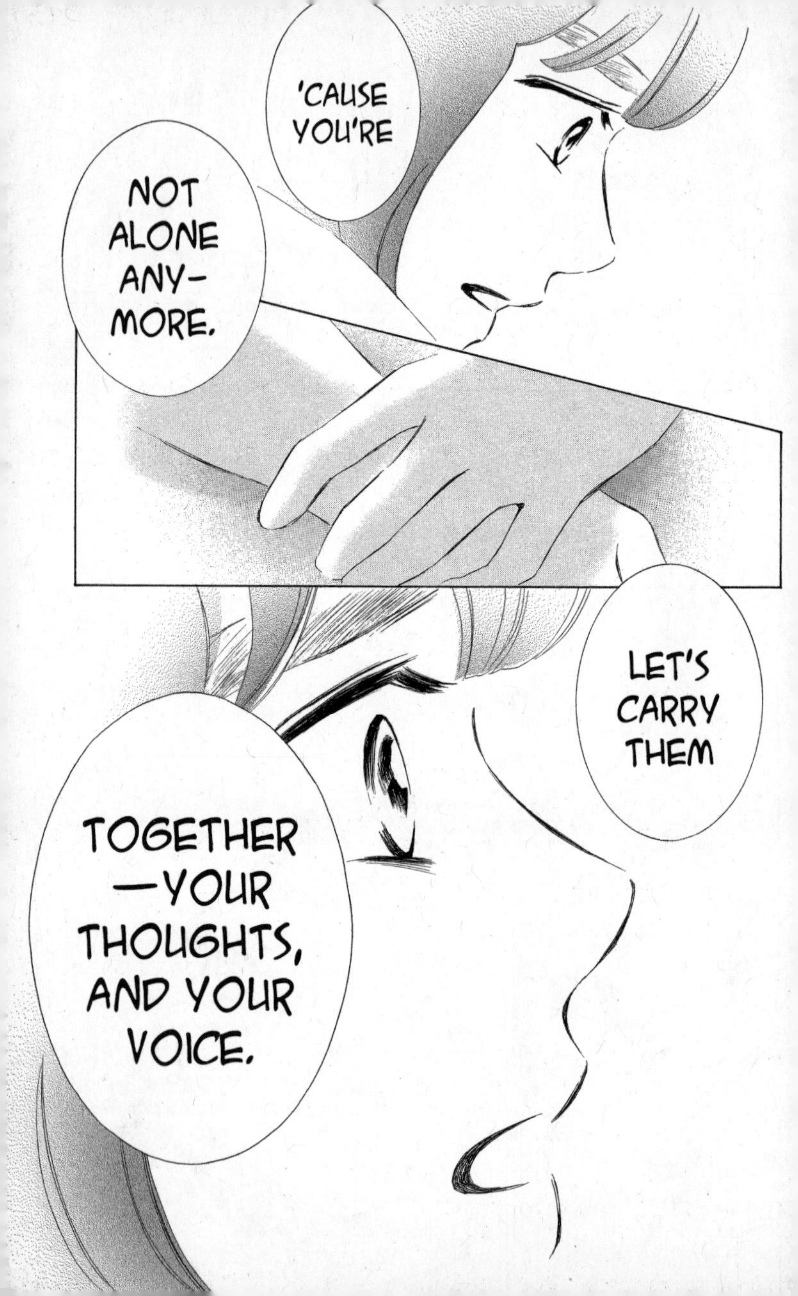
'CAUSE YOU'RE
NOT ALONE ANY-MORE.
LET'S CARRY THEM
TOGETHER—YOUR THOUGHTS, AND YOUR VOICE.

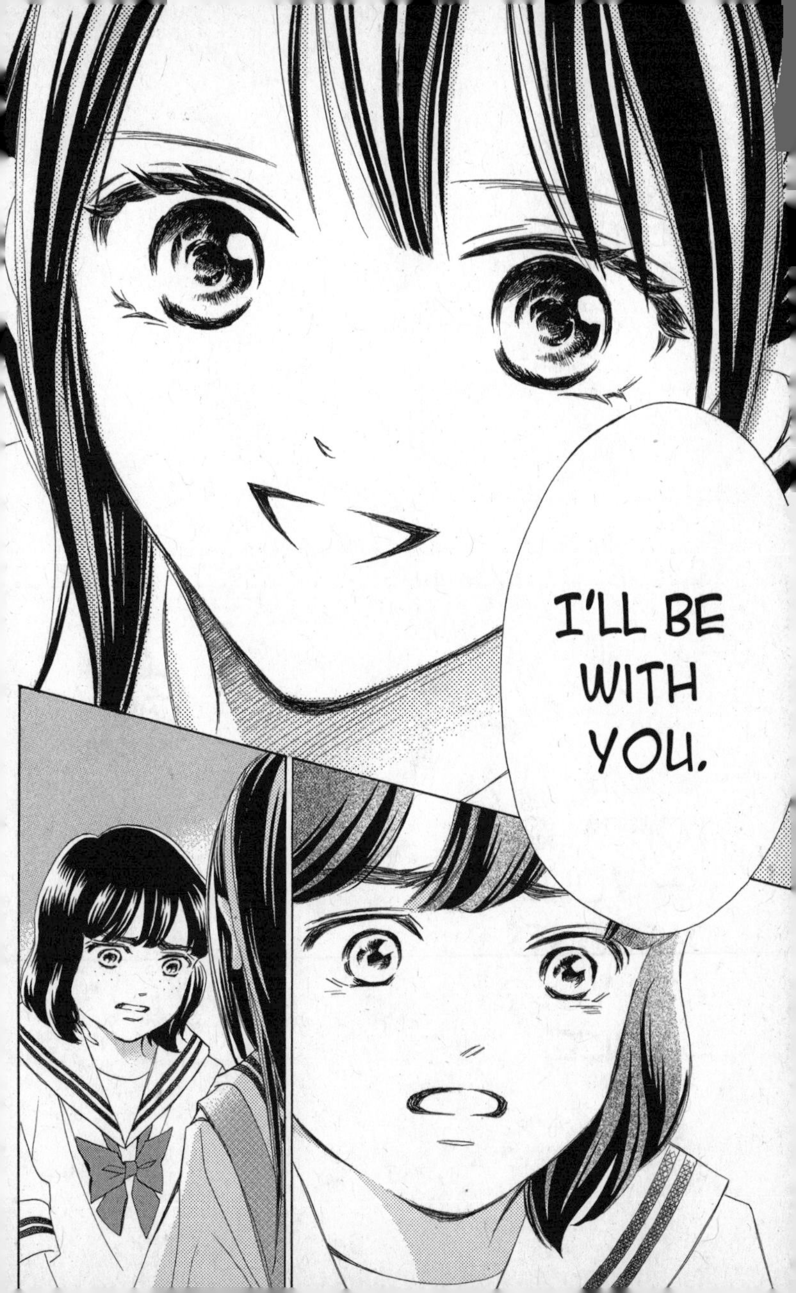
I'LL BE WITH YOU.

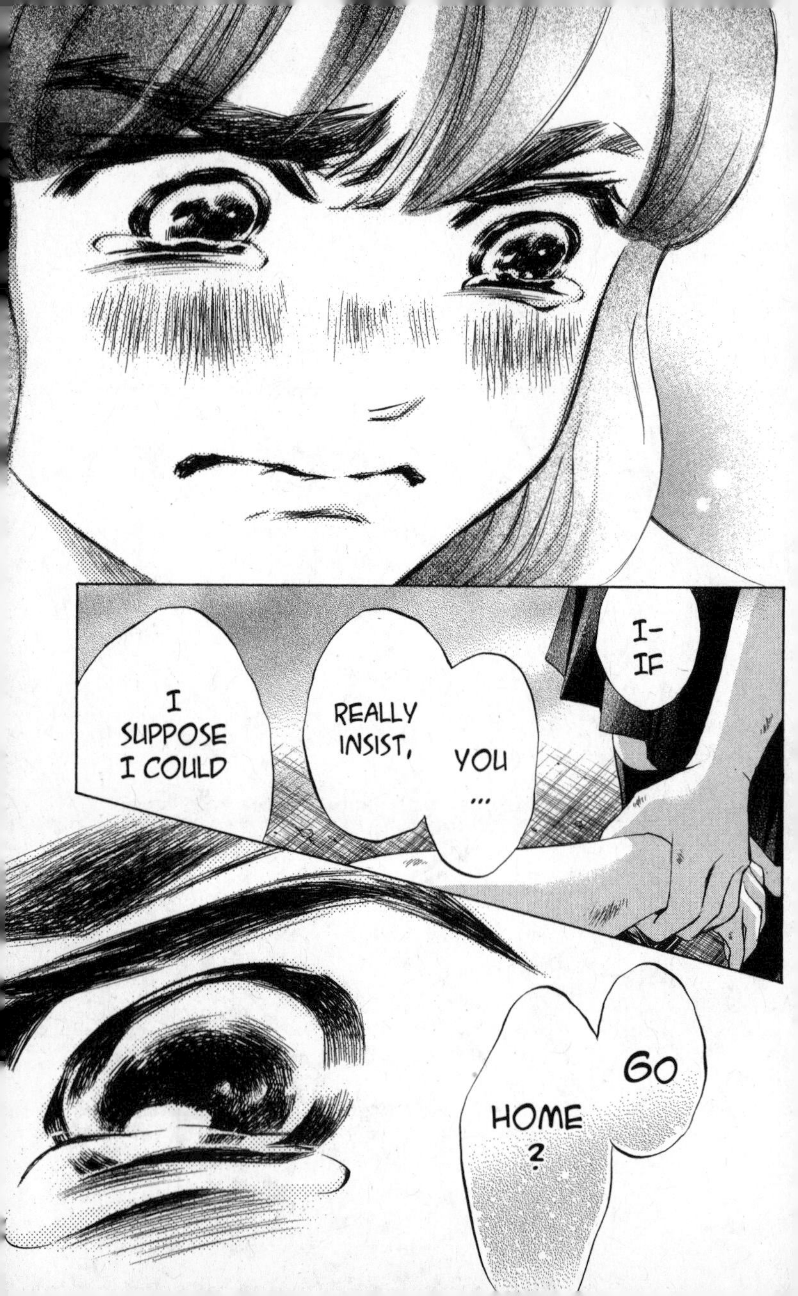
I-IF
YOU ...
REALLY INSIST,
I SUPPOSE I COULD
GO HOME?

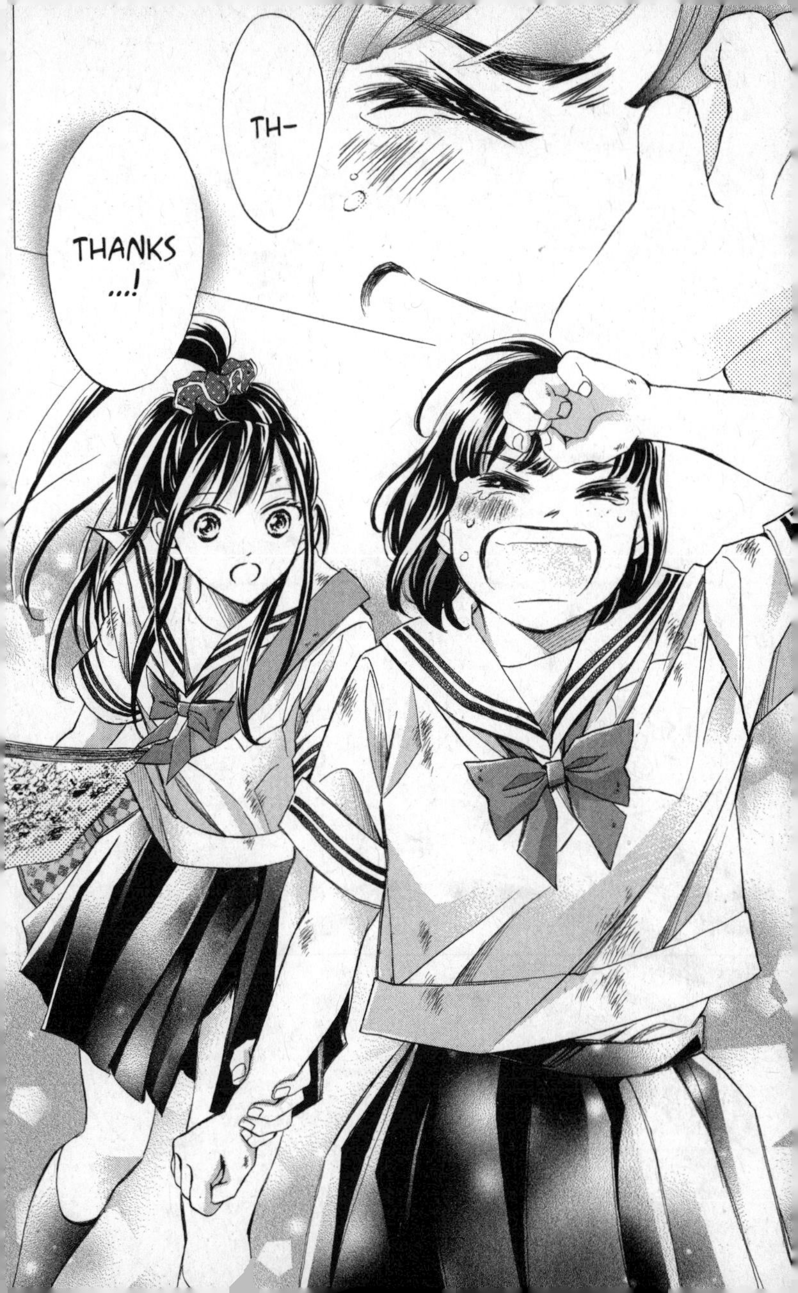
TH-
THANKS ...!

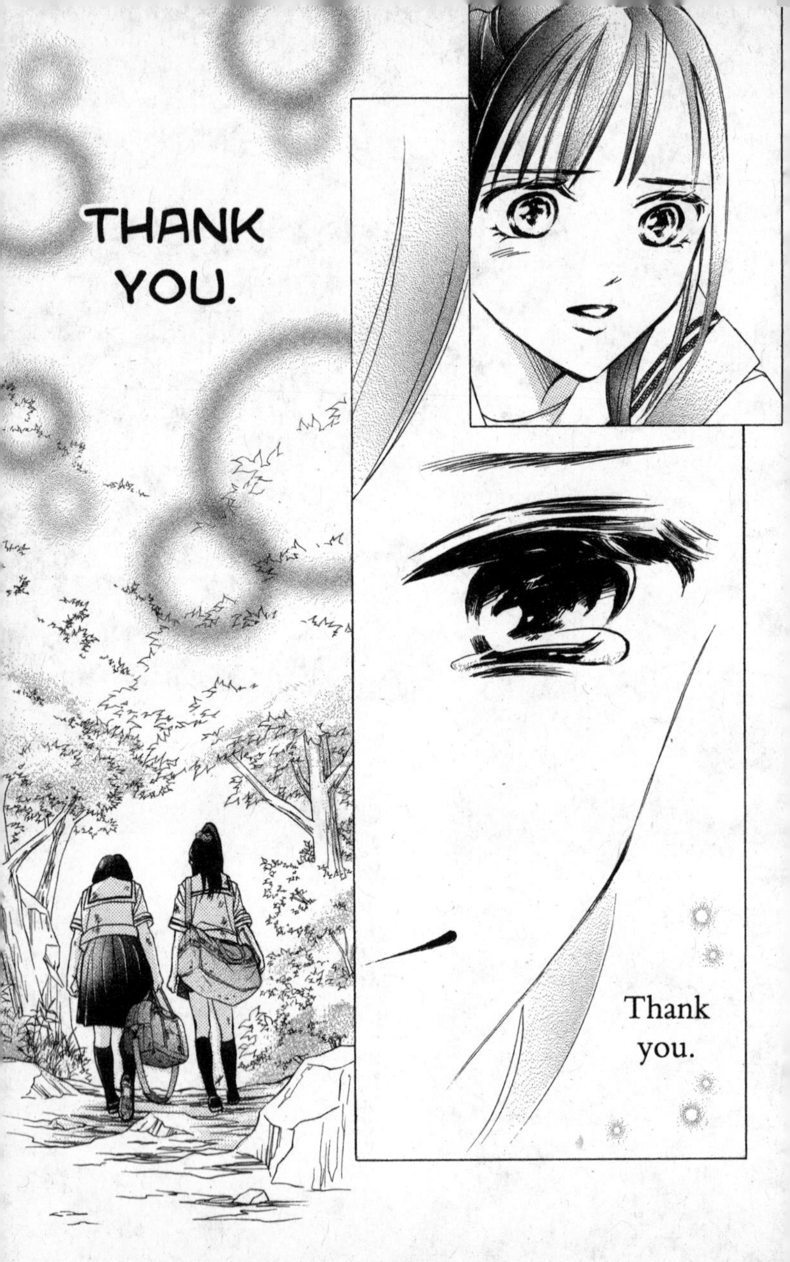
Thank you.
THANK YOU.

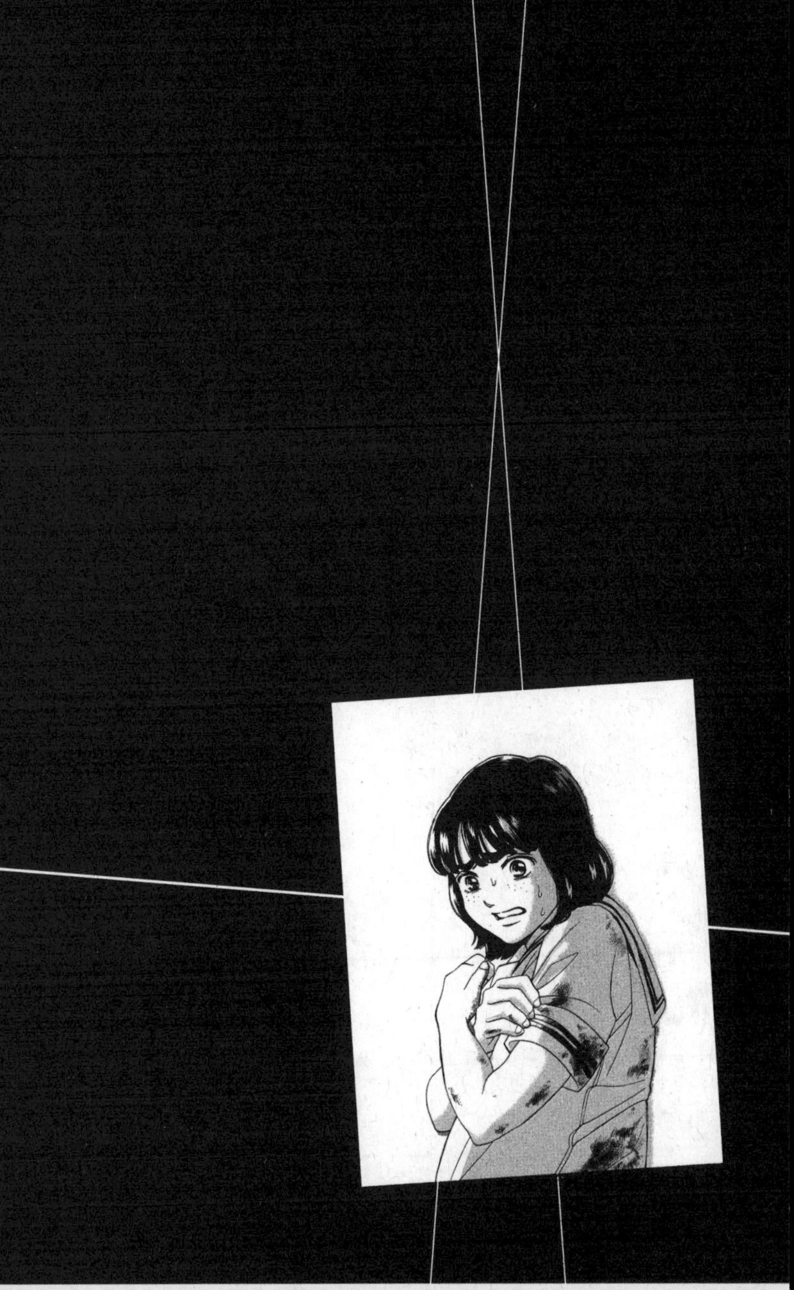

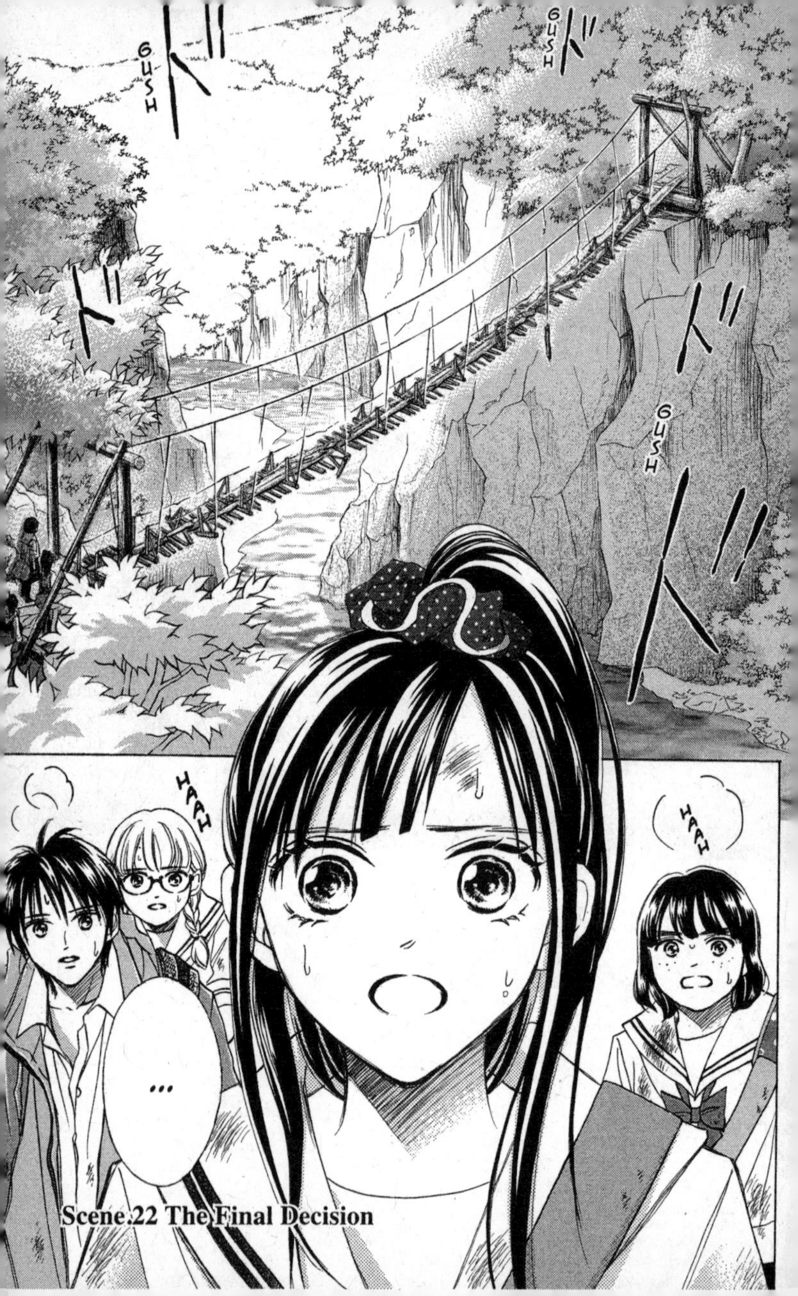
GUSH
GUSH
GUSH
HAAH
HAAH
...

Scene.22 The Final Decision

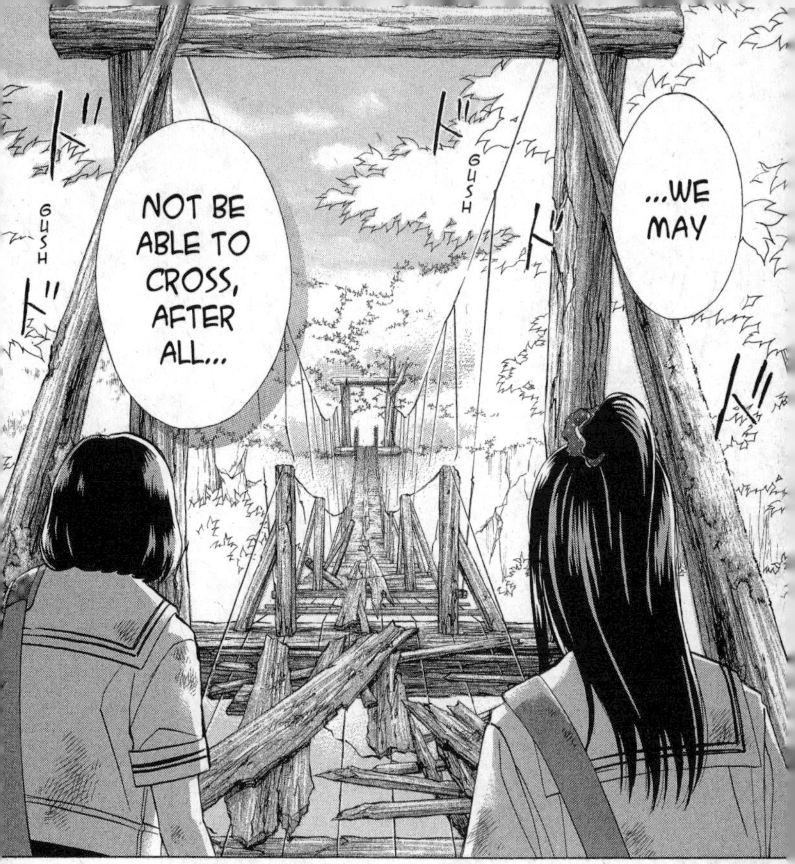
...WE MAY
GUSH
NOT BE ABLE TO CROSS, AFTER ALL...
GUSH

LIMIT

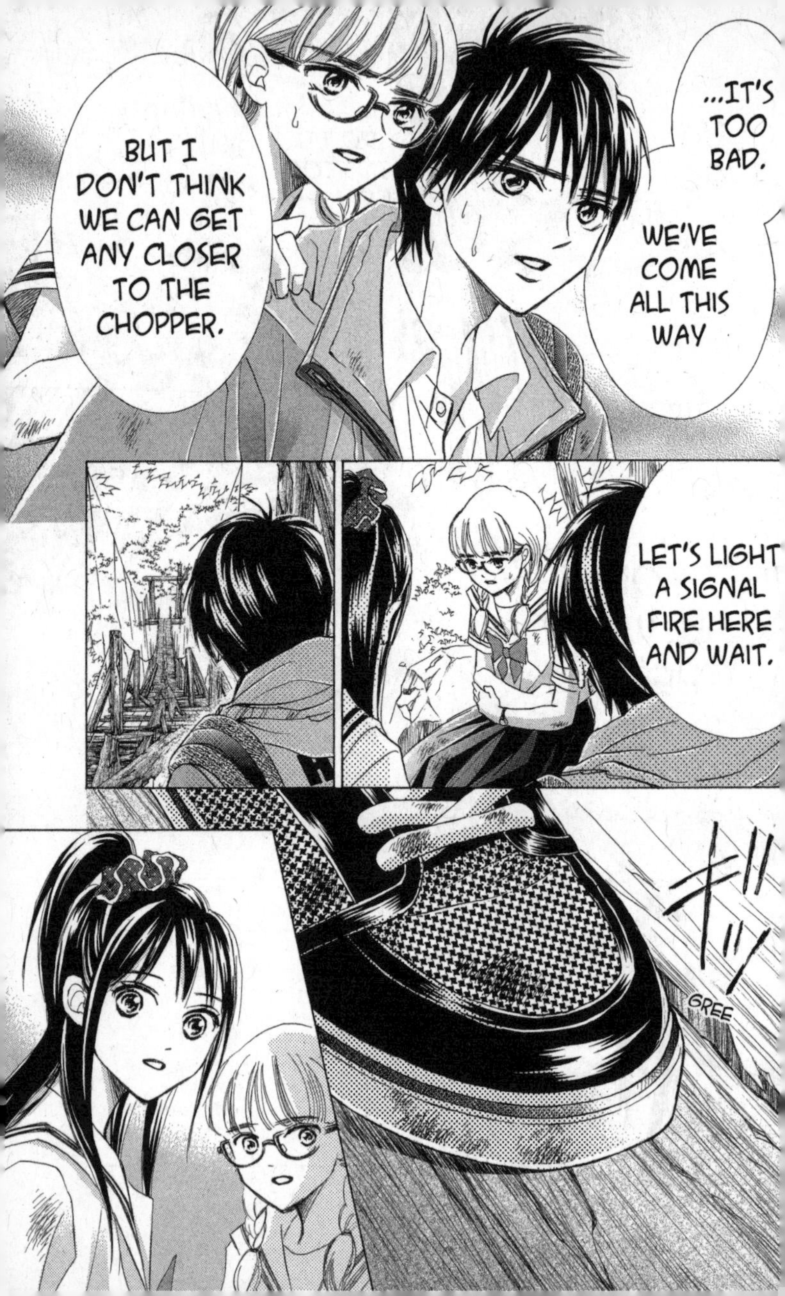
...IT'S TOO BAD.
WE'VE COME ALL THIS WAY
BUT I DON'T THINK WE CAN GET ANY CLOSER TO THE CHOPPER.
LET'S LIGHT A SIGNAL FIRE HERE AND WAIT.
GREE

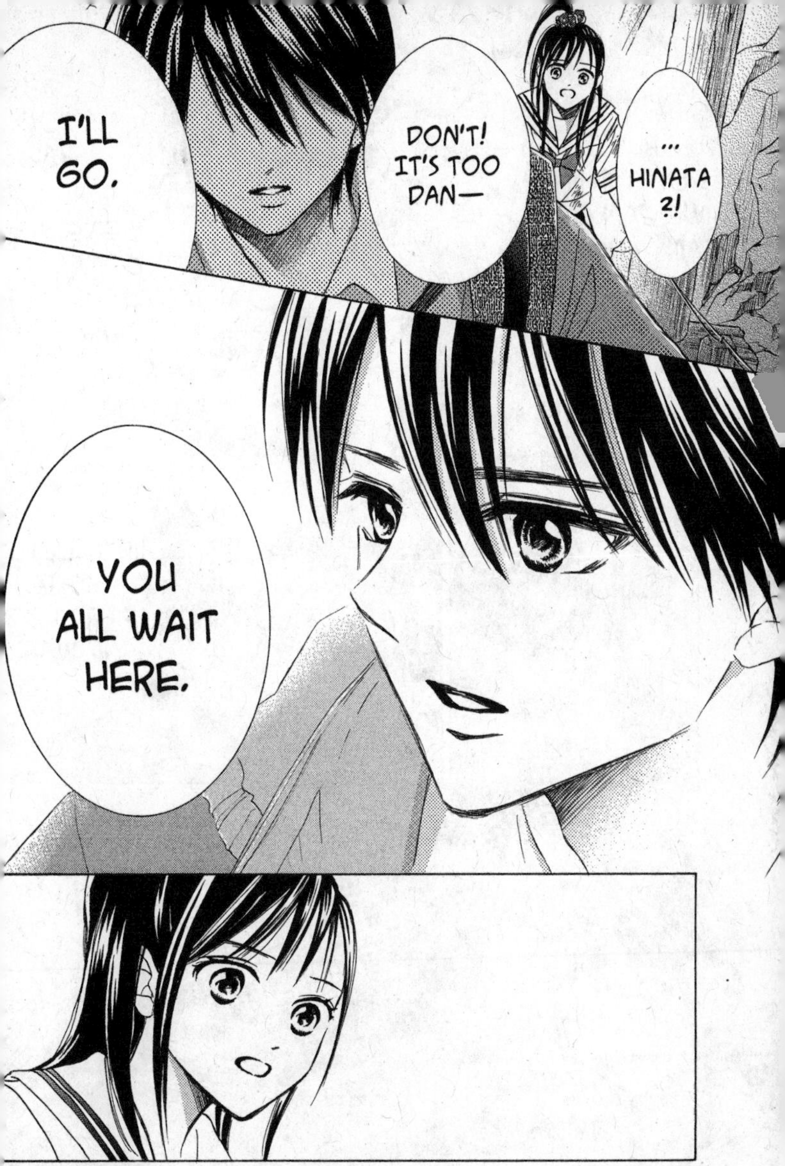
... HINATA ?!
DON'T! IT'S TOO DAN—
I'LL GO.
YOU ALL WAIT HERE.

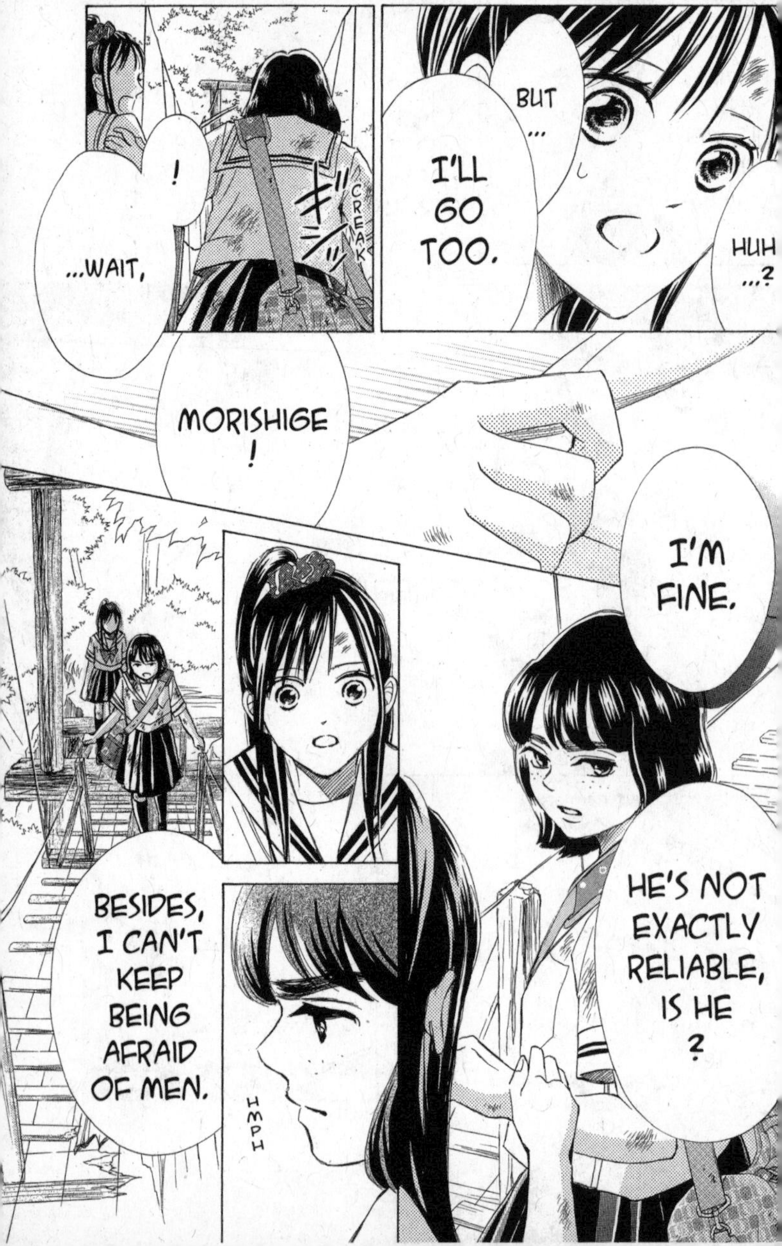
HUH ...?
BUT ...
I'LL GO TOO.
CREAK
!
...WAIT,
MORISHIGE !
I'M FINE.
HE'S NOT EXACTLY RELIABLE, IS HE ?
HMPH
BESIDES, I CAN'T KEEP BEING AFRAID OF MEN.

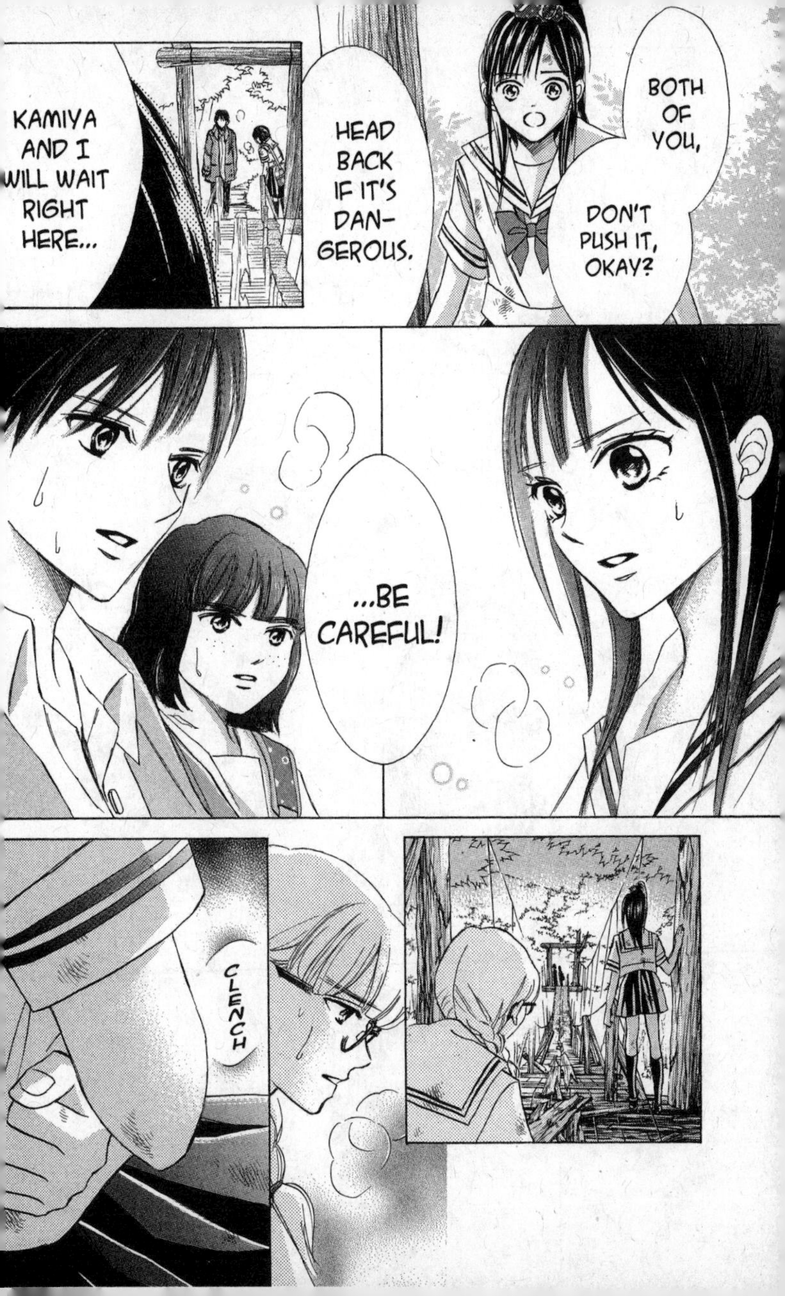
BOTH OF YOU,
DON'T PUSH IT, OKAY?
HEAD BACK IF IT'S DAN-GEROUS.
KAMIYA AND I WILL WAIT RIGHT HERE...
...BE CAREFUL!
CLENCH

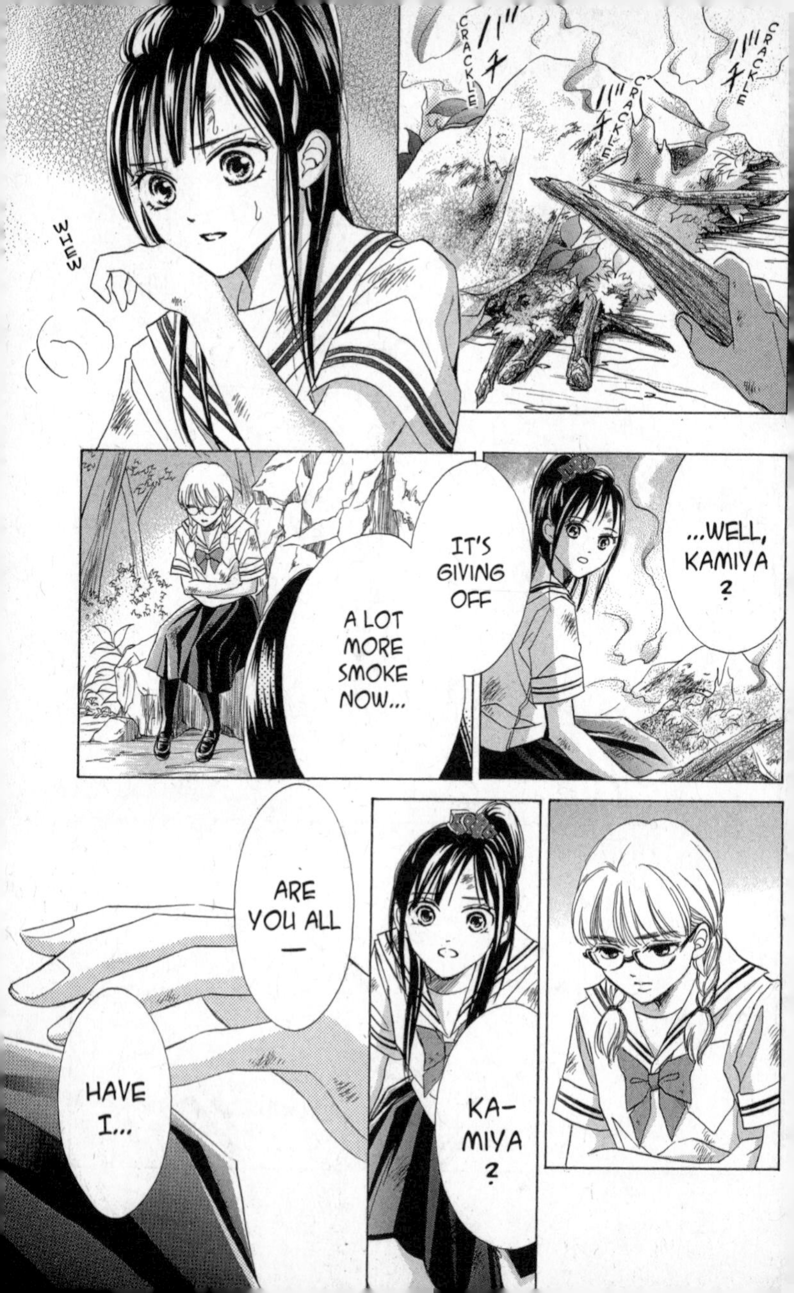

バチ
CRACKLE
バチ
CRACKLE
バチ
CRACKLE
WHEW
...WELL, KAMIYA?
IT'S GIVING OFF
A LOT MORE SMOKE NOW...
KA-MIYA?
ARE YOU ALL —
HAVE I...

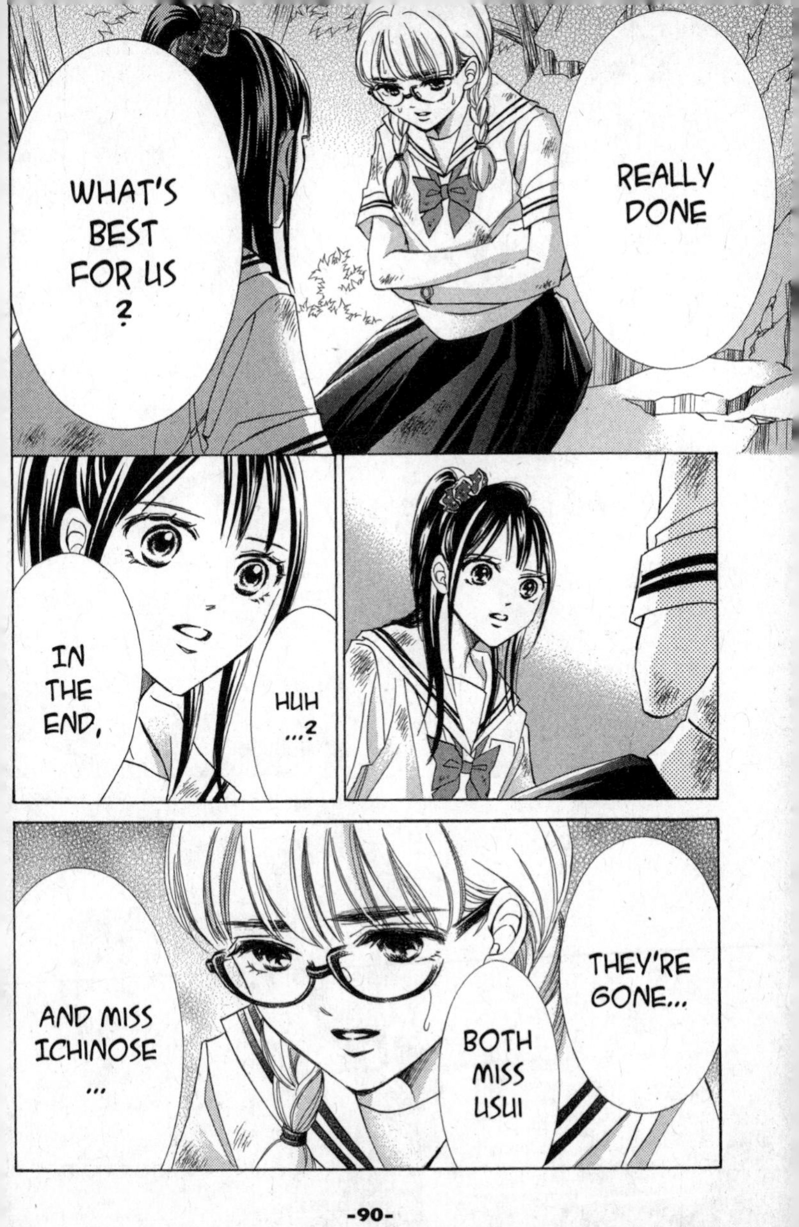
REALLY DONE
WHAT'S BEST FOR US ?
HUH ...?
IN THE END,
THEY'RE GONE...
BOTH MISS USUI
AND MISS ICHINOSE ...

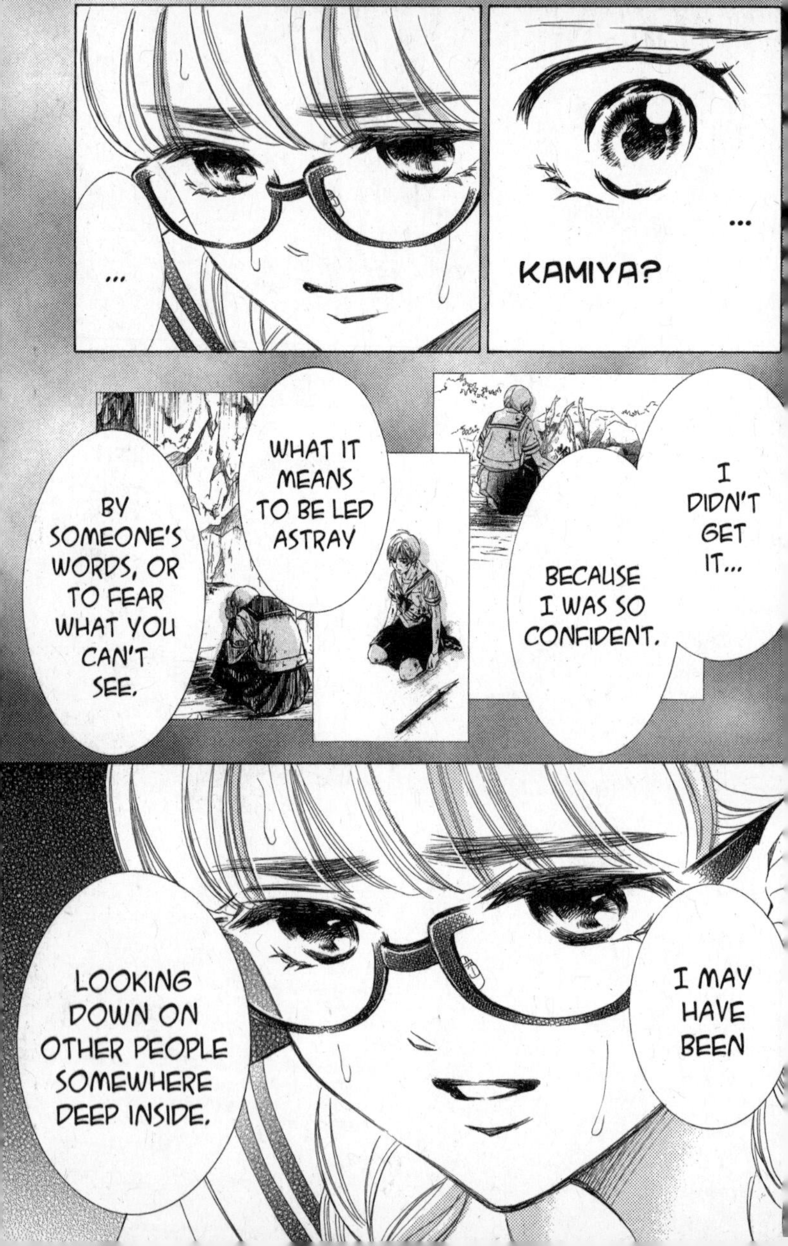
...
KAMIYA?
...
I DIDN'T GET IT...
BECAUSE I WAS SO CONFIDENT.
WHAT IT MEANS TO BE LED ASTRAY
BY SOMEONE'S WORDS, OR TO FEAR WHAT YOU CAN'T SEE.
I MAY HAVE BEEN
LOOKING DOWN ON OTHER PEOPLE SOMEWHERE DEEP INSIDE.

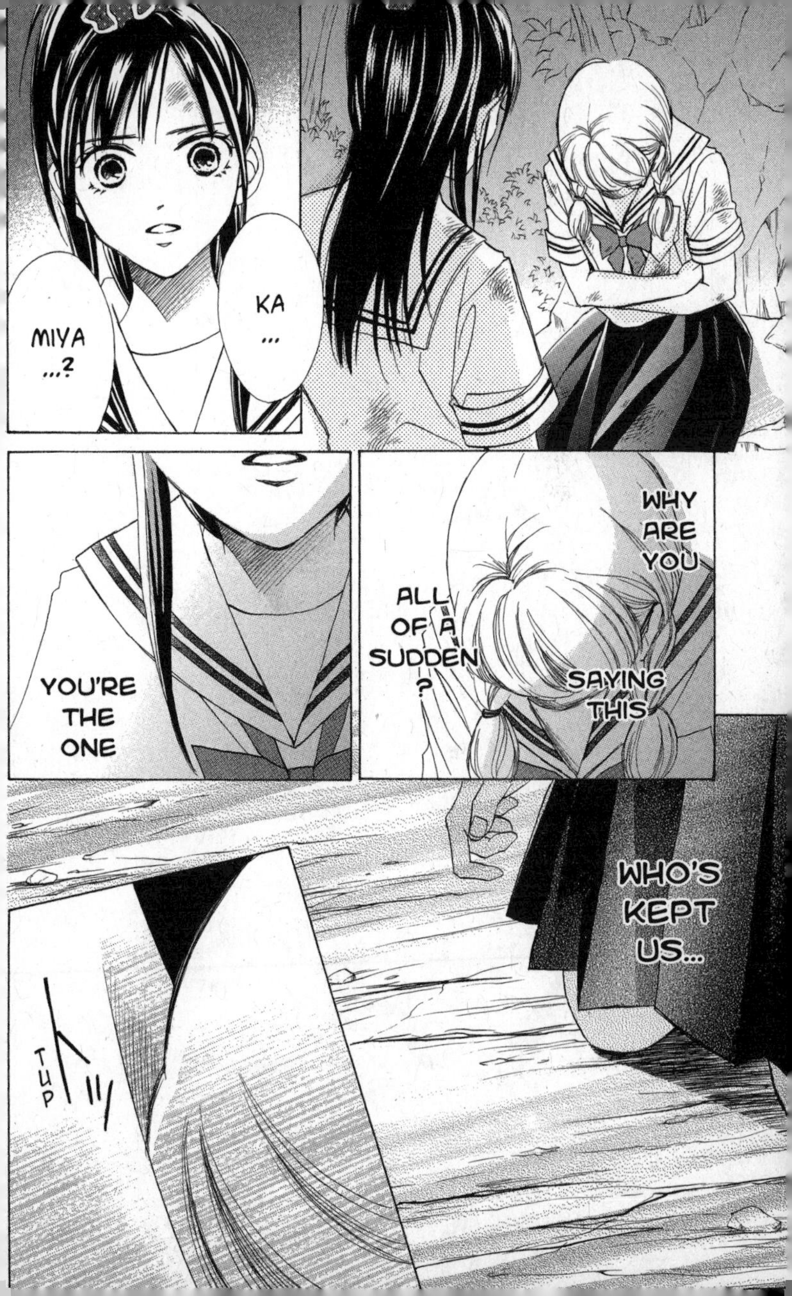
KA ...
MIYA ...?
WHY ARE YOU SAYING THIS
ALL OF A SUDDEN ?
YOU'RE THE ONE
WHO'S KEPT US...
TUP

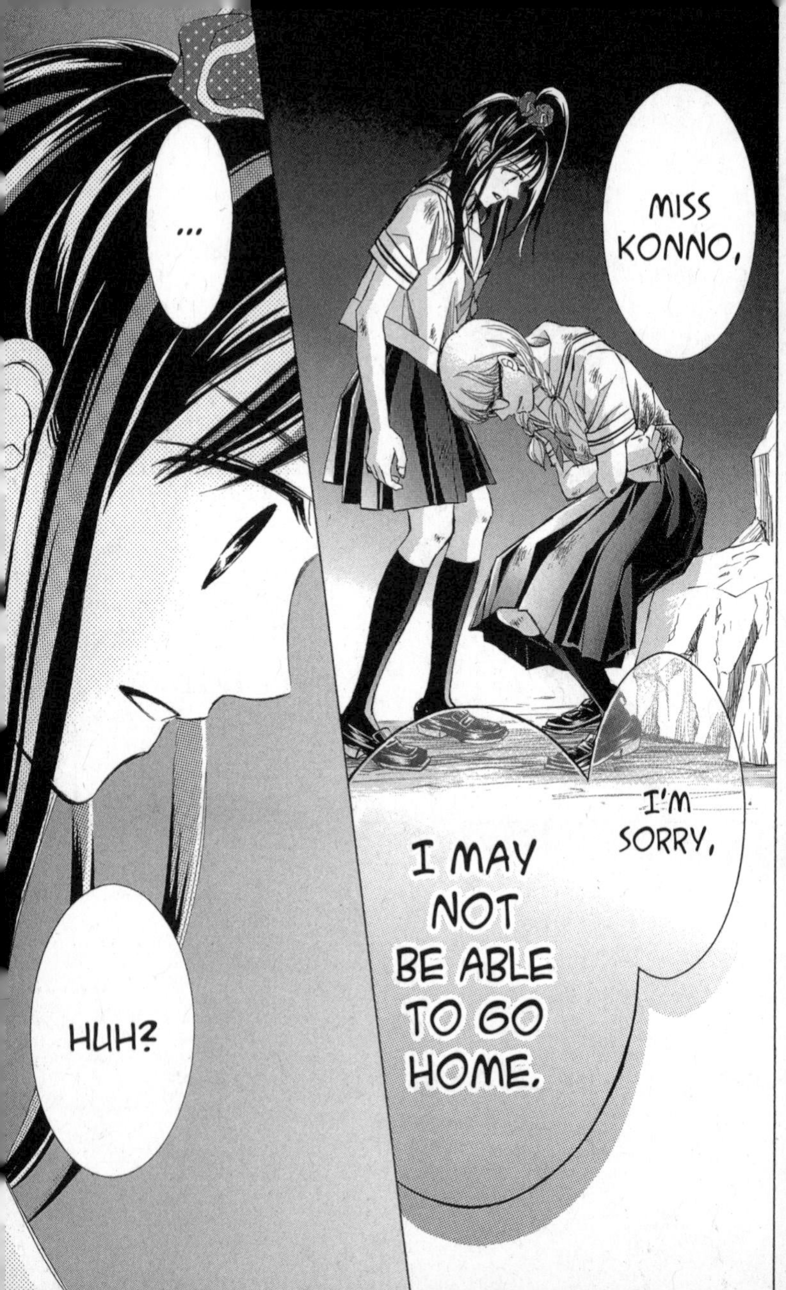
MISS KONNO,
I'M SORRY,
I MAY NOT BE ABLE TO GO HOME.
...
HUH?

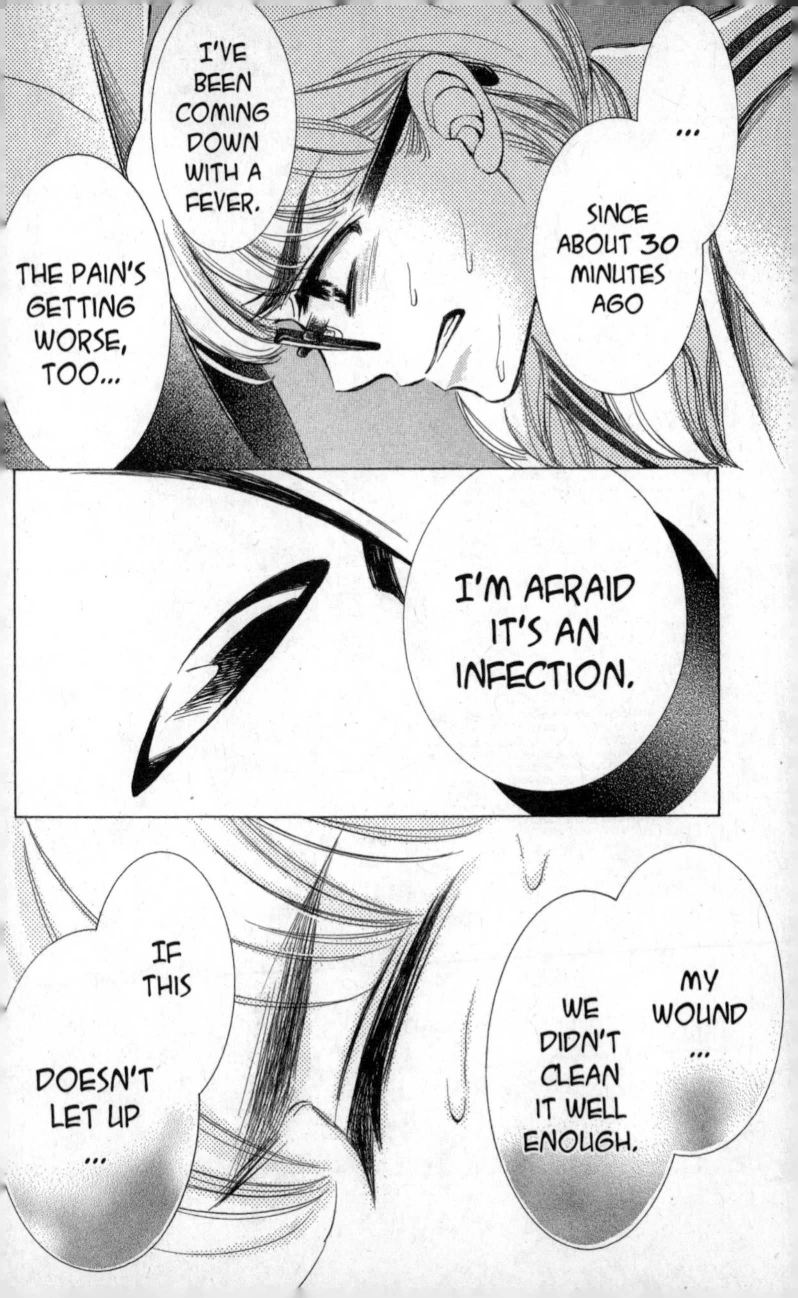
...
SINCE ABOUT 30 MINUTES AGO
I'VE BEEN COMING DOWN WITH A FEVER.
THE PAIN'S GETTING WORSE, TOO...
I'M AFRAID IT'S AN INFECTION.
MY WOUND ...
WE DIDN'T CLEAN IT WELL ENOUGH.
IF THIS
DOESN'T LET UP ...

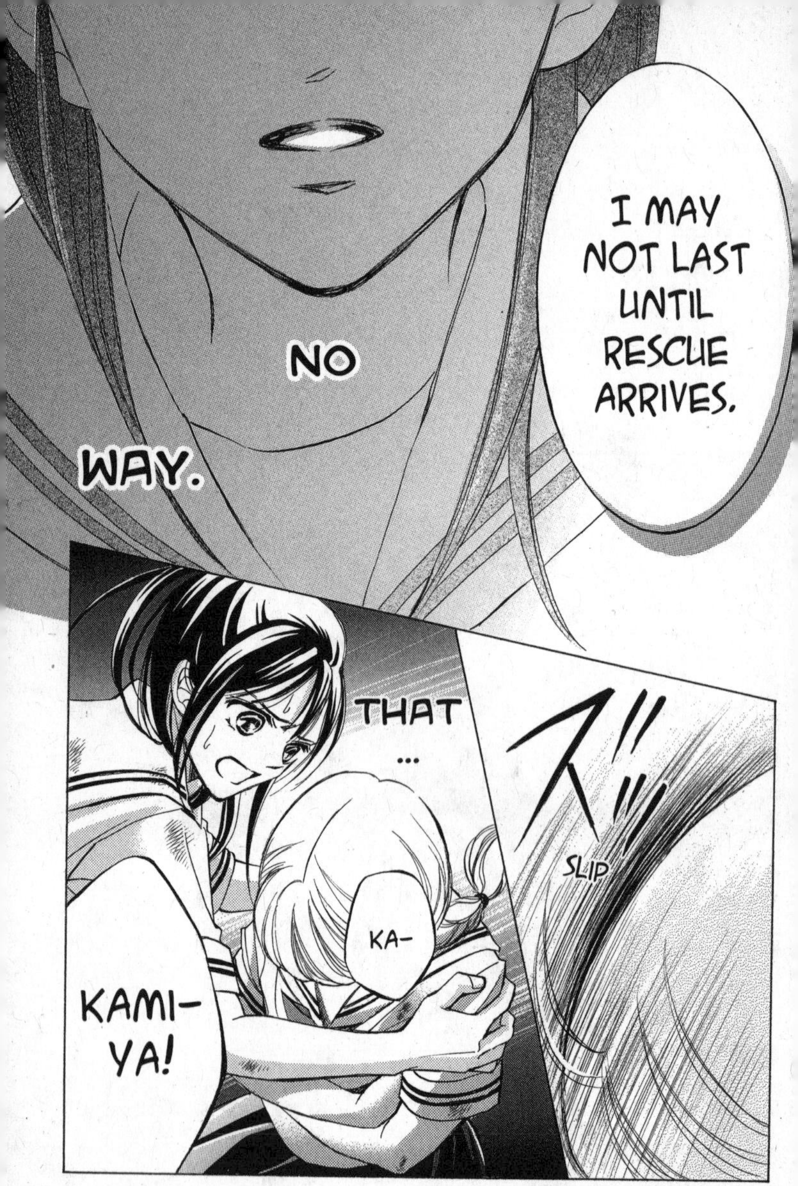
I MAY NOT LAST UNTIL RESCUE ARRIVES.
NO
WAY.
ズ
SLIP
THAT ...
KA-
KAMI-YA!

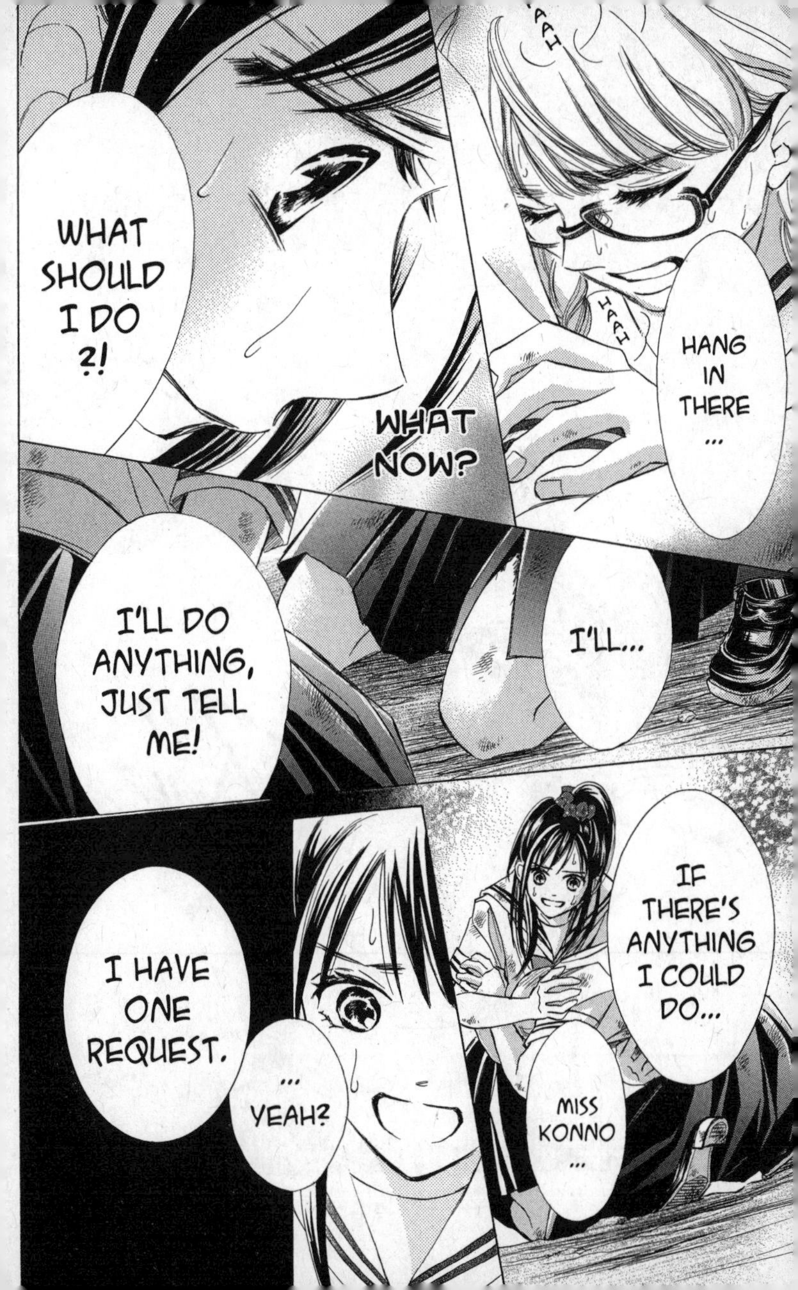
HAAH
HAAH
HANG IN THERE ...
WHAT SHOULD I DO ?!
WHAT NOW?
I'LL...
I'LL DO ANYTHING, JUST TELL ME!
IF THERE'S ANYTHING I COULD DO...
MISS KONNO ...
... YEAH?
I HAVE ONE REQUEST.

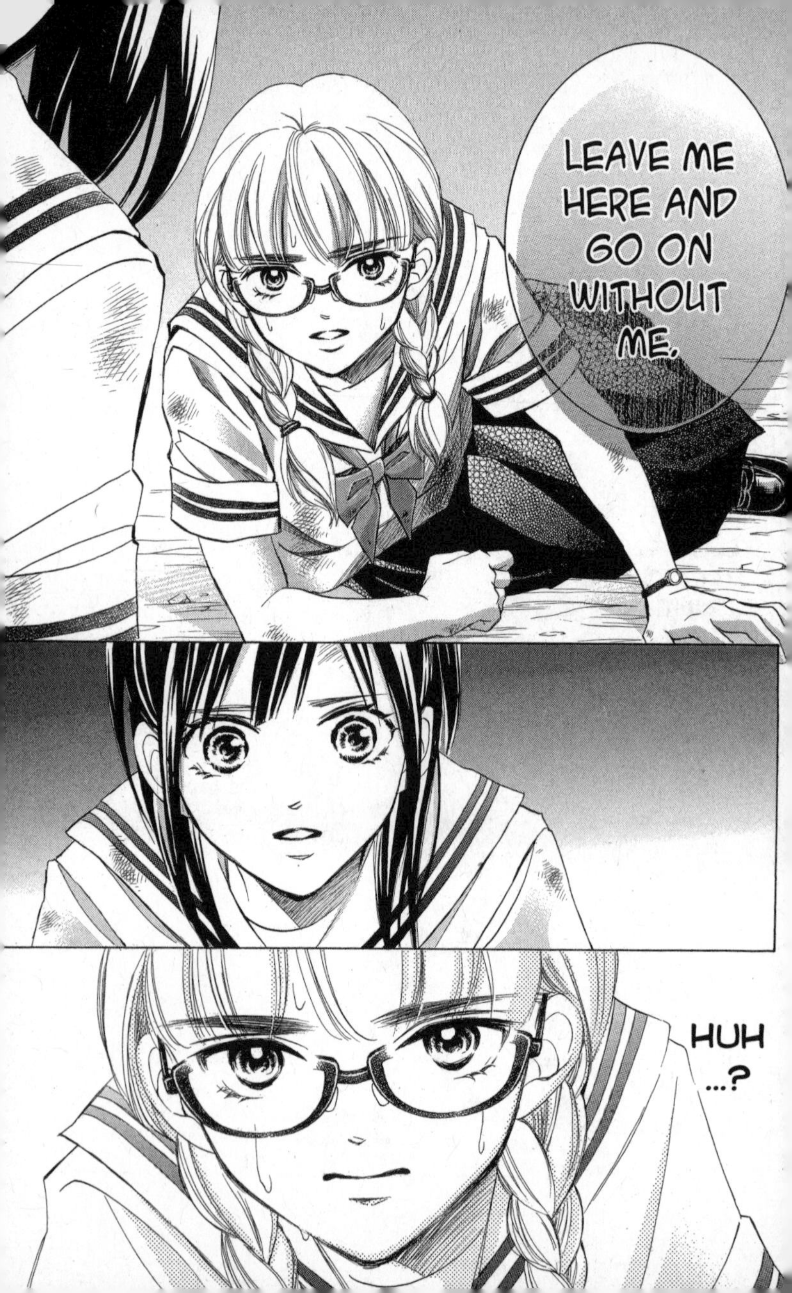
LEAVE ME HERE AND GO ON WITHOUT ME.
HUH ...?

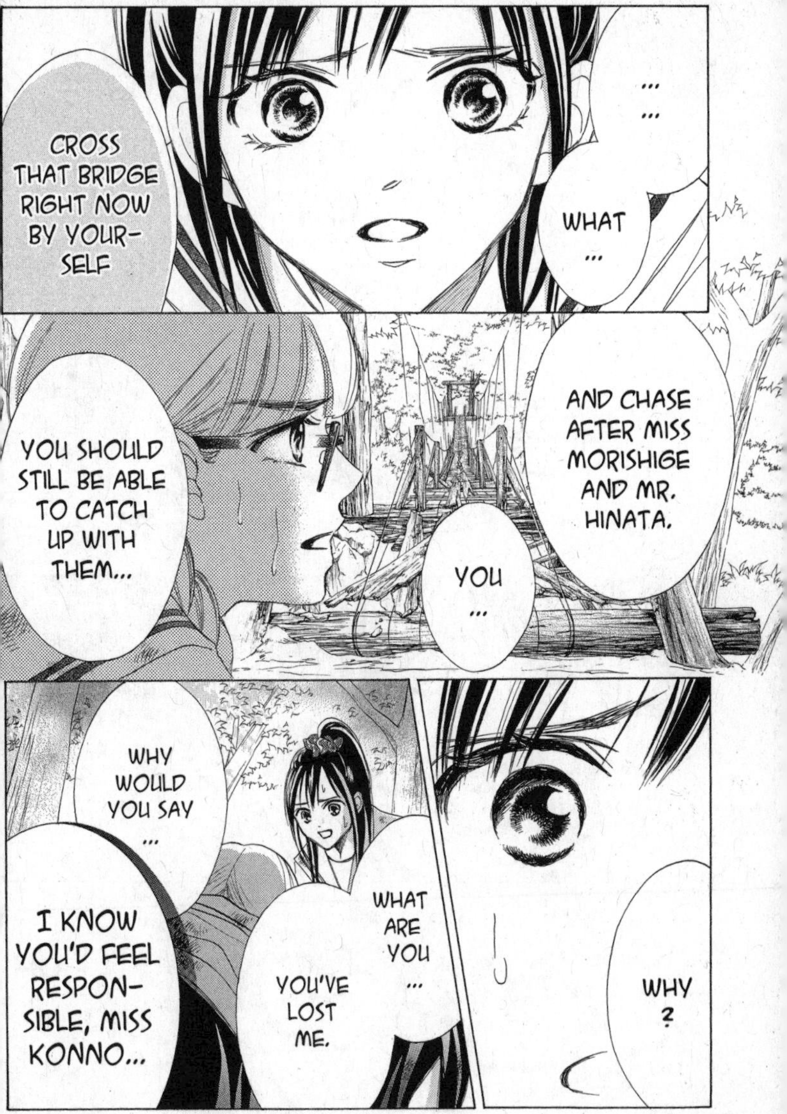
... ...
WHAT ...
CROSS THAT BRIDGE RIGHT NOW BY YOURSELF
AND CHASE AFTER MISS MORISHIGE AND MR. HINATA.
YOU ...
YOU SHOULD STILL BE ABLE TO CATCH UP WITH THEM...
WHY ?
WHY WOULD YOU SAY ...
WHAT ARE YOU ...
YOU'VE LOST ME.
I KNOW YOU'D FEEL RESPONSIBLE, MISS KONNO...

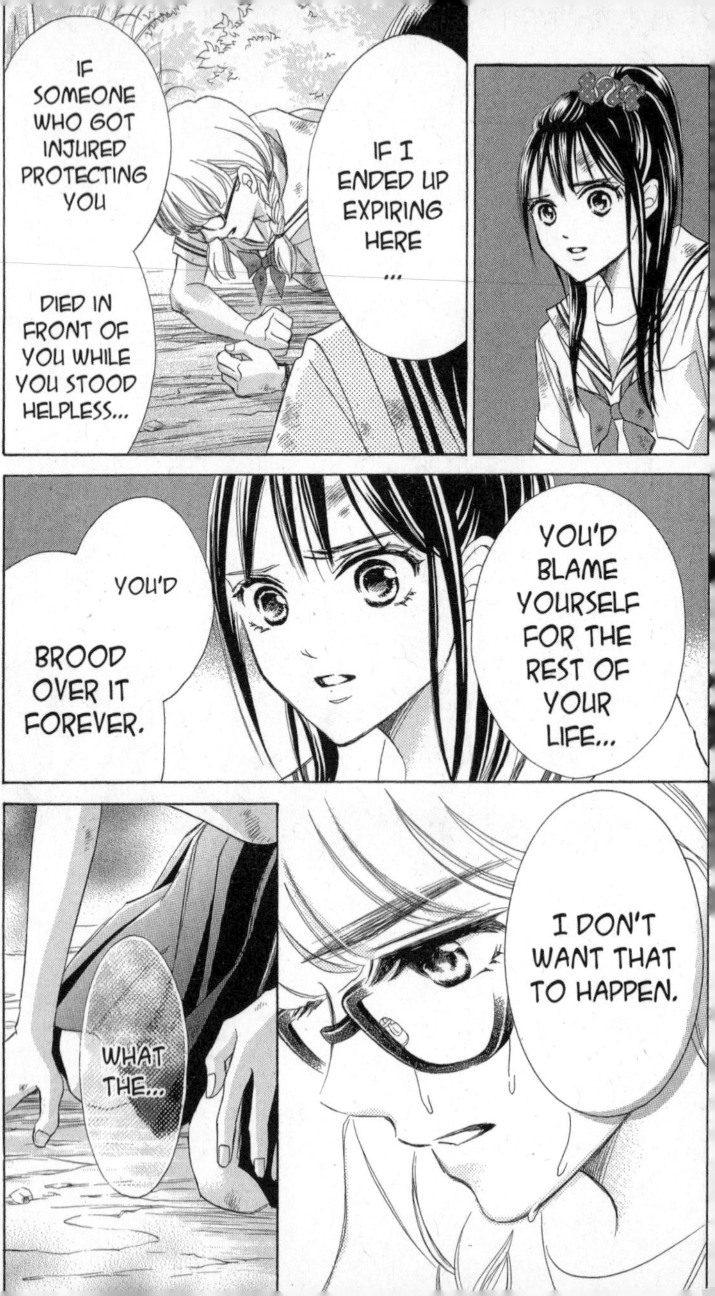
IF I ENDED UP EXPIRING HERE ...
IF SOMEONE WHO GOT INJURED PROTECTING YOU
DIED IN FRONT OF YOU WHILE YOU STOOD HELPLESS...
YOU'D BLAME YOURSELF FOR THE REST OF YOUR LIFE...
YOU'D
BROOD OVER IT FOREVER.
I DON'T WANT THAT TO HAPPEN.
WHAT THE...

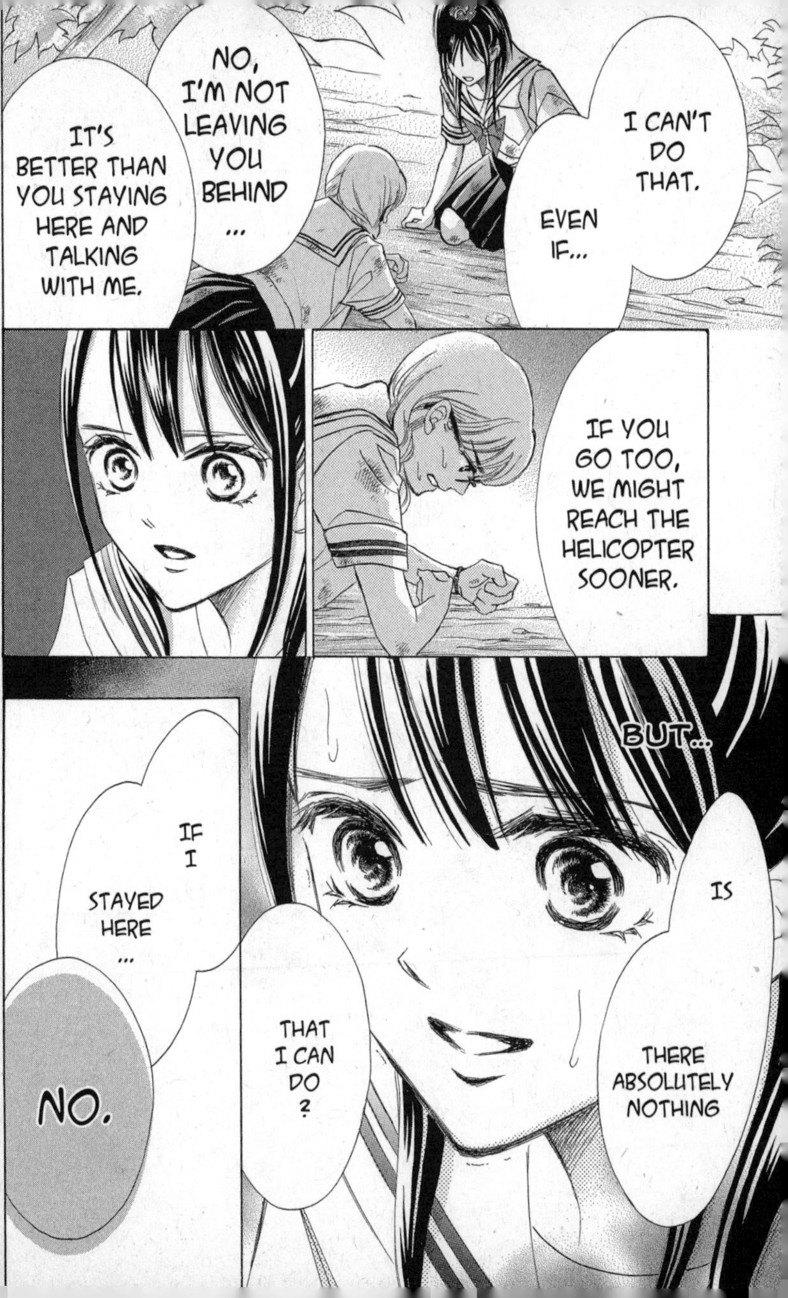
I CAN'T DO THAT.
EVEN IF...
NO, I'M NOT LEAVING YOU BEHIND ...
IT'S BETTER THAN YOU STAYING HERE AND TALKING WITH ME.
IF YOU GO TOO, WE MIGHT REACH THE HELICOPTER SOONER.
BUT...
IS THERE ABSOLUTELY NOTHING
THAT I CAN DO ?
IF I STAYED HERE ...
NO.

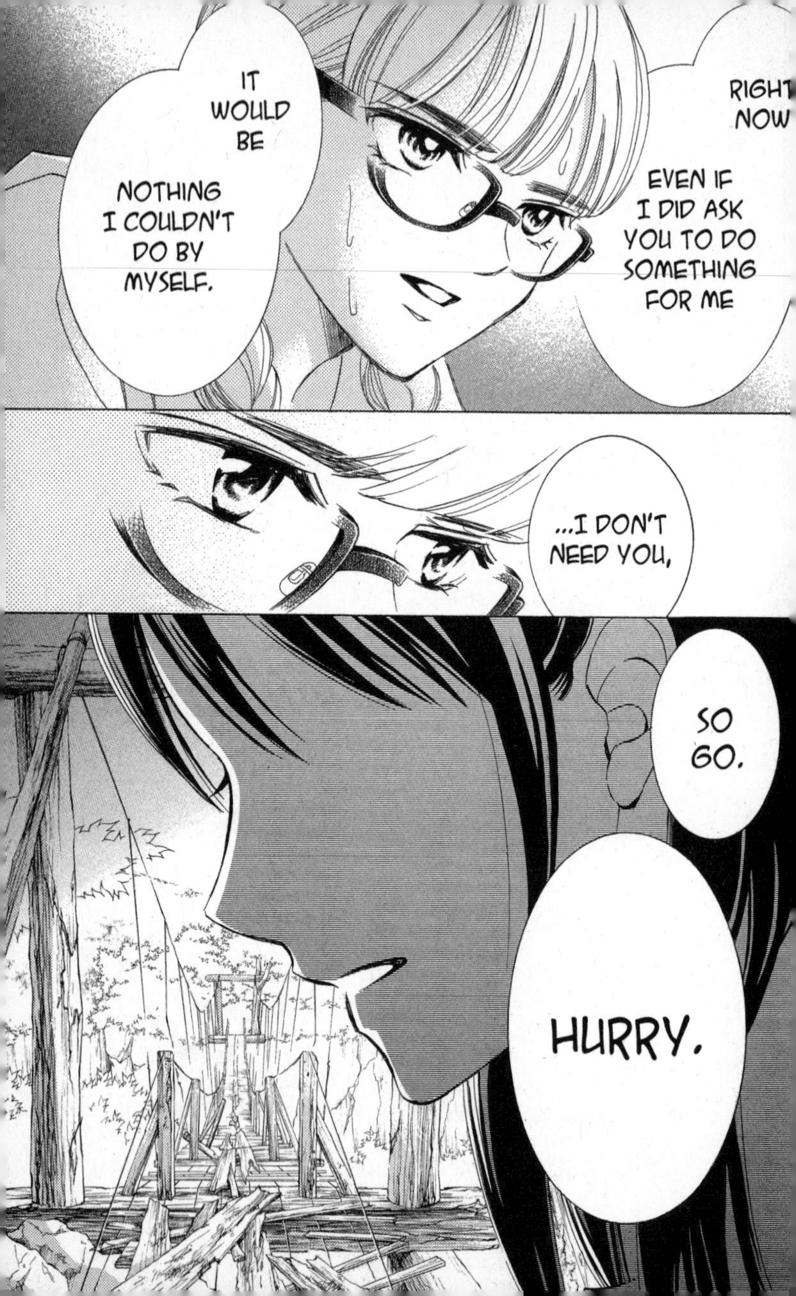
RIGHT NOW
EVEN IF I DID ASK YOU TO DO SOMETHING FOR ME
IT WOULD BE
NOTHING I COULDN'T DO BY MYSELF.
...I DON'T NEED YOU,
SO GO.
HURRY.

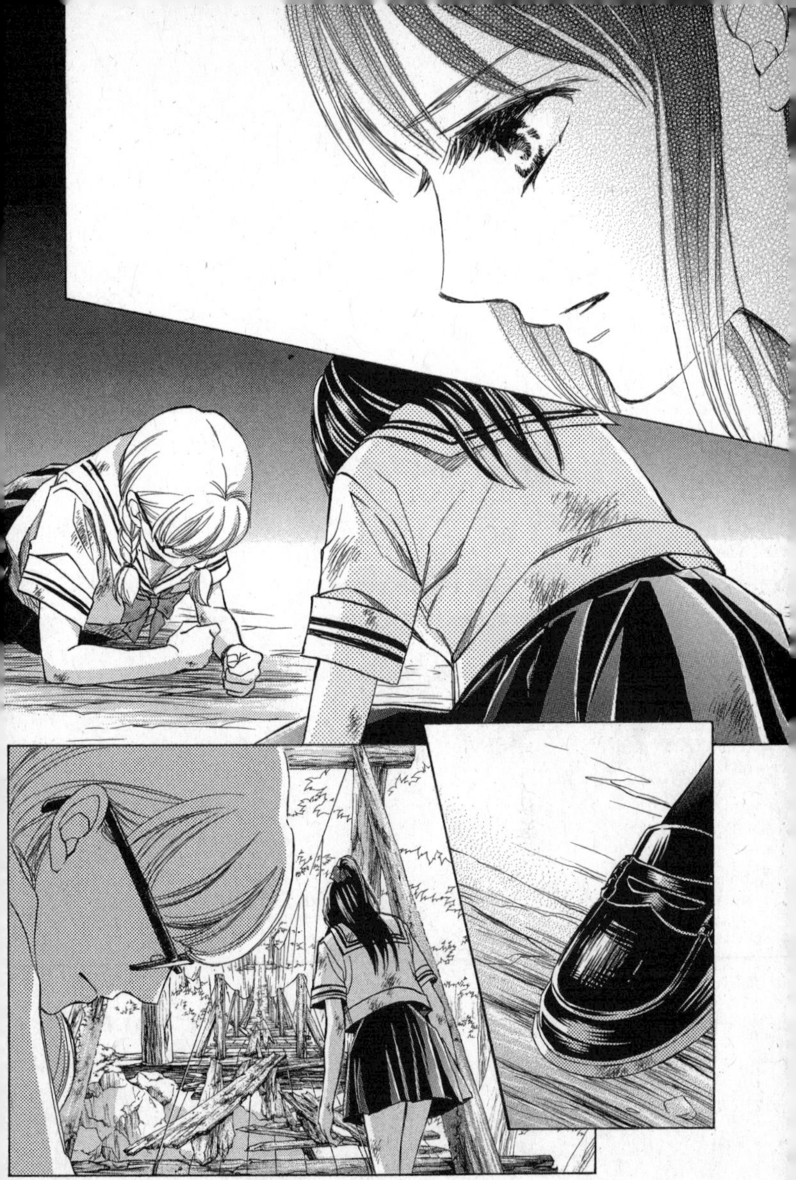

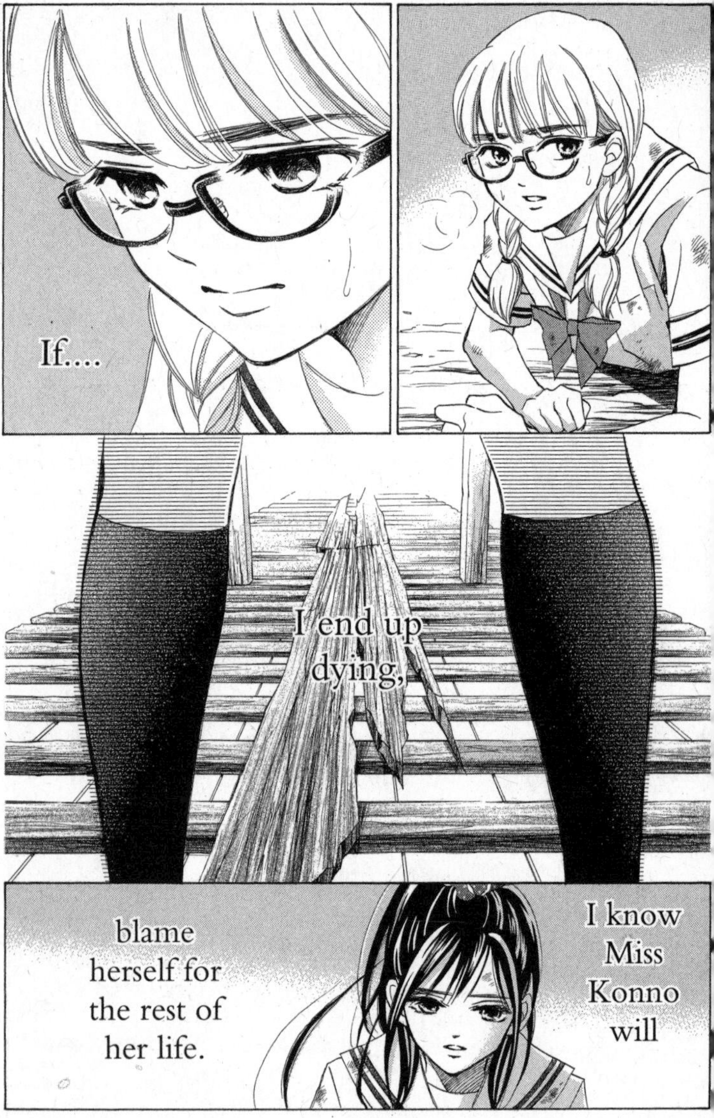
If....
I end up dying,
I know Miss Konno will
blame herself for the rest of her life.

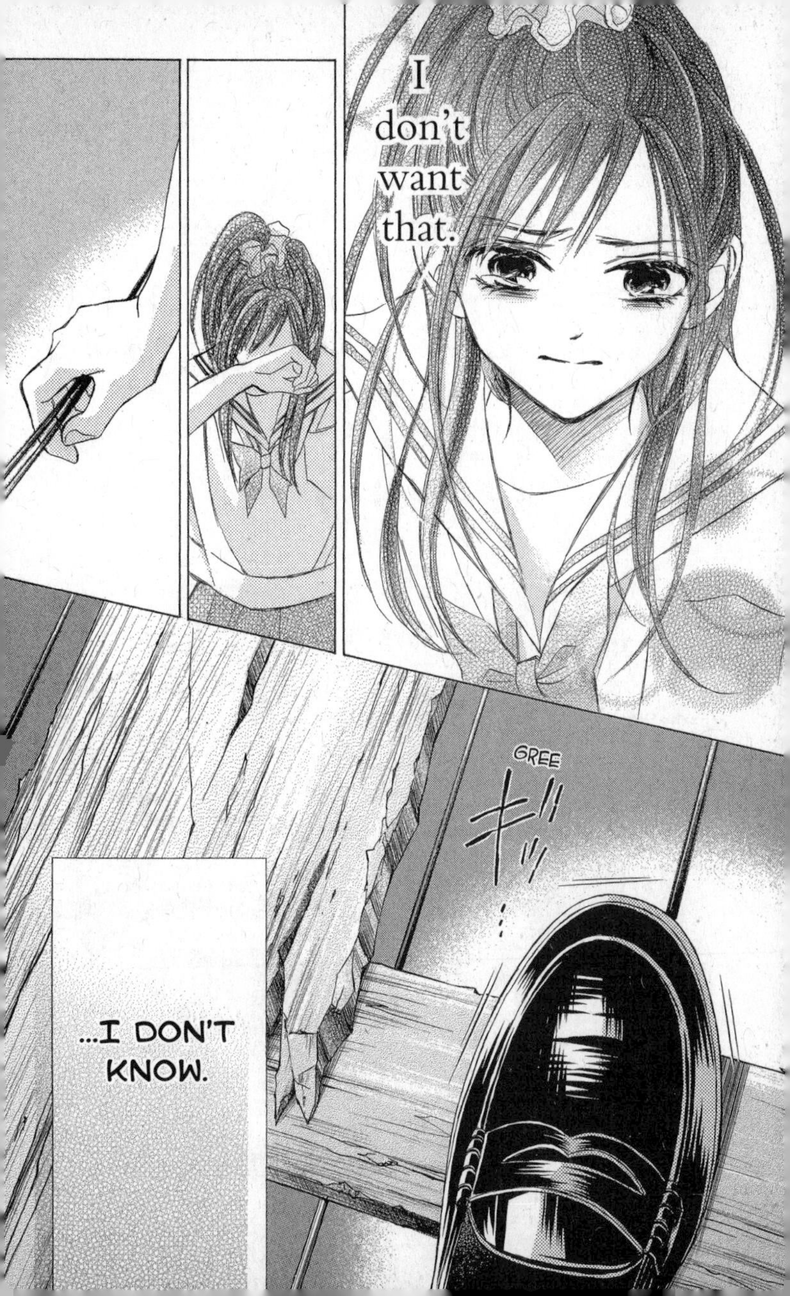
I don't want that.
GREE
...I DON'T KNOW.

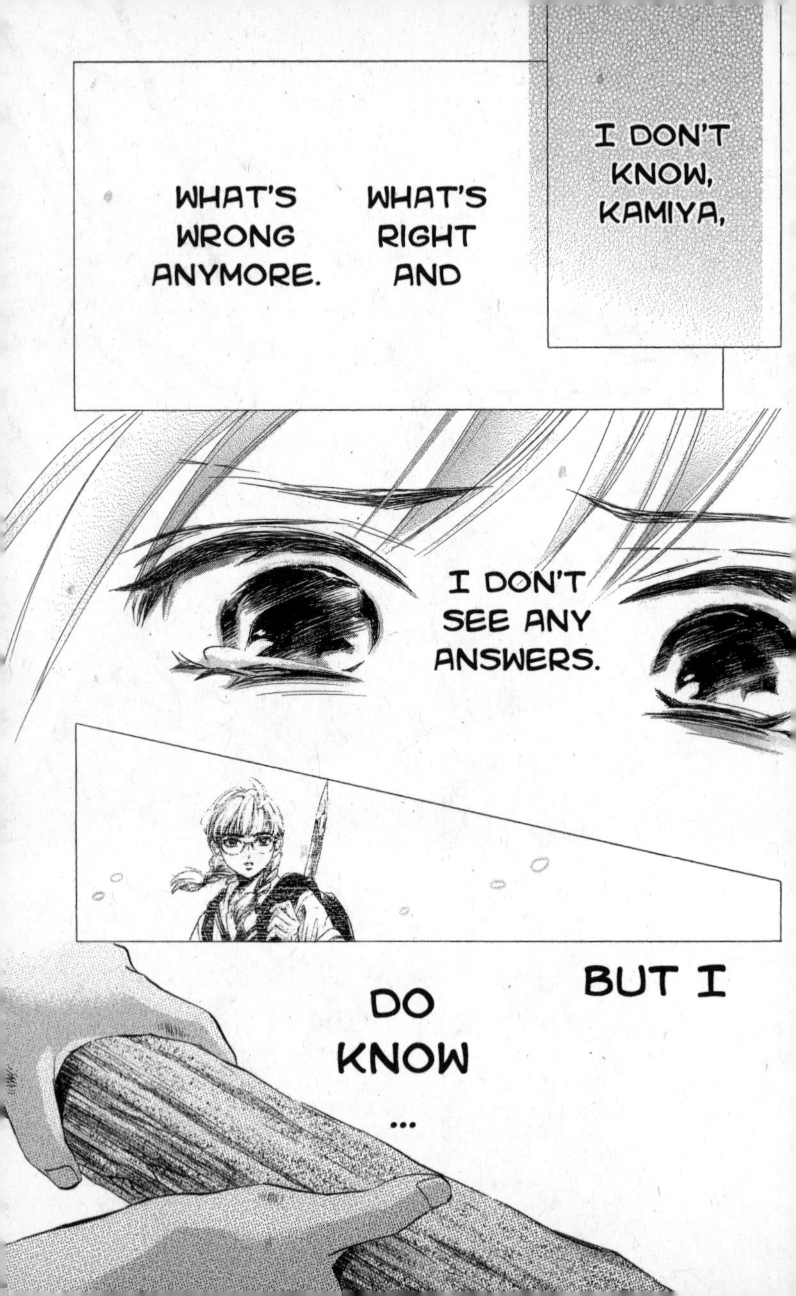
I DON'T KNOW, KAMIYA,
WHAT'S RIGHT AND
WHAT'S WRONG ANYMORE.
I DON'T SEE ANY ANSWERS.
BUT I
DO KNOW ...

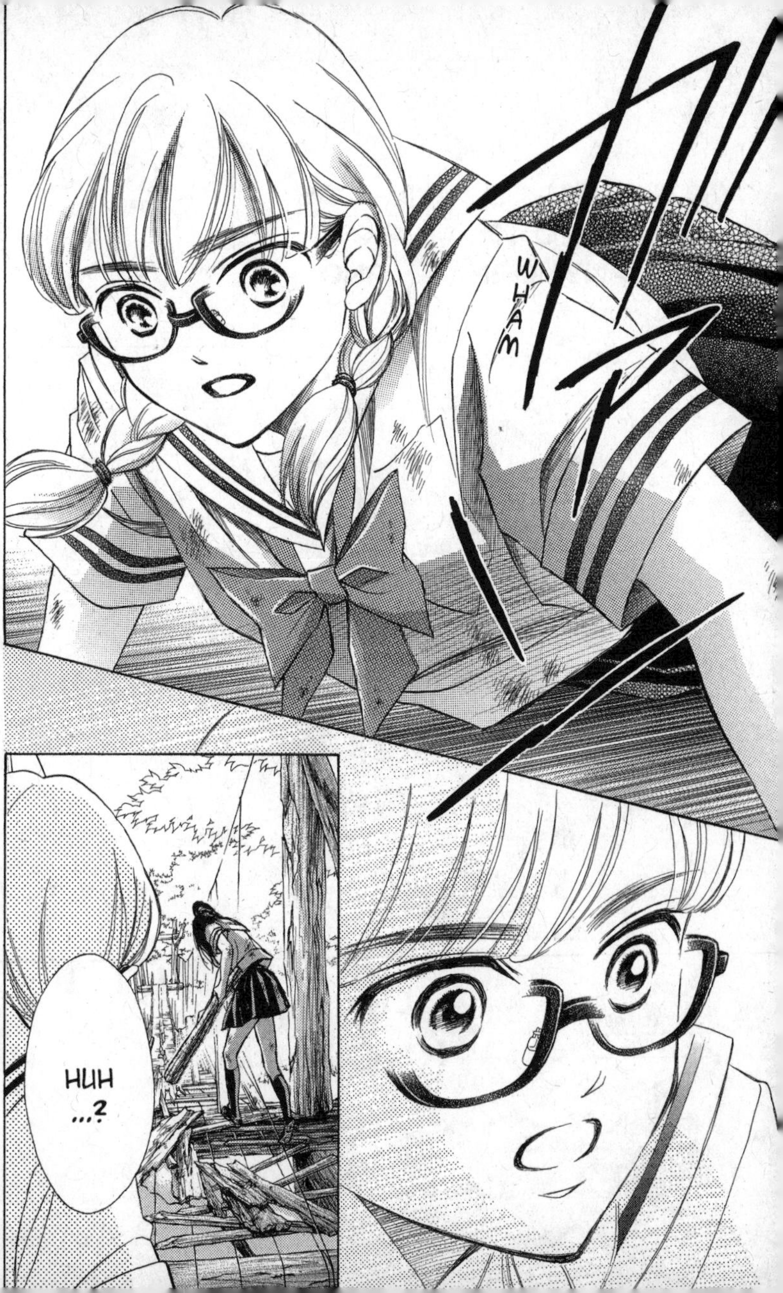
WHAM
HUH
...?

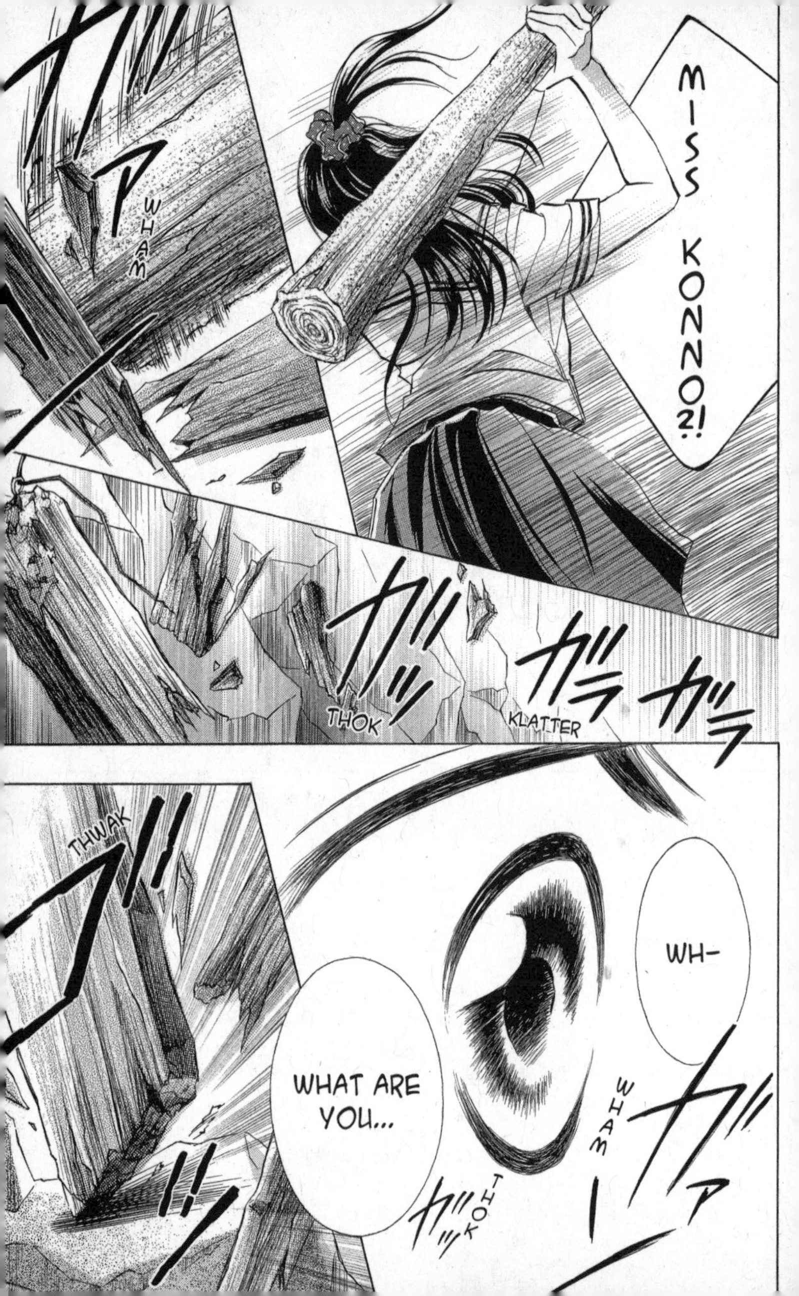
MISS KONNO?!
WHAM
KLATTER
THOK
WH-
WHAM
WHAT ARE YOU...
THOK
THWAK

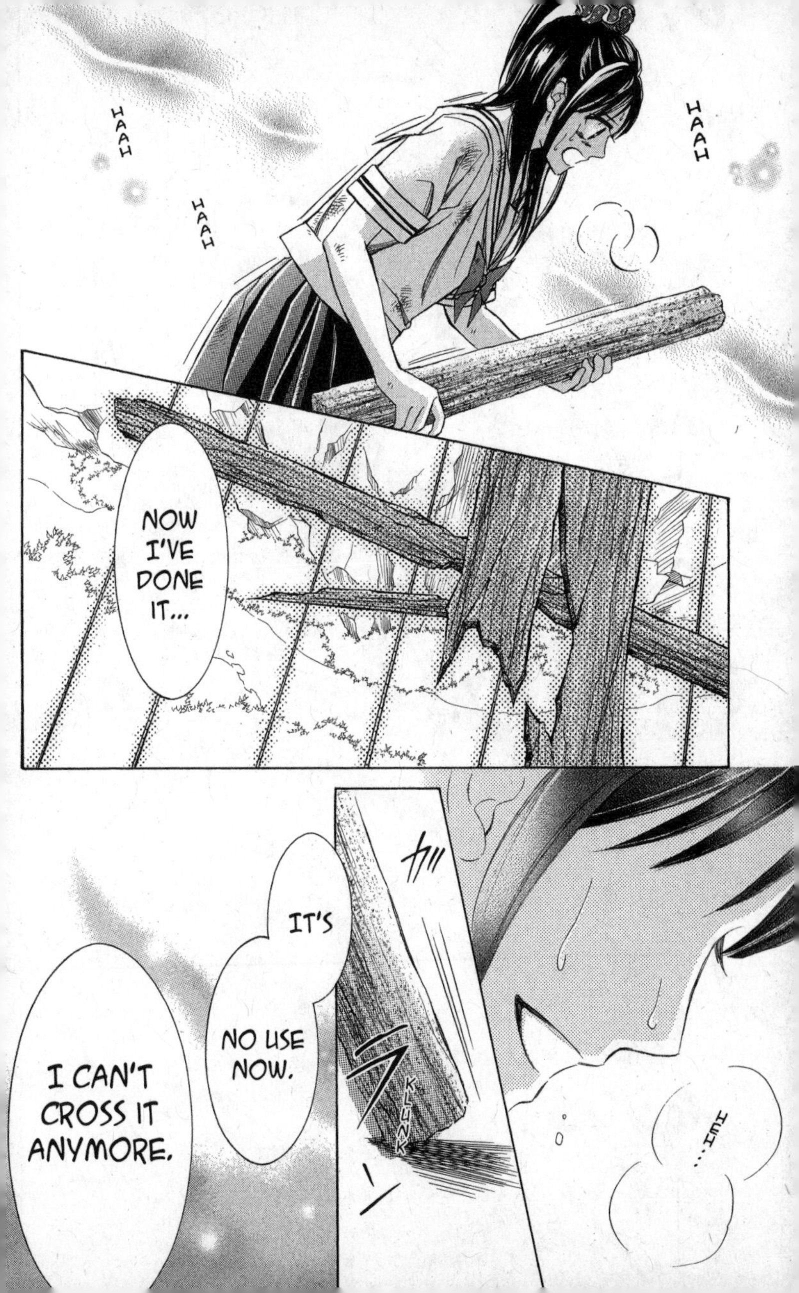
HAAH
HAAH
HAAH
NOW I'VE DONE IT...
HEH...
KLUNK
IT'S
NO USE NOW.
I CAN'T CROSS IT ANYMORE.

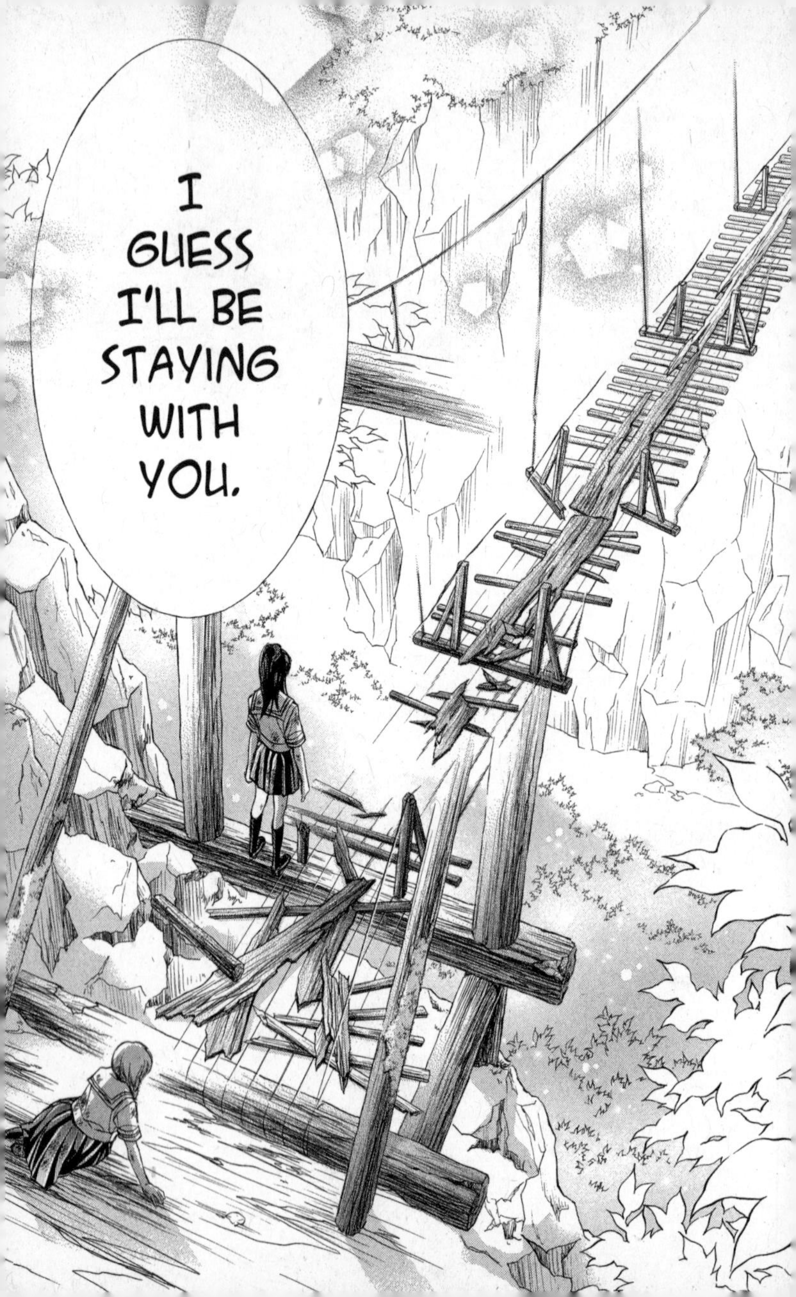
I GUESS I'LL BE STAYING WITH YOU.

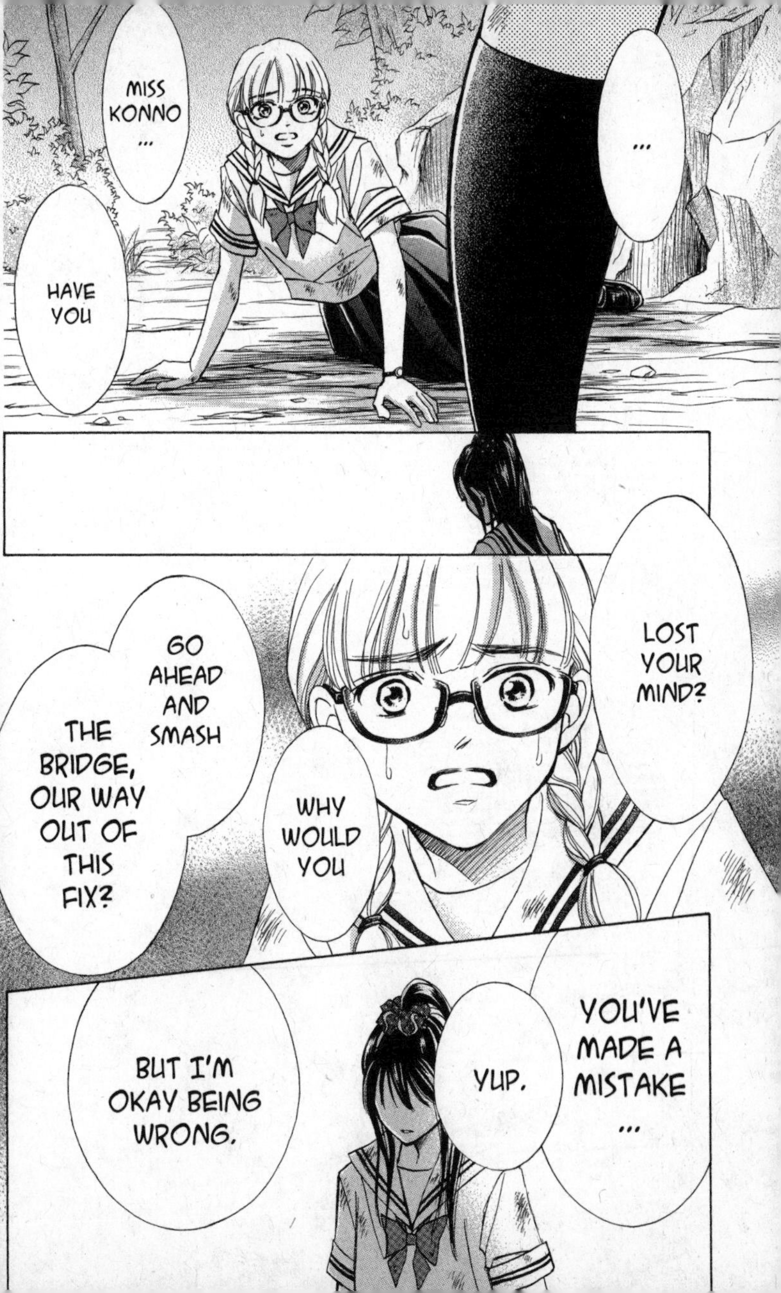
...
MISS KONNO ...
HAVE YOU
LOST YOUR MIND?
WHY WOULD YOU
GO AHEAD AND SMASH THE BRIDGE, OUR WAY OUT OF THIS FIX?
YOU'VE MADE A MISTAKE ...
YUP.
BUT I'M OKAY BEING WRONG.

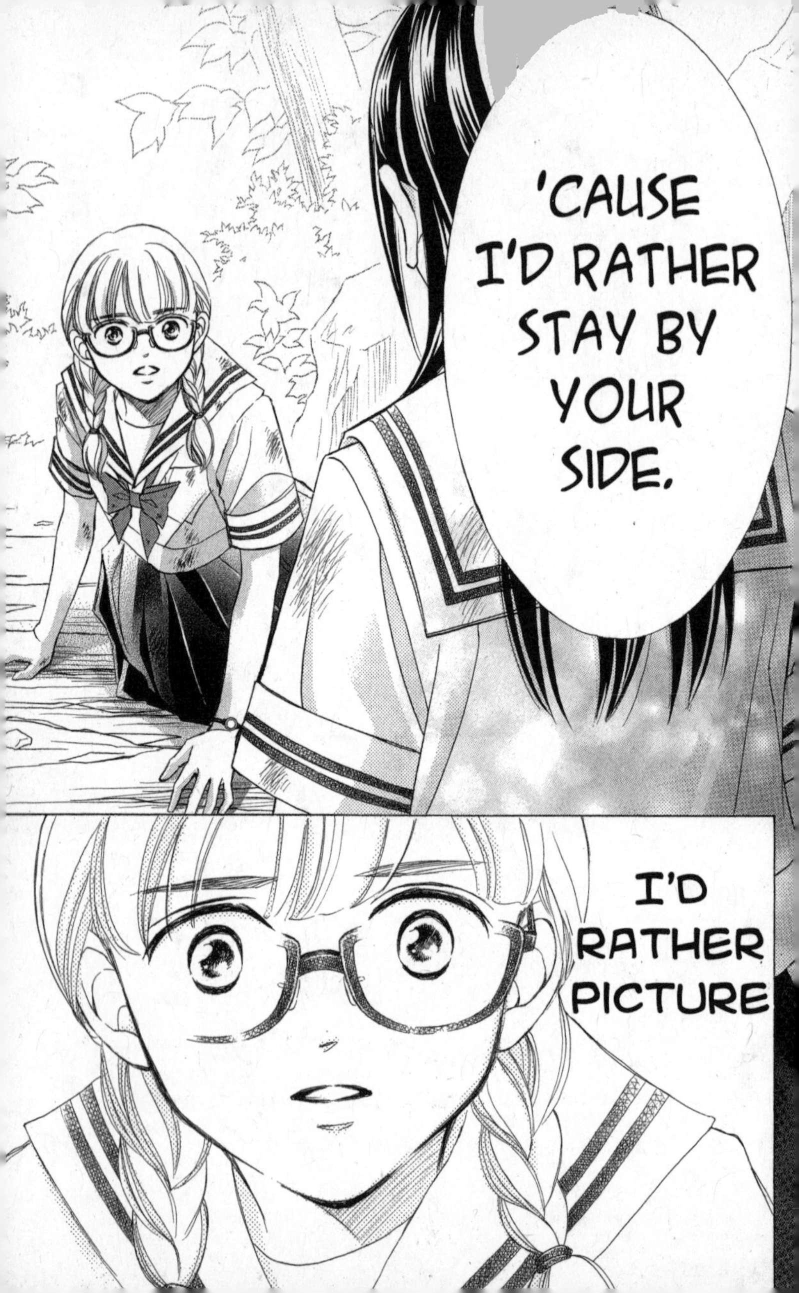
'CAUSE I'D RATHER STAY BY YOUR SIDE.
I'D RATHER PICTURE

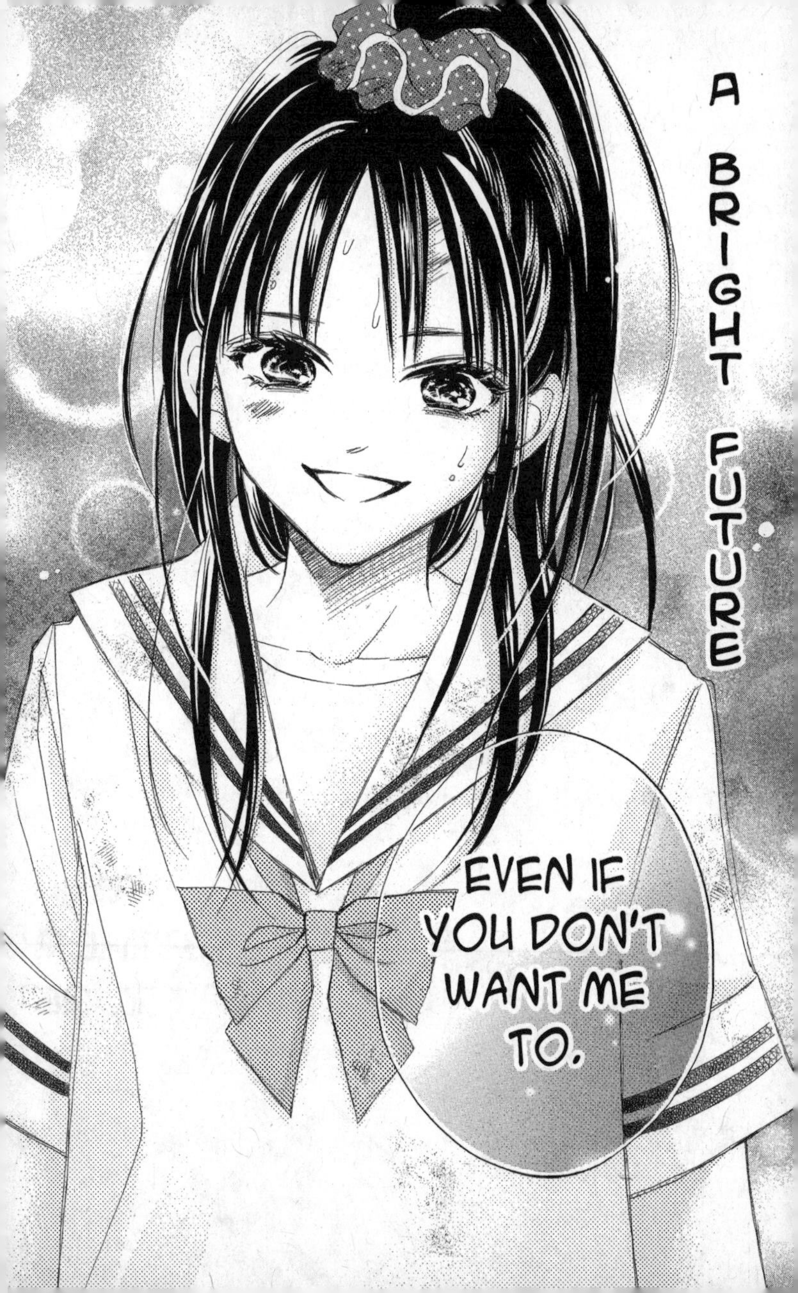
A BRIGHT FUTURE
EVEN IF YOU DON'T WANT ME TO.

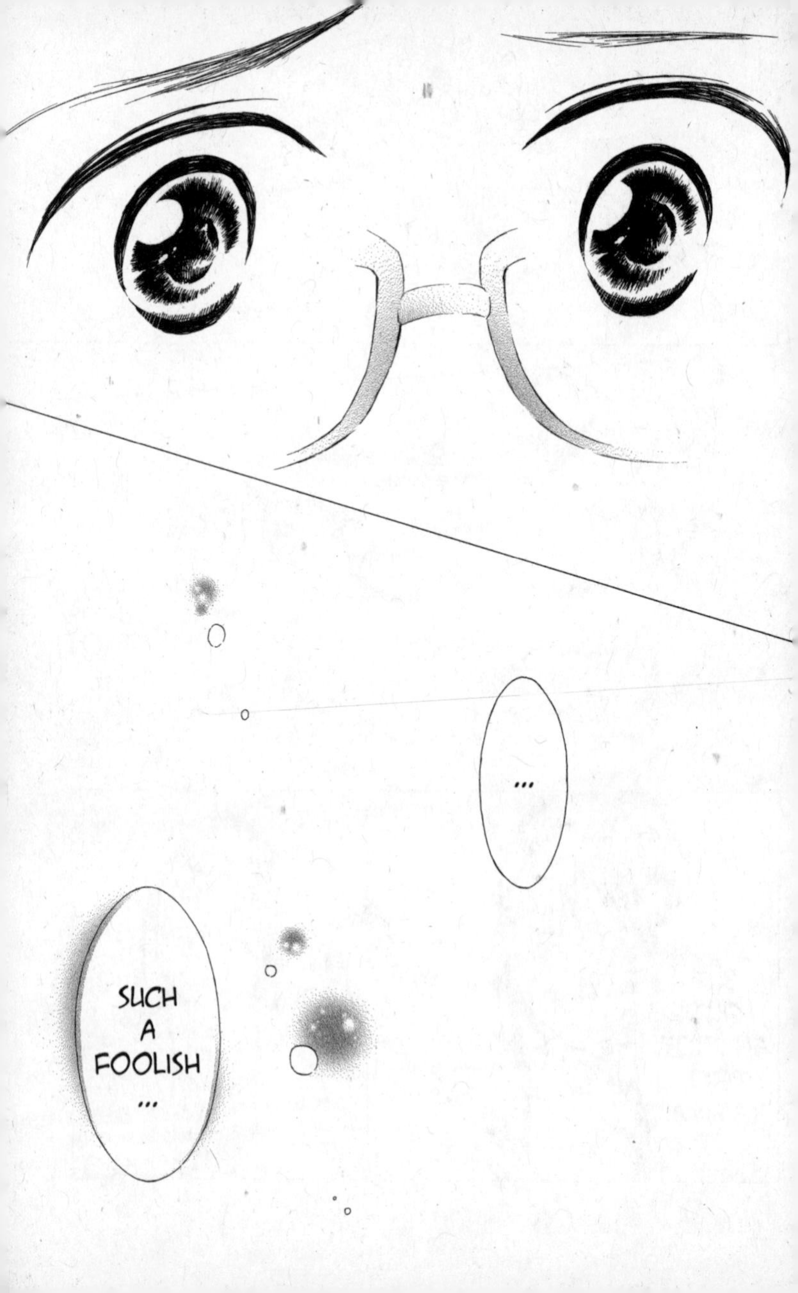
...
SUCH A FOOLISH ...

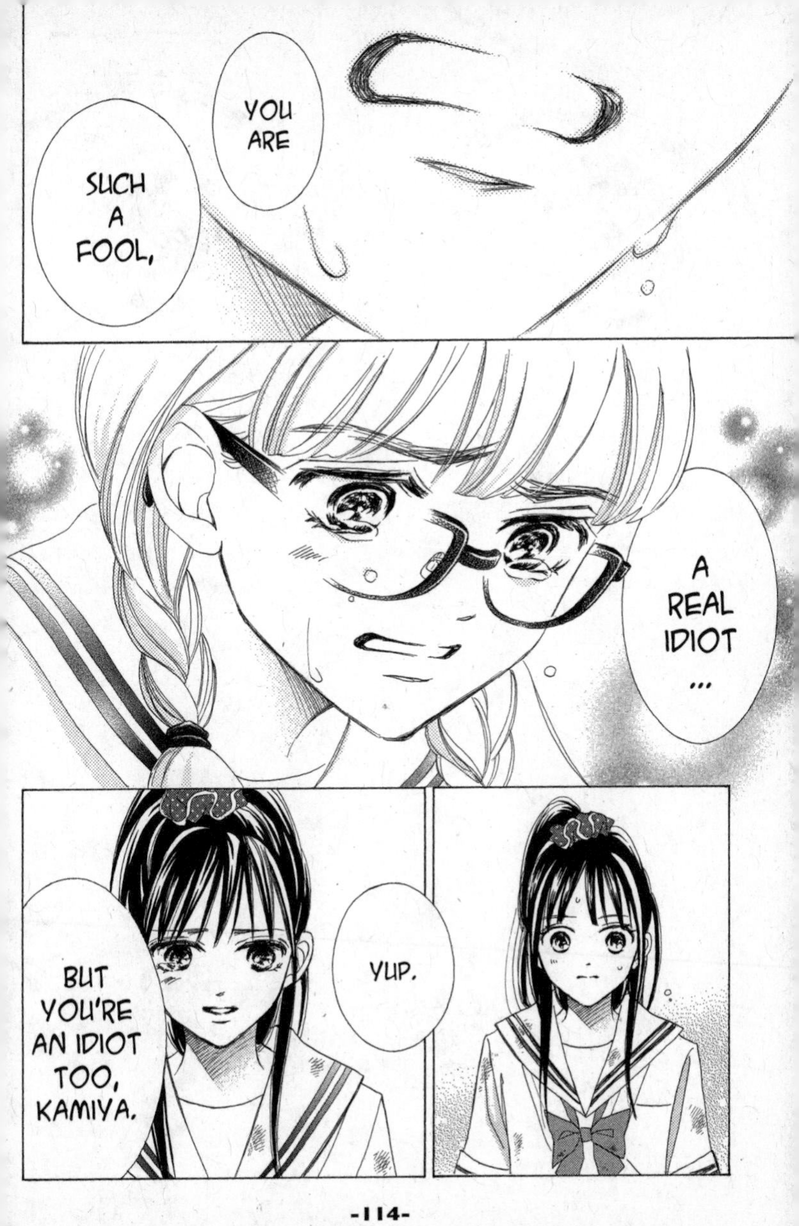
YOU ARE
SUCH A FOOL,
A REAL IDIOT ...
YUP.
BUT YOU'RE AN IDIOT TOO, KAMIYA.

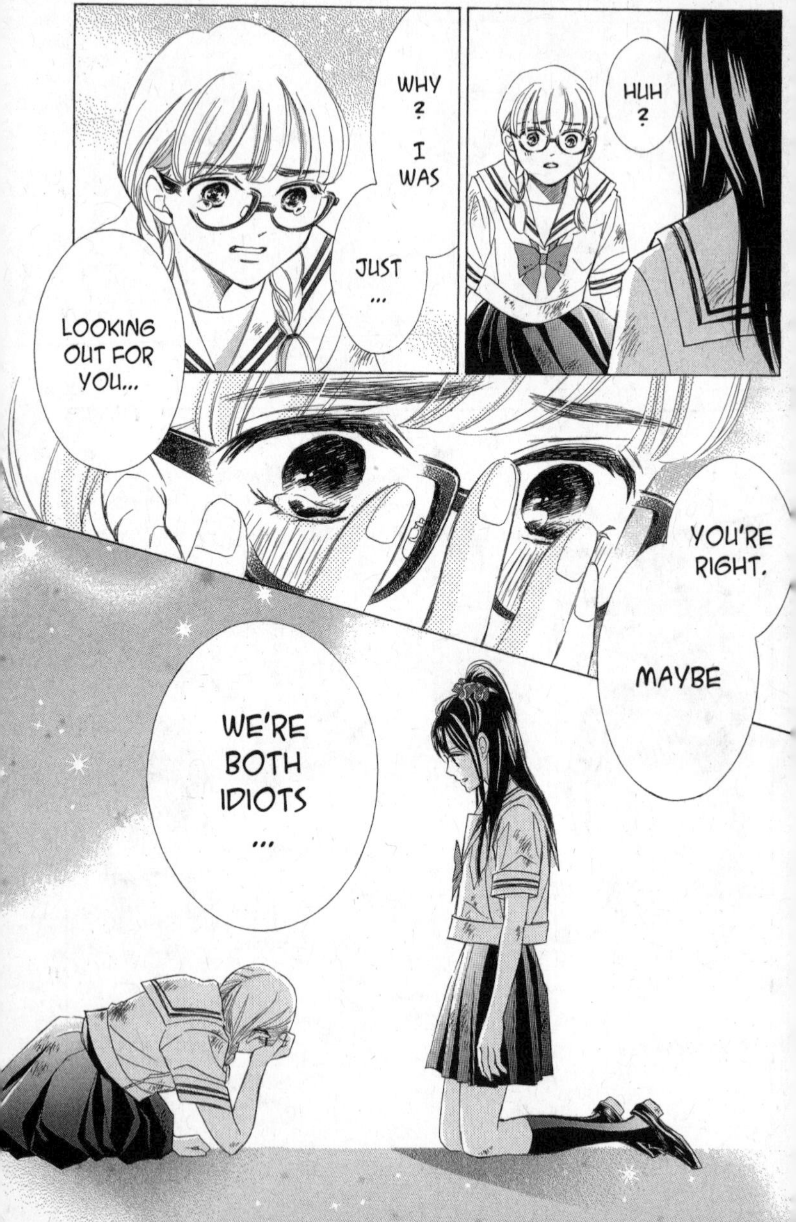
HUH?
WHY? I WAS
JUST...
LOOKING OUT FOR YOU...
YOU'RE RIGHT.
MAYBE
WE'RE BOTH IDIOTS ...

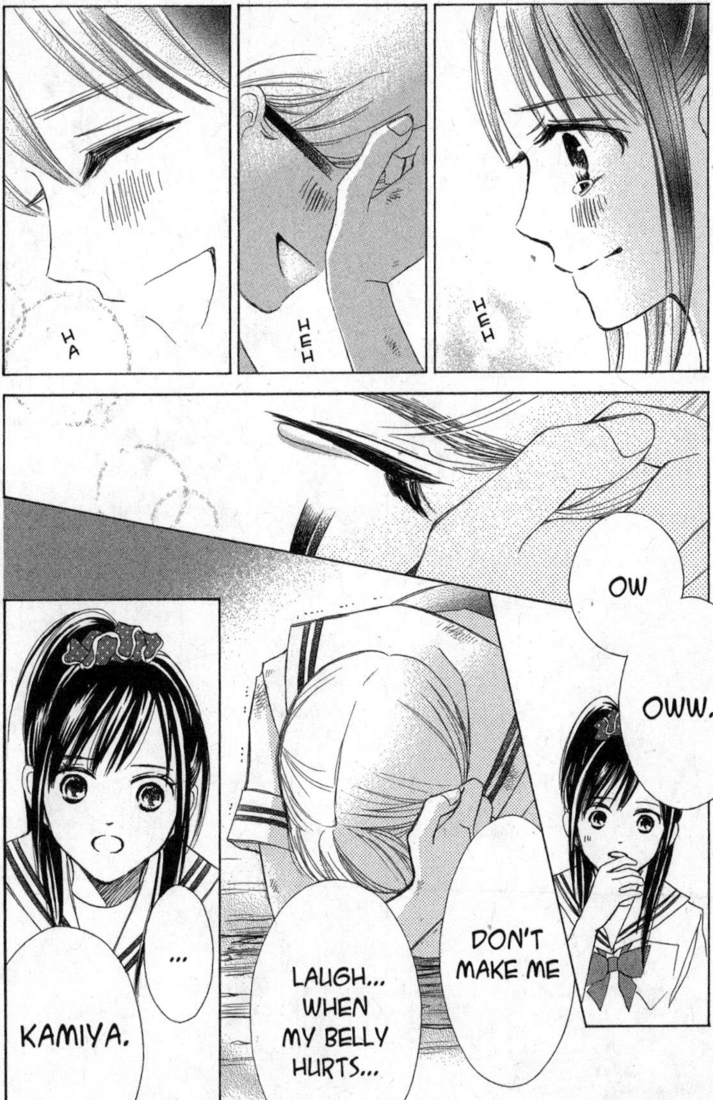
HEH
HEH
HA
OW
OWW...
DON'T MAKE ME
LAUGH... WHEN MY BELLY HURTS...
...
KAMIYA.

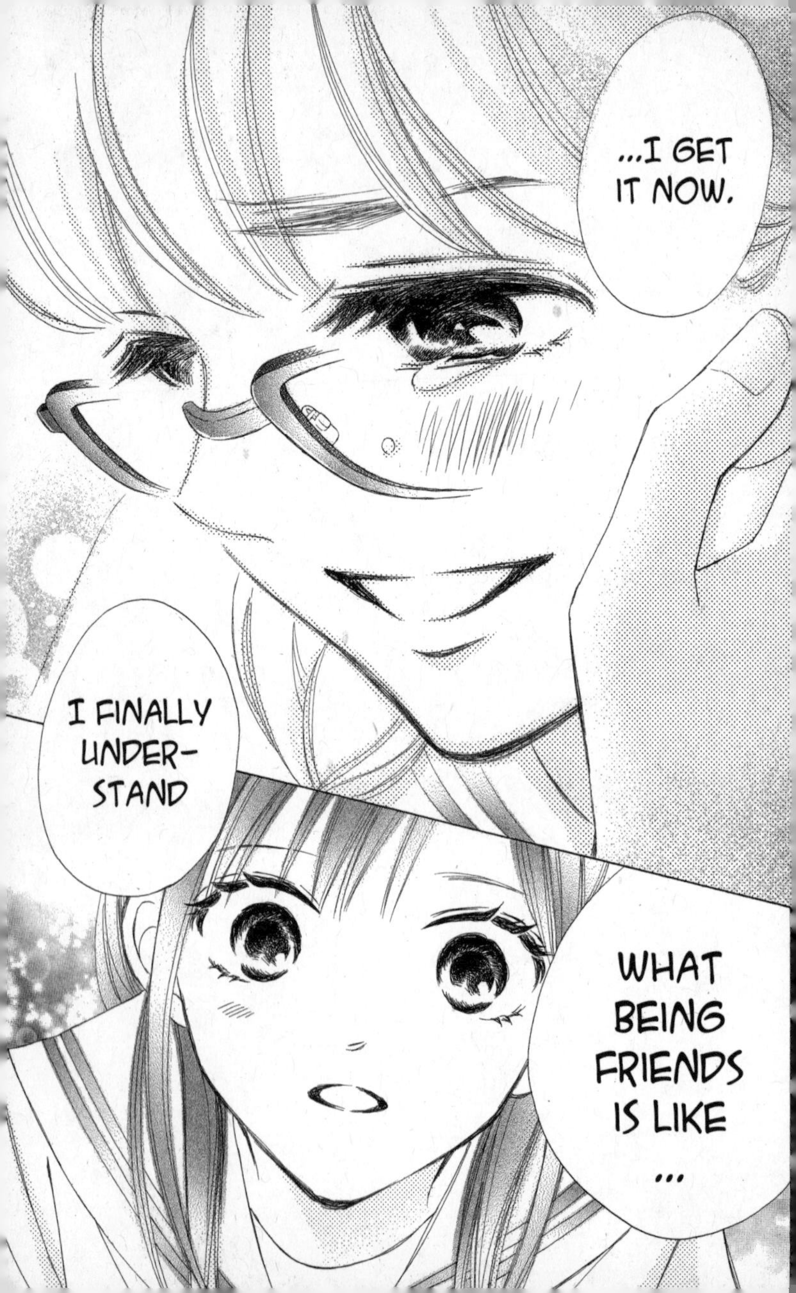
...I GET IT NOW.
WHAT BEING FRIENDS IS LIKE ...
I FINALLY UNDER-STAND

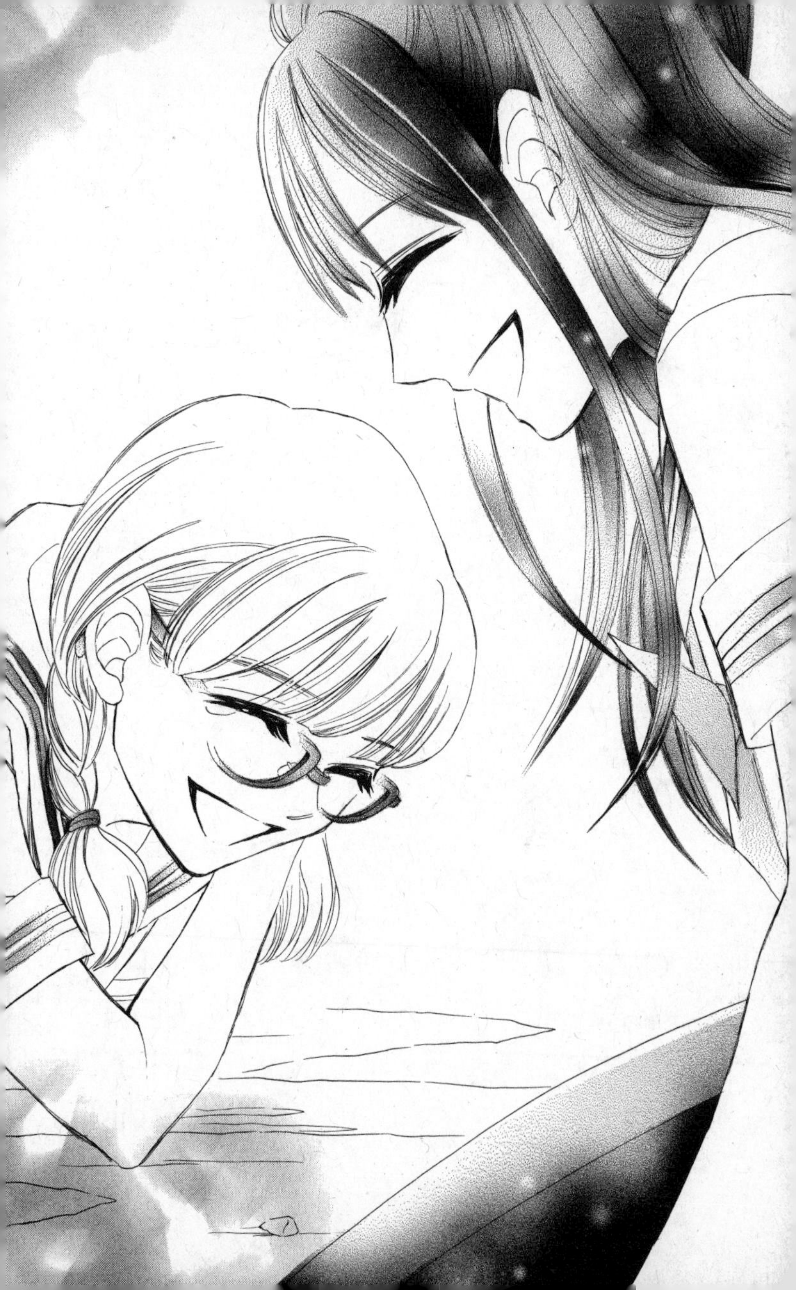

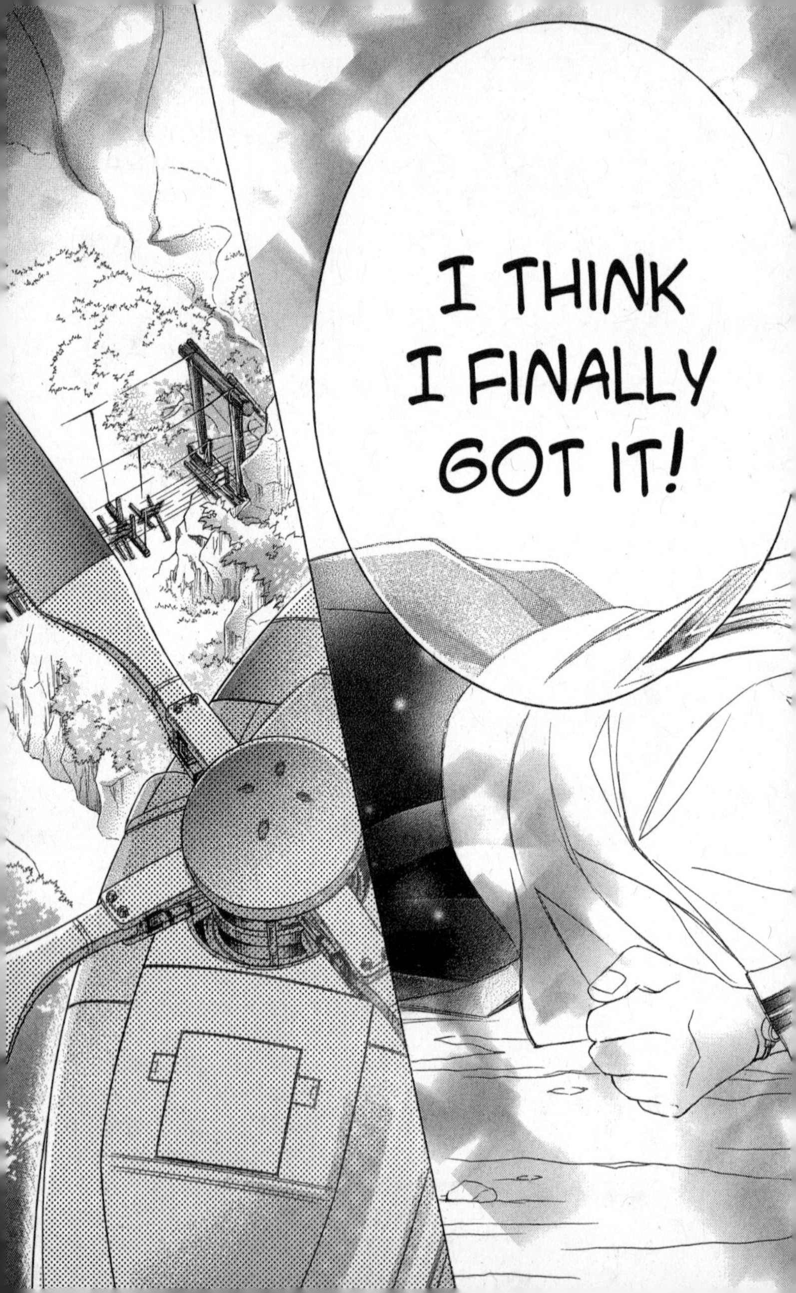
I THINK I FINALLY GOT IT!

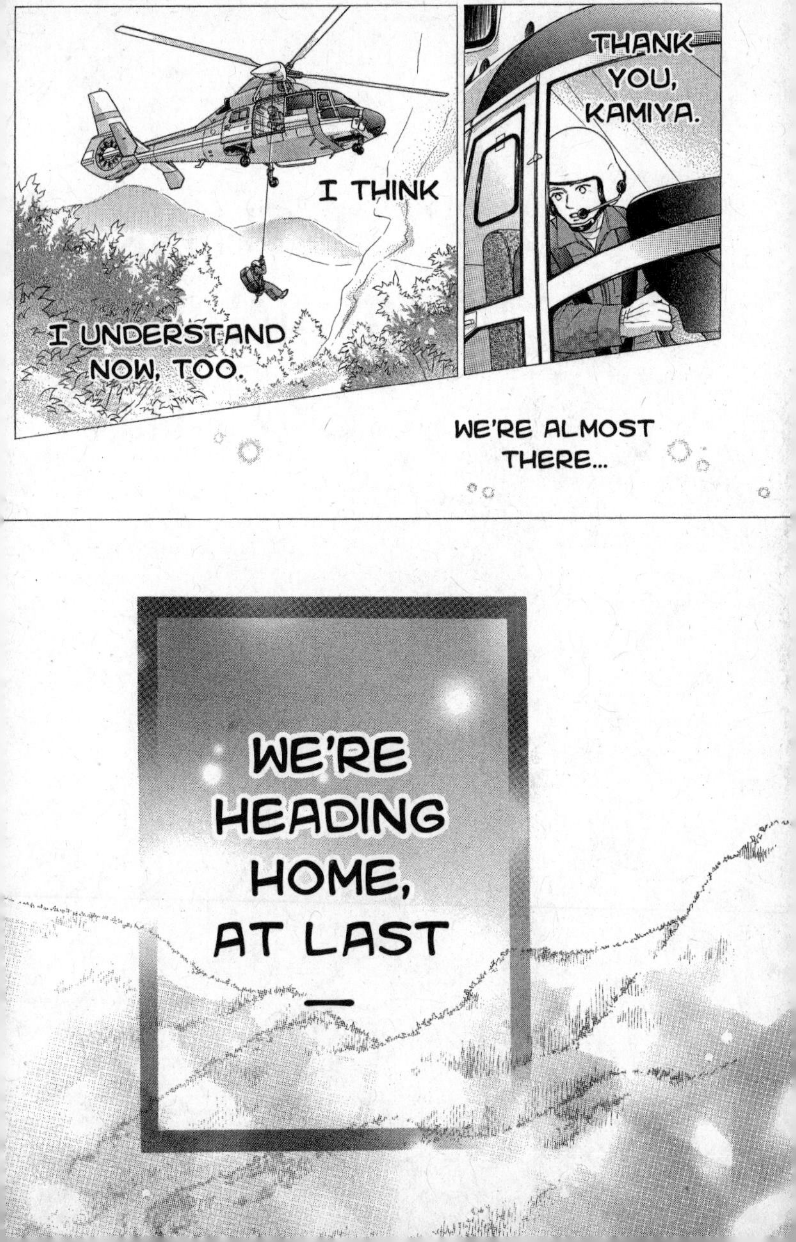
THANK YOU, KAMIYA.
I THINK
I UNDERSTAND NOW, TOO.
WE'RE ALMOST THERE...
WE'RE HEADING HOME, AT LAST —

L
I
M
I
T

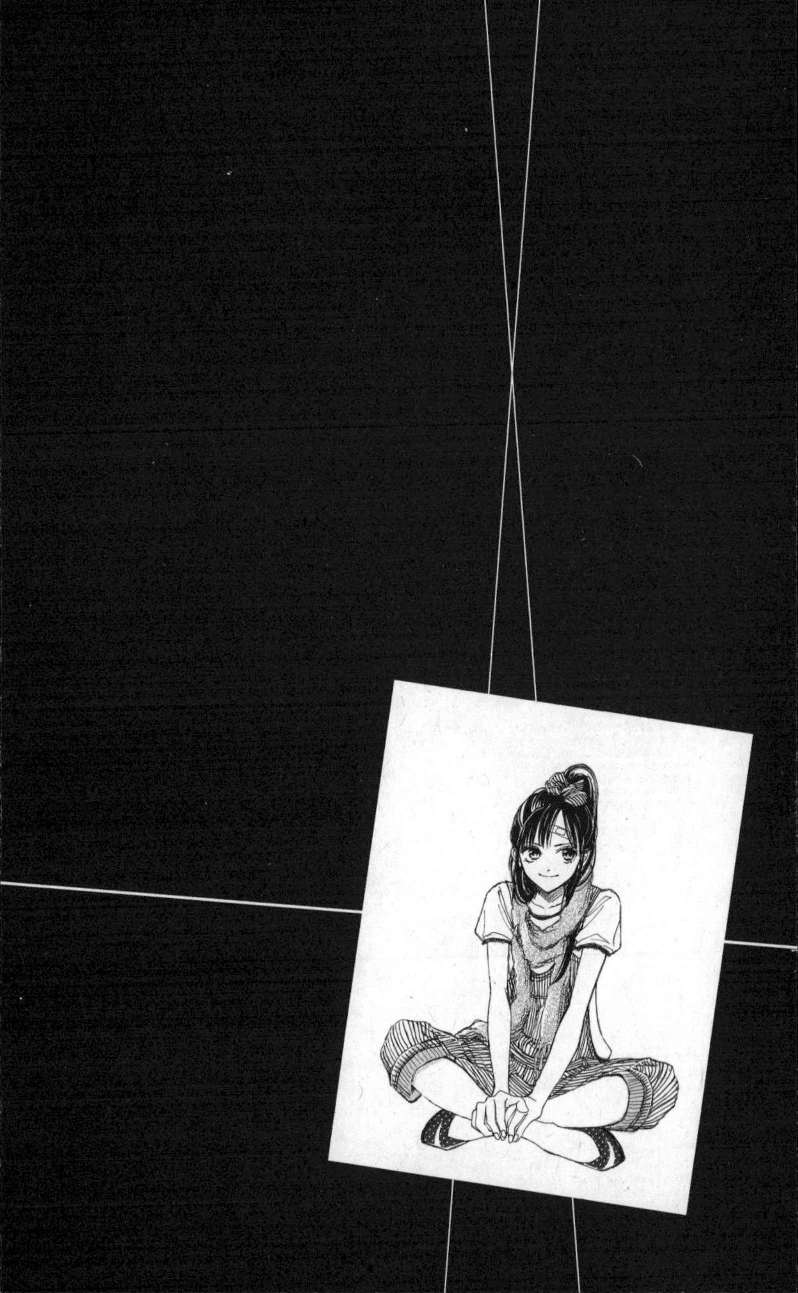

Last Scene. Onward, Towards Tomorrow...

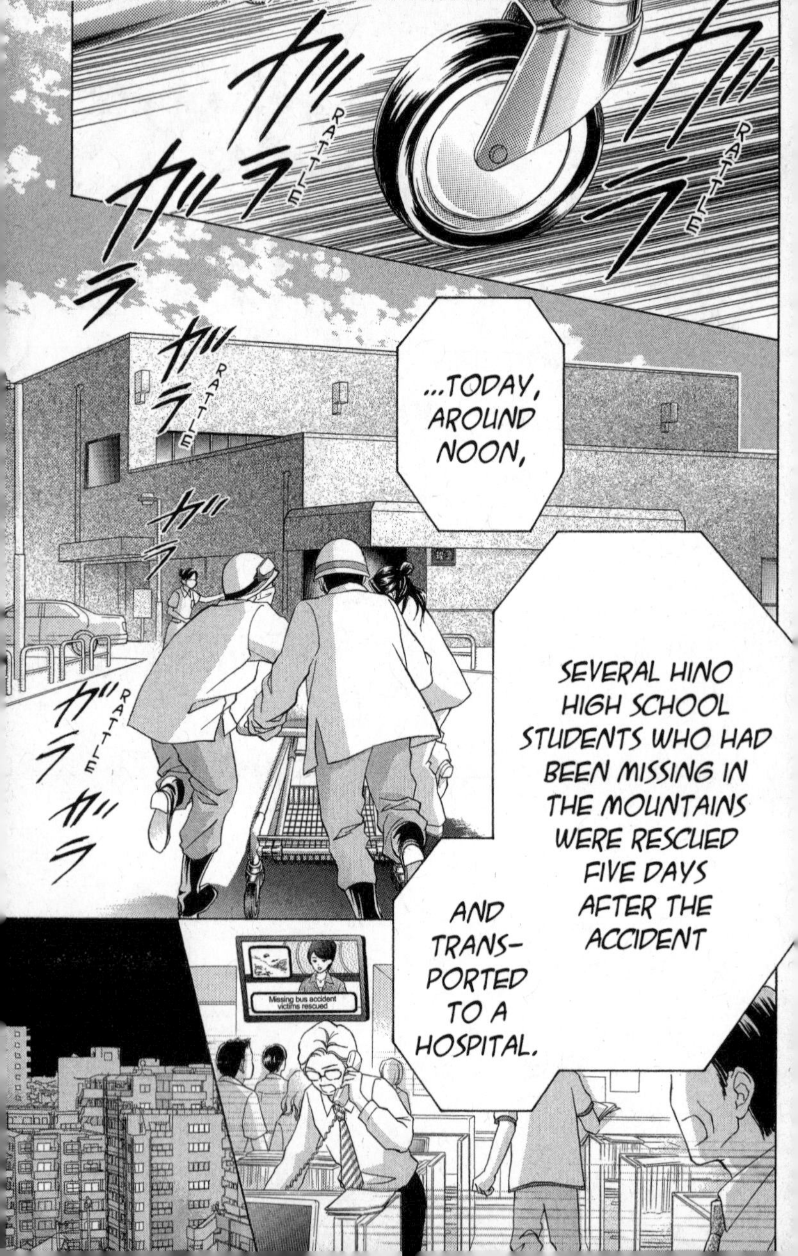

ガラ
RATTLE
ガラ
RATTLE
ガラ
ガラ
RATTLE
ガラ
ガラ
RATTLE
ガラ
...TODAY, AROUND NOON,
SEVERAL HINO HIGH SCHOOL STUDENTS WHO HAD BEEN MISSING IN THE MOUNTAINS WERE RESCUED FIVE DAYS AFTER THE ACCIDENT
AND TRANS-PORTED TO A HOSPITAL.
Missing bus accident victims rescued

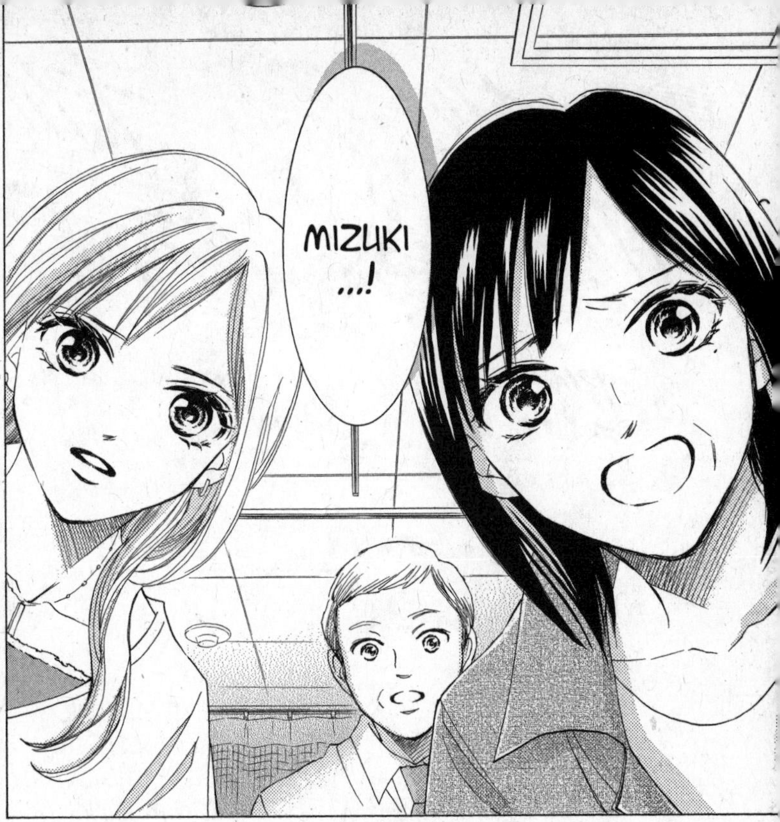
MIZUKI ...!

LIMIT

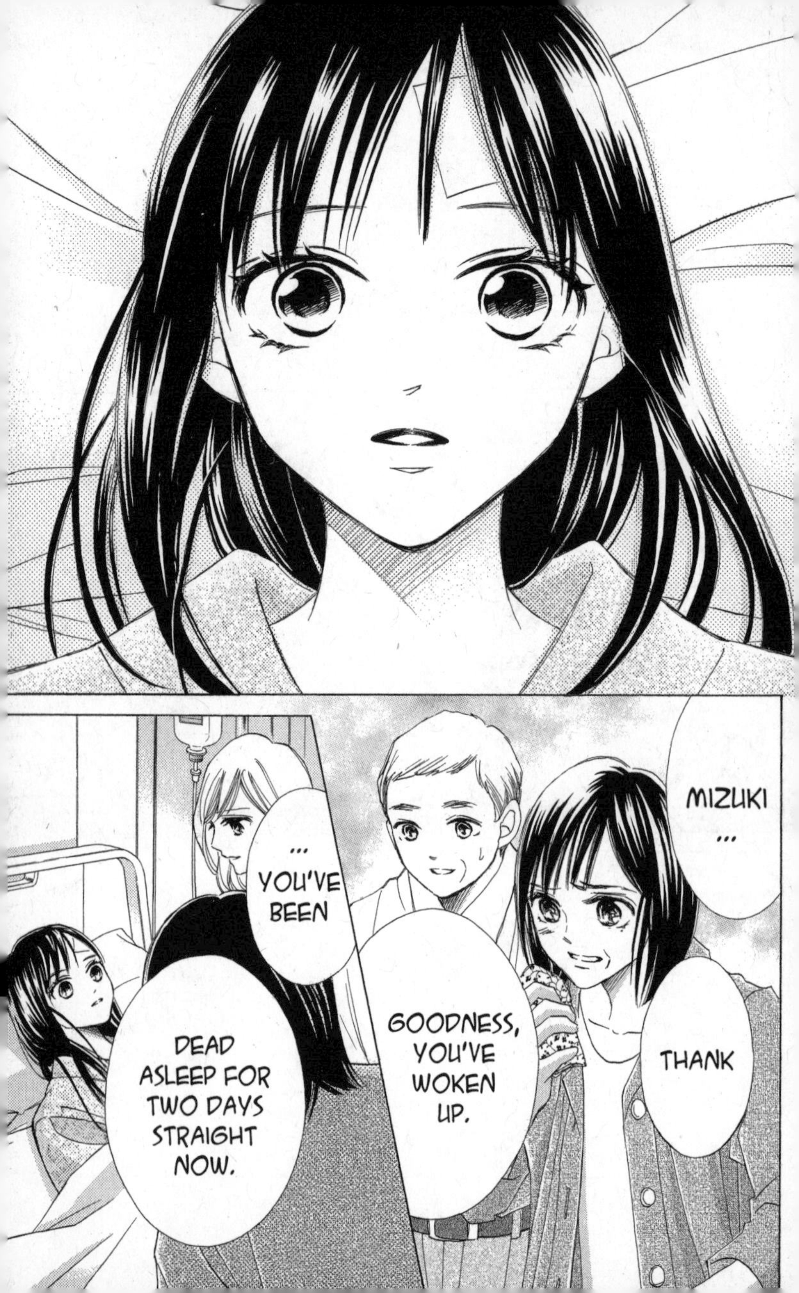
MIZUKI ...
THANK
GOODNESS, YOU'VE WOKEN UP.
... YOU'VE BEEN
DEAD ASLEEP FOR TWO DAYS STRAIGHT NOW.

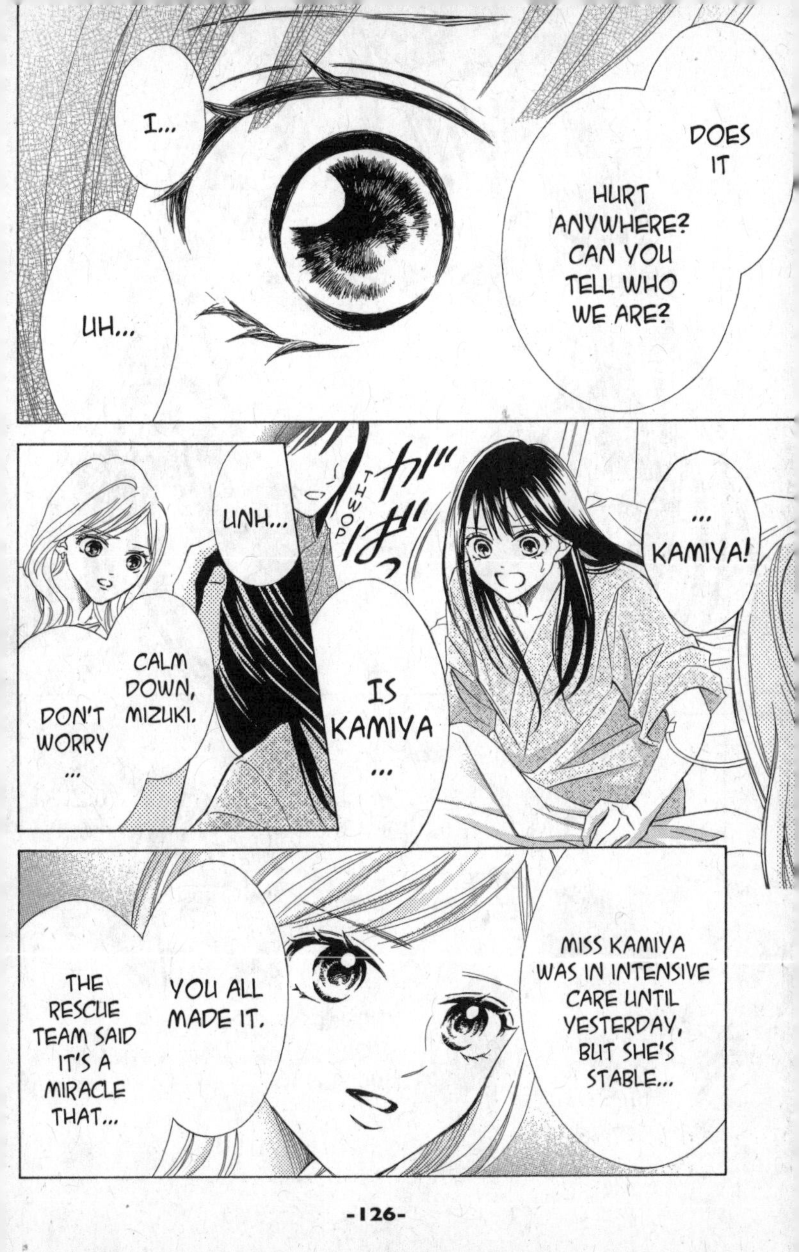
DOES IT HURT ANYWHERE? CAN YOU TELL WHO WE ARE?
I...
UH...
... KAMIYA!
THWOP
がばっ
IS KAMIYA ...
UNH...
CALM DOWN, MIZUKI.
DON'T WORRY ...
MISS KAMIYA WAS IN INTENSIVE CARE UNTIL YESTERDAY, BUT SHE'S STABLE...
YOU ALL MADE IT.
THE RESCUE TEAM SAID IT'S A MIRACLE THAT...

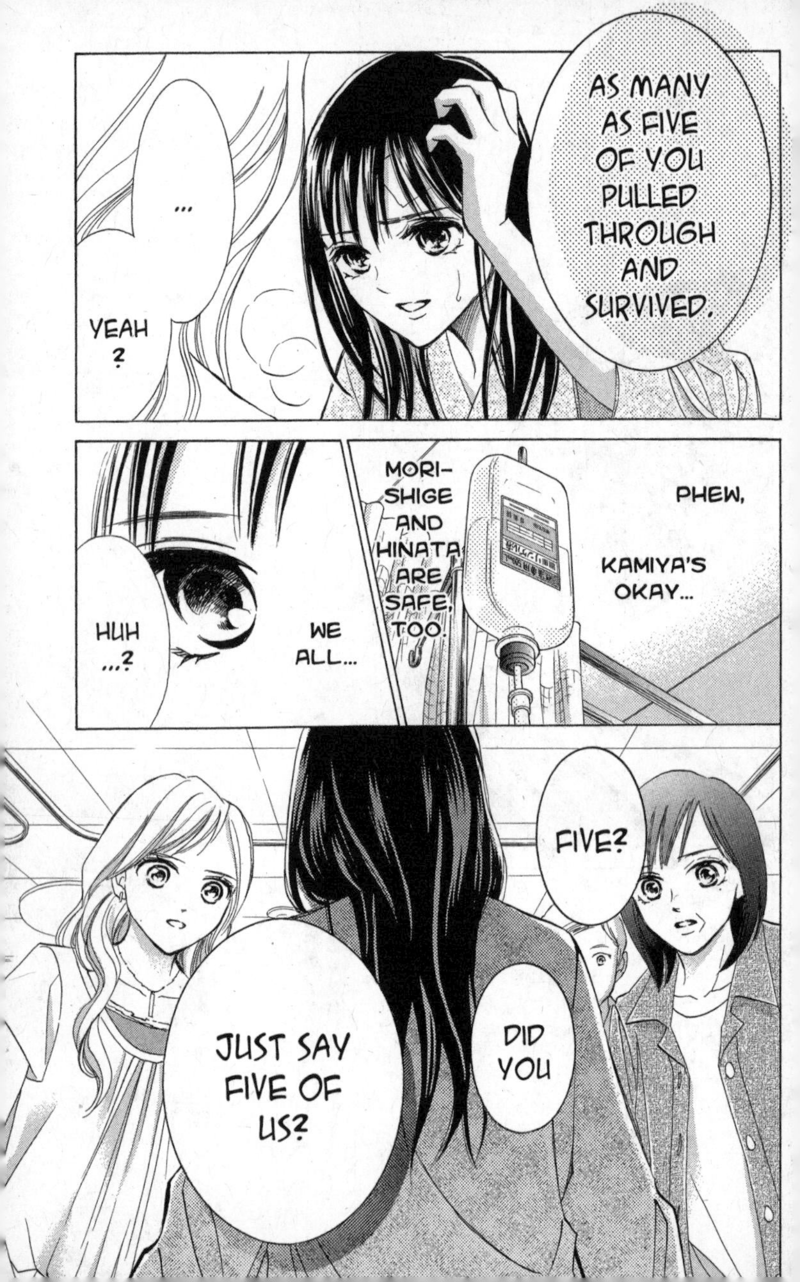
AS MANY AS FIVE OF YOU PULLED THROUGH AND SURVIVED.
...
YEAH?
PHEW,
KAMIYA'S OKAY...
MORI-SHIGE AND HINATA ARE SAFE, TOO.
WE ALL...
HUH...?
FIVE?
DID YOU
JUST SAY FIVE OF US?

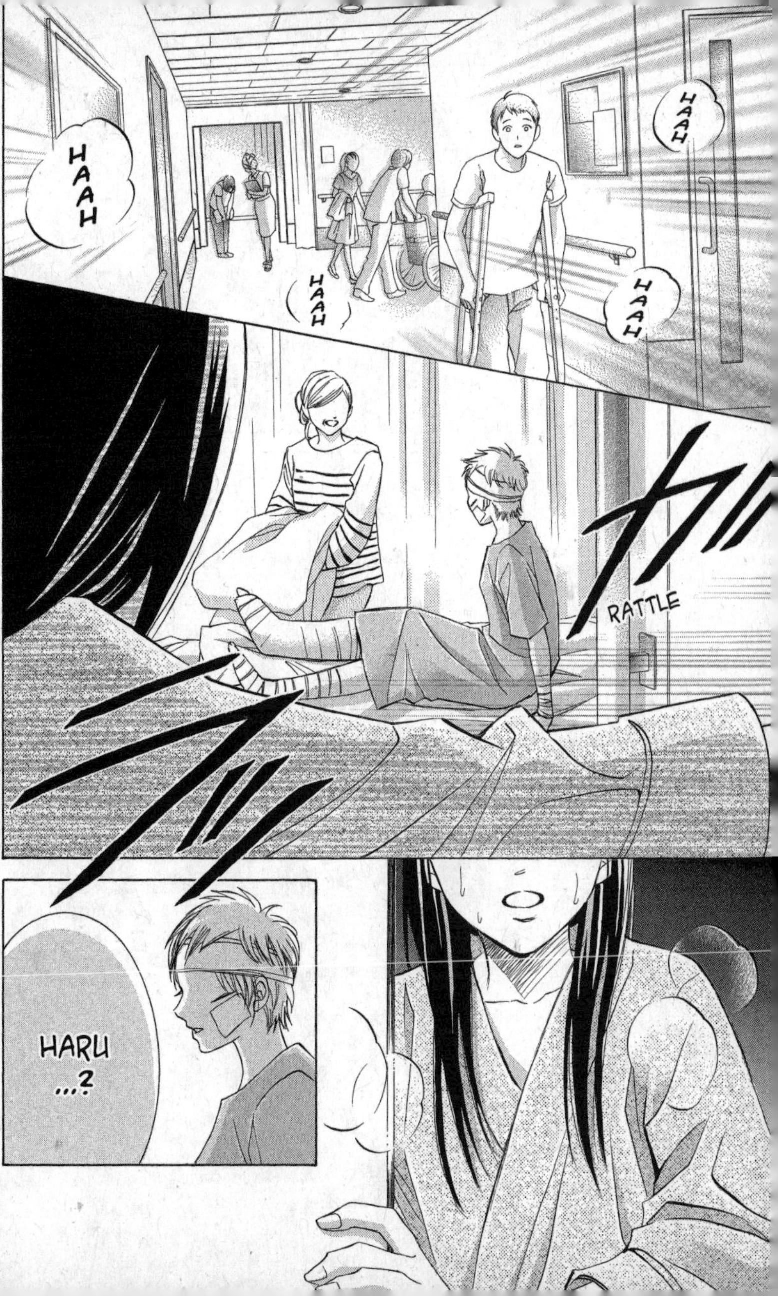
HAAH
HAAH
HAAH
HAAH
RATTLE
HARU ...?

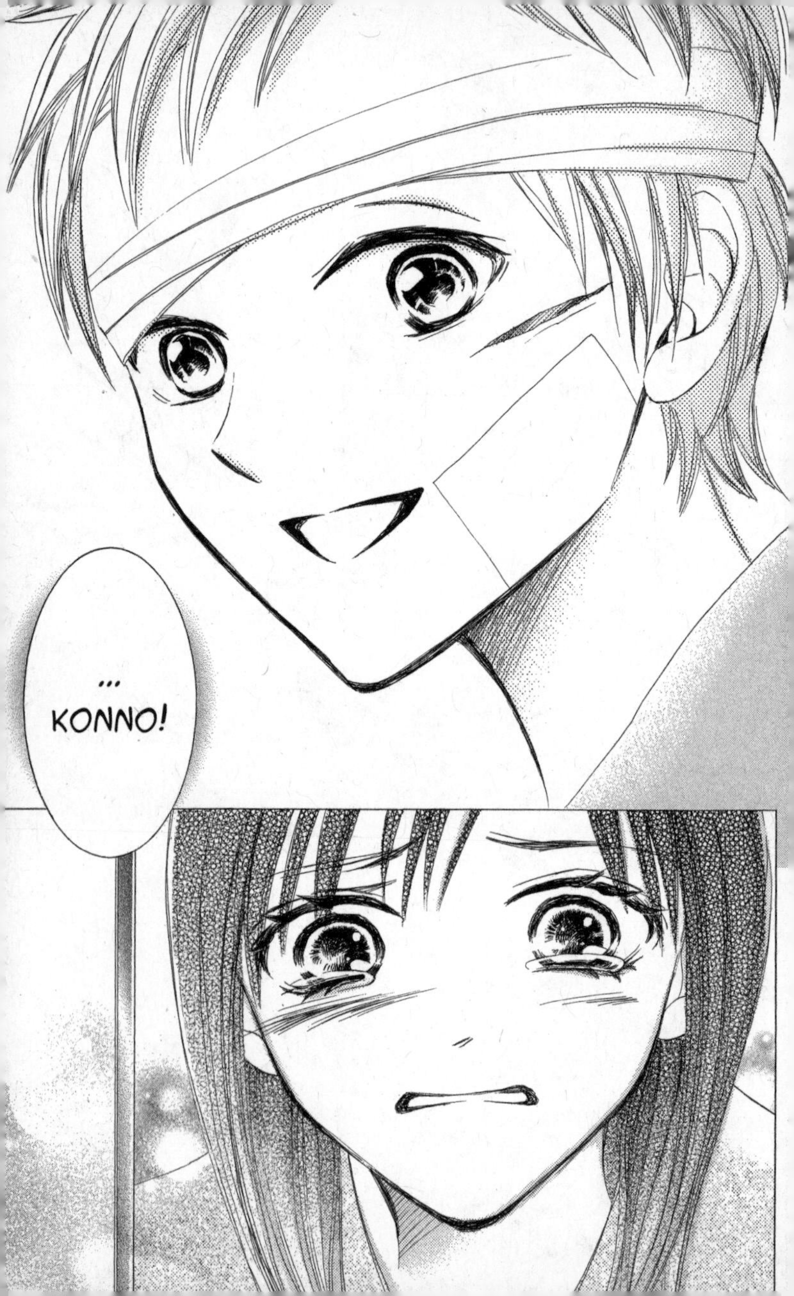
...
KONNO!

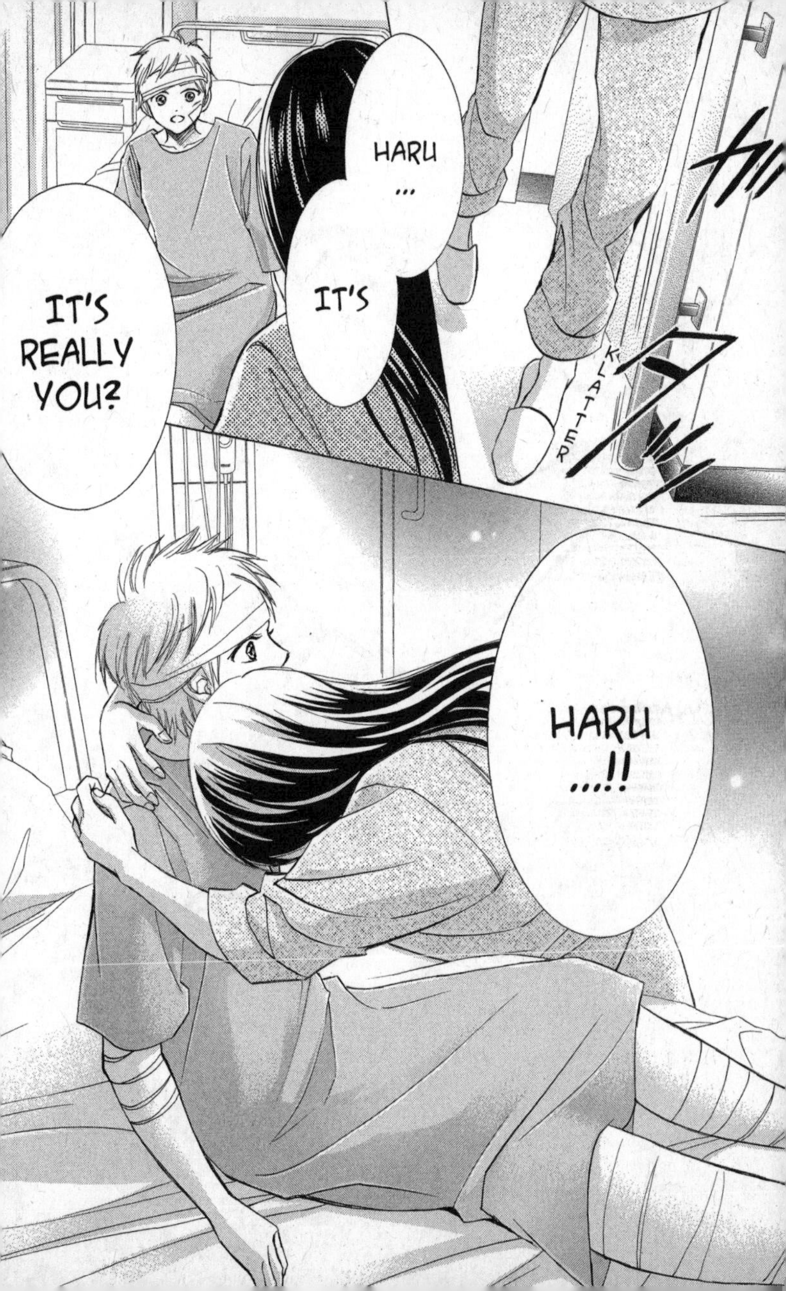
KLATTER
HARU ...
IT'S
IT'S REALLY YOU?
HARU ...!!

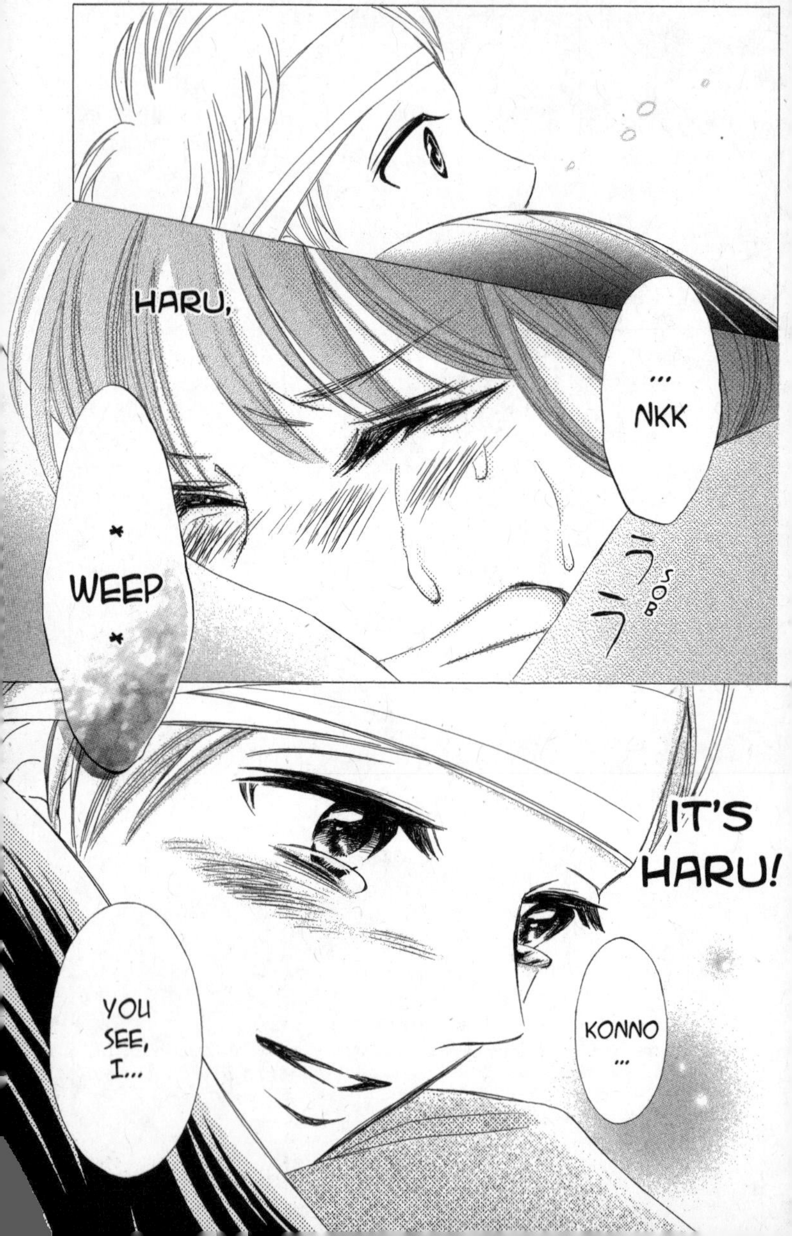
... NKK
SOB
HARU,
* WEEP *
IT'S HARU!
KONNO ...
YOU SEE, I...

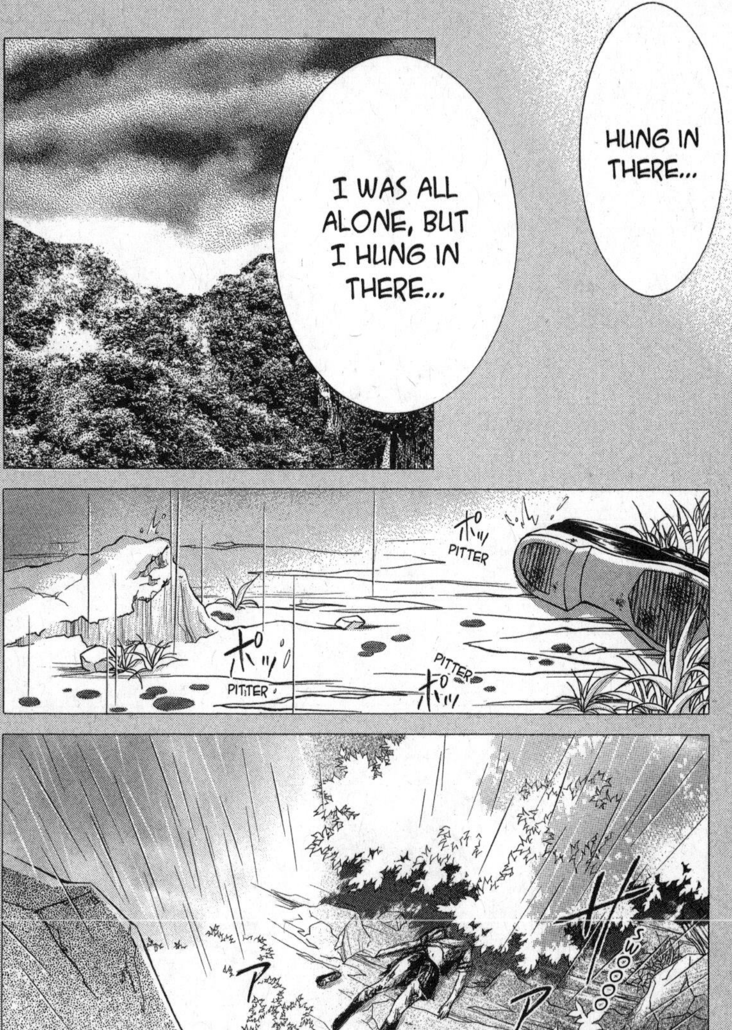
HUNG IN THERE...
I WAS ALL ALONE, BUT I HUNG IN THERE...
PITTER
PITTER
PITTER
SWOOOOO

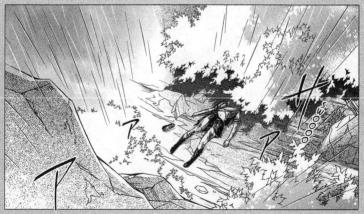

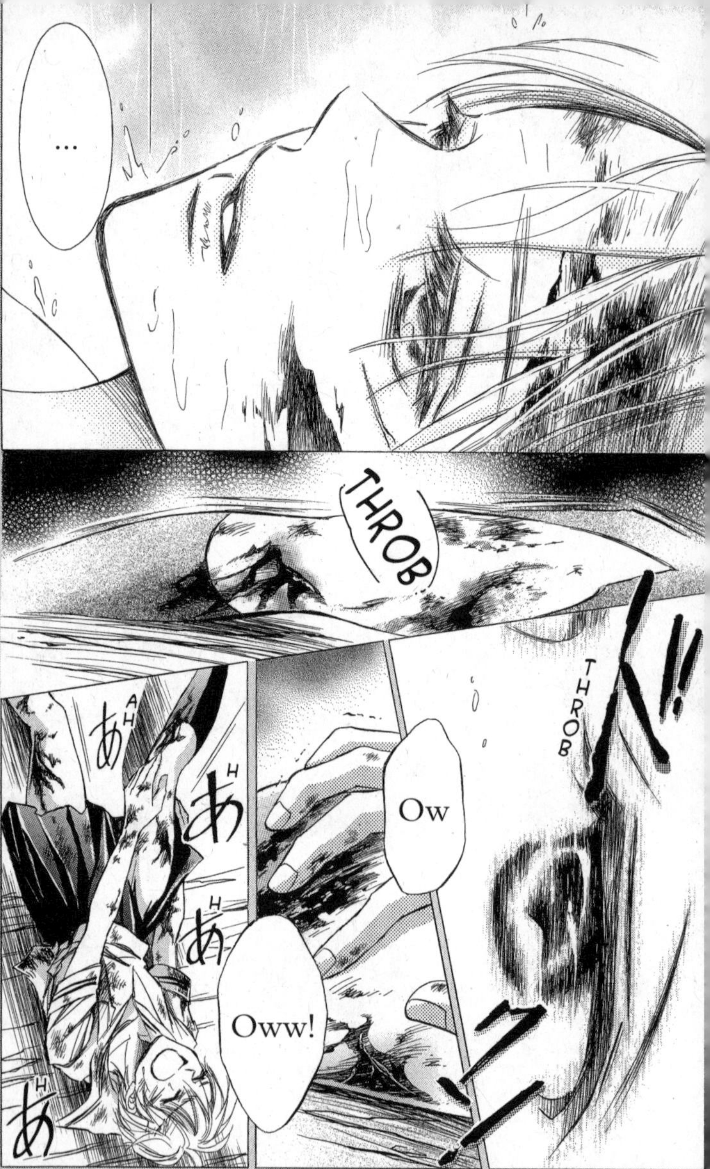
...
THROB
THROB
Ow
Oww!
あ AH
あ H
あ H
あ H

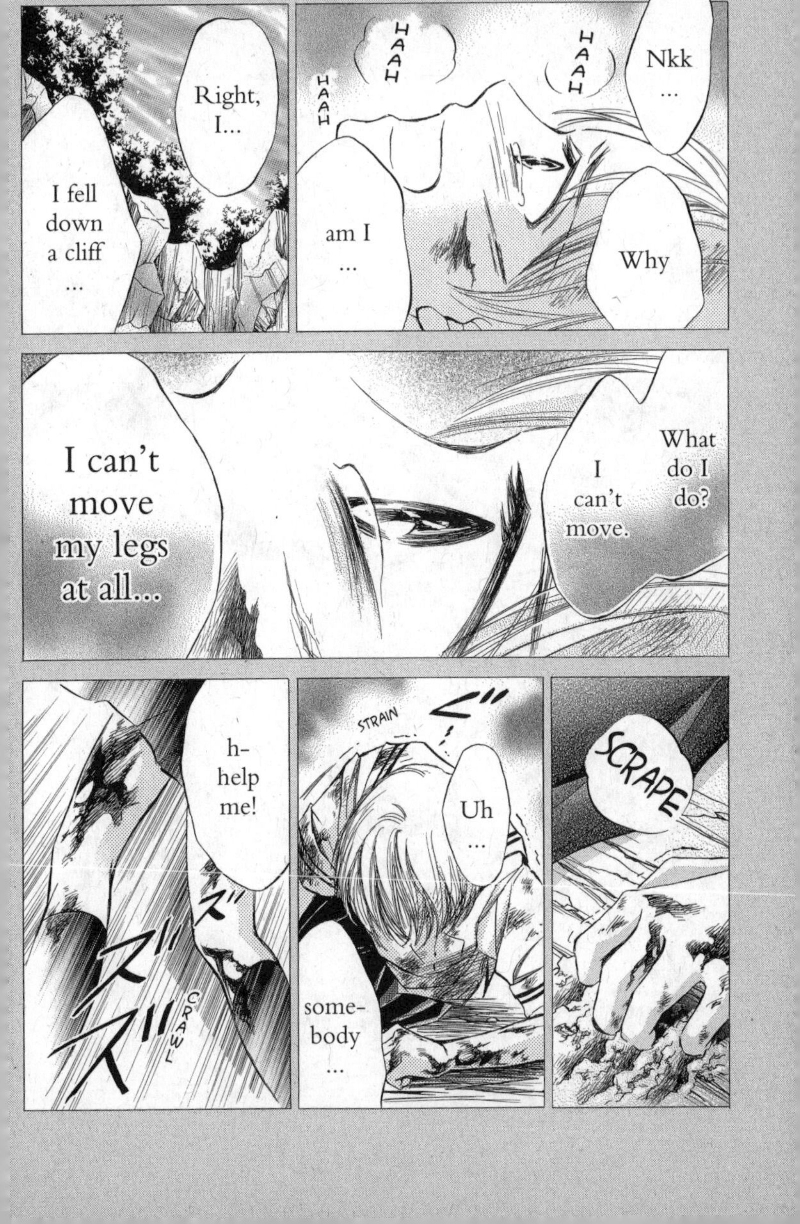
Nkk ...
HAAH
HAAH
HAAH
Why
am I ...
Right, I...
I fell down a cliff ...
What do I do?
I can't move.
I can't move my legs at all...
SCRAPE
STRAIN
Uh ...
somebody ...
h-help me!
CRAWL

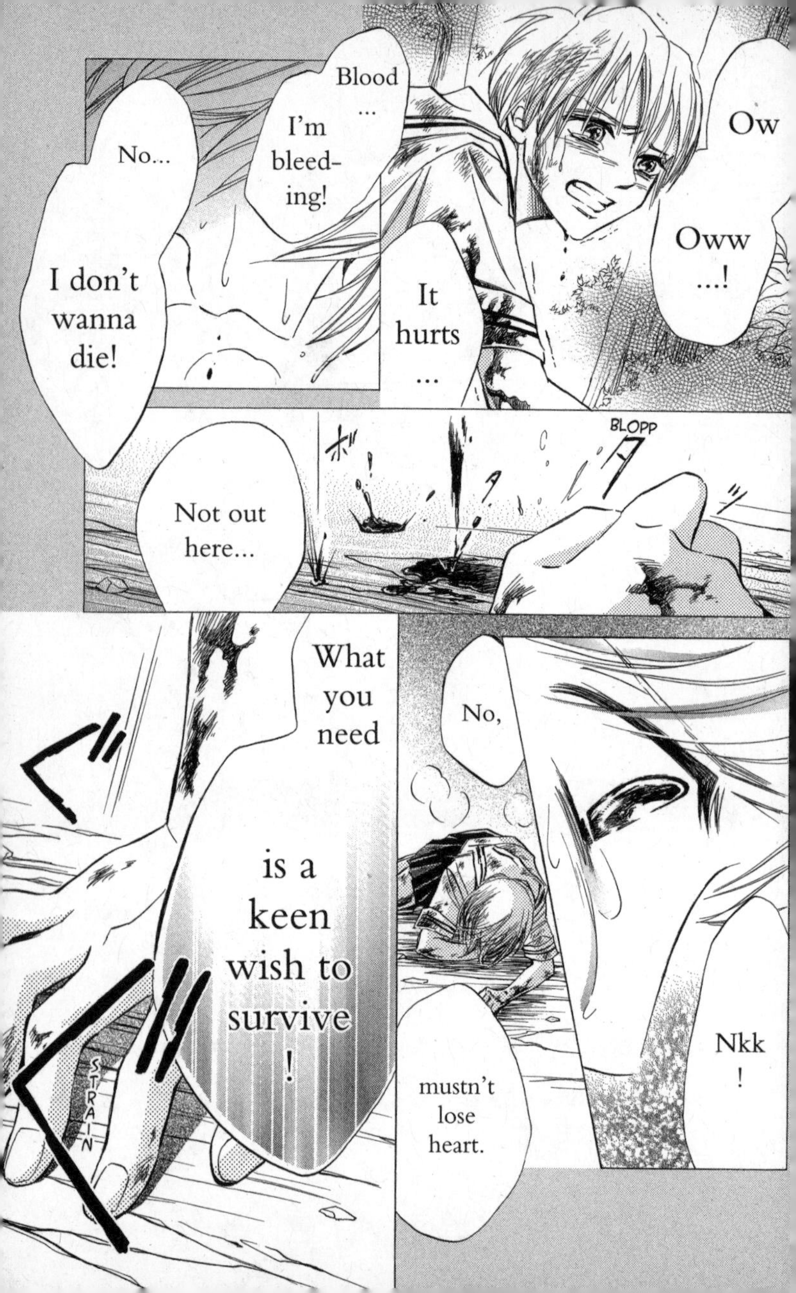
Ow
Oww ...!
Blood ... I'm bleed-ing!
It hurts ...
No...
I don't wanna die!
BLOPP
Not out here...
Nkk !
No,
mustn't lose heart.
What you need
is a keen wish to survive !
STRAIN

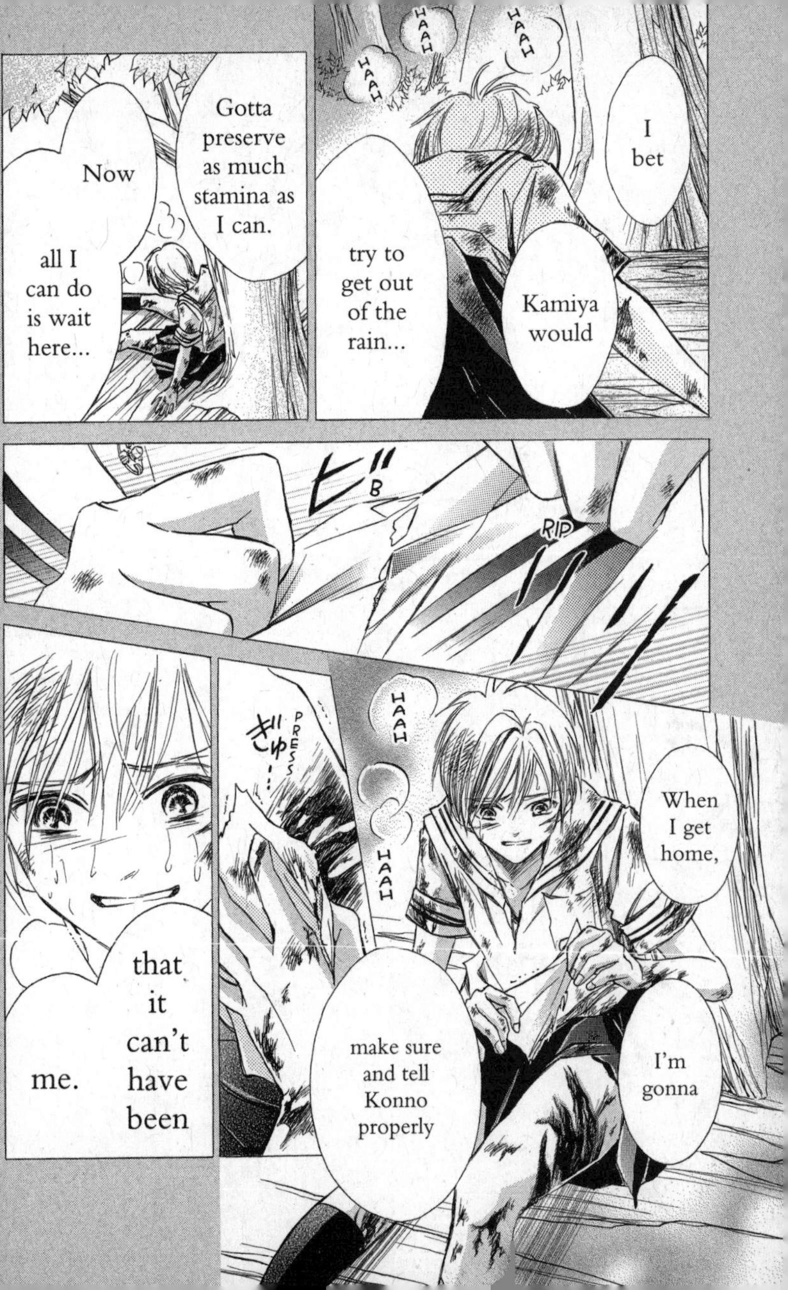
HAAH
HAAH
HAAH
I bet
Kamiya would
try to get out of the rain...
Gotta preserve as much stamina as I can.
Now
all I can do is wait here...
B
RIP
HAAH
When I get home,
I'm gonna
make sure and tell Konno properly
HAAH
PRESS
that it can't have been
me.

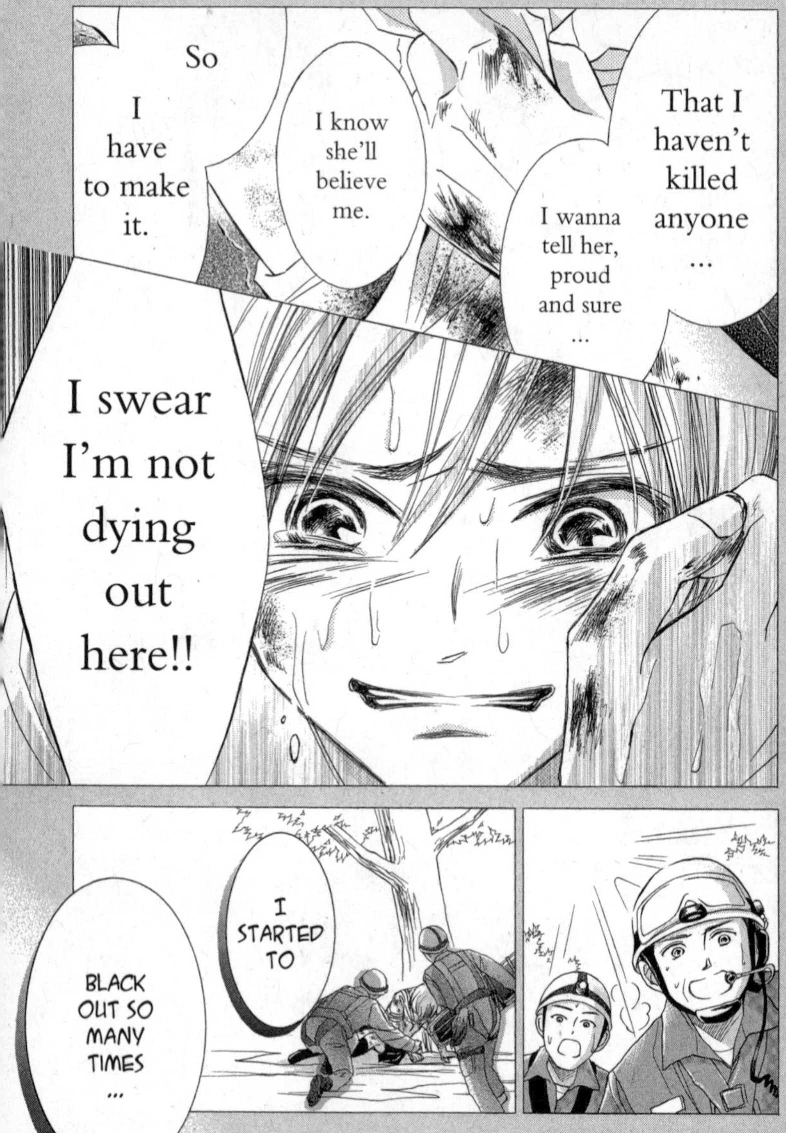
That I haven't killed anyone ...
I wanna tell her, proud and sure ...
I know she'll believe me.
So I have to make it.
I swear I'm not dying out here!!
I STARTED TO
BLACK OUT SO MANY TIMES ...

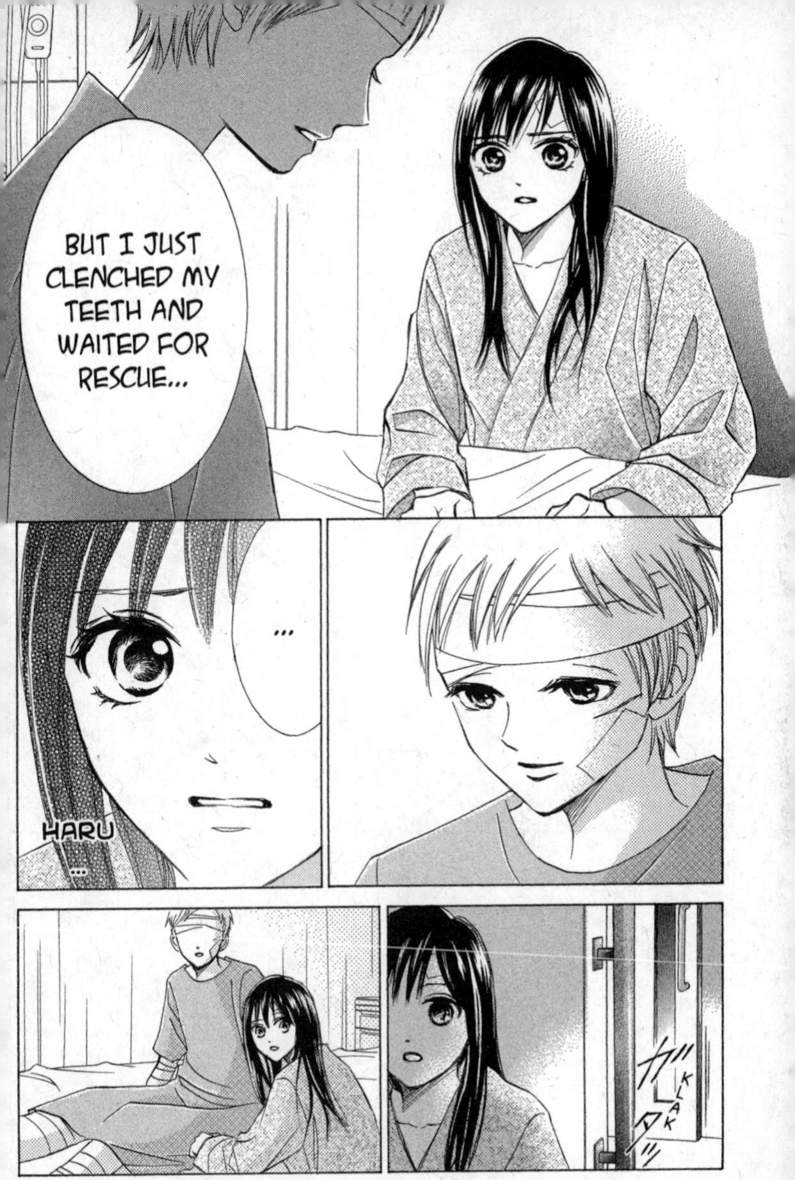
BUT I JUST CLENCHED MY TEETH AND WAITED FOR RESCUE...
...
HARU ...
KLAK

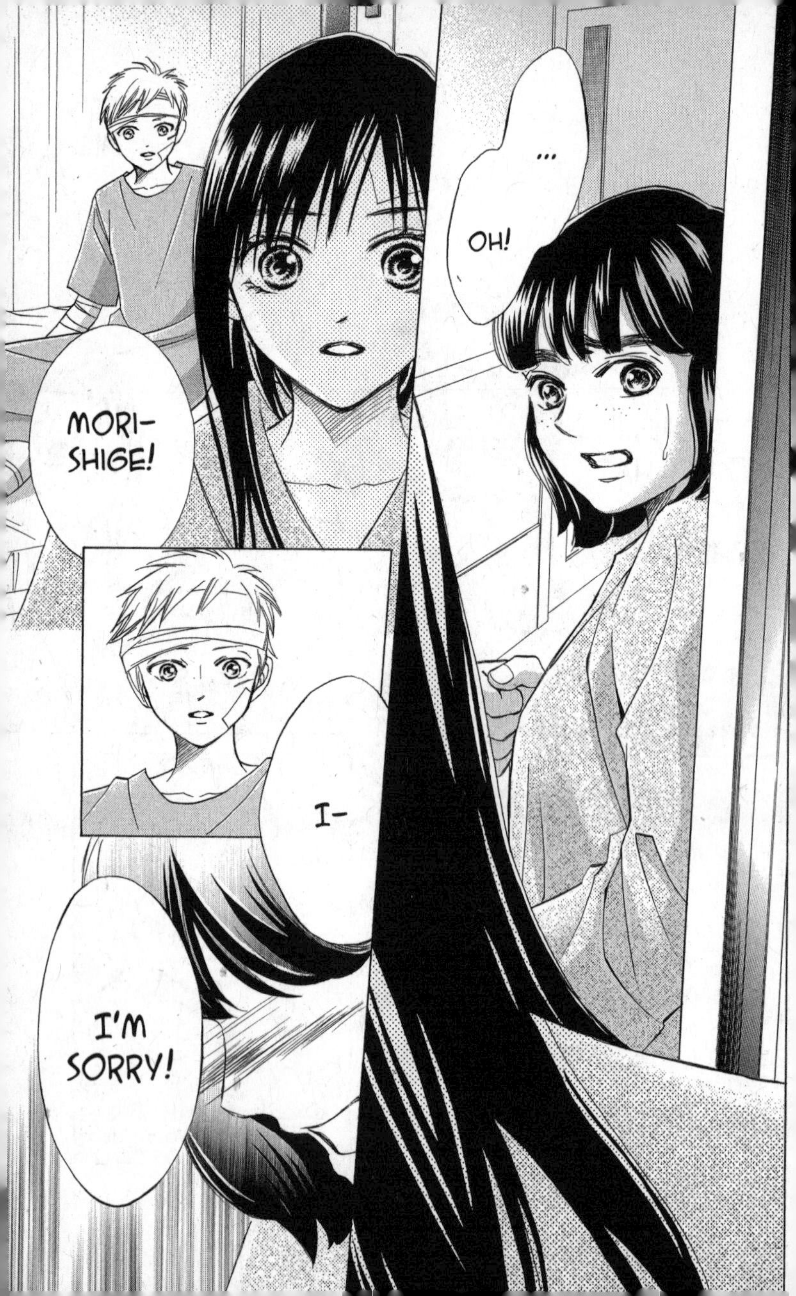
...
OH!
MORI-SHIGE!
I-
I'M SORRY!

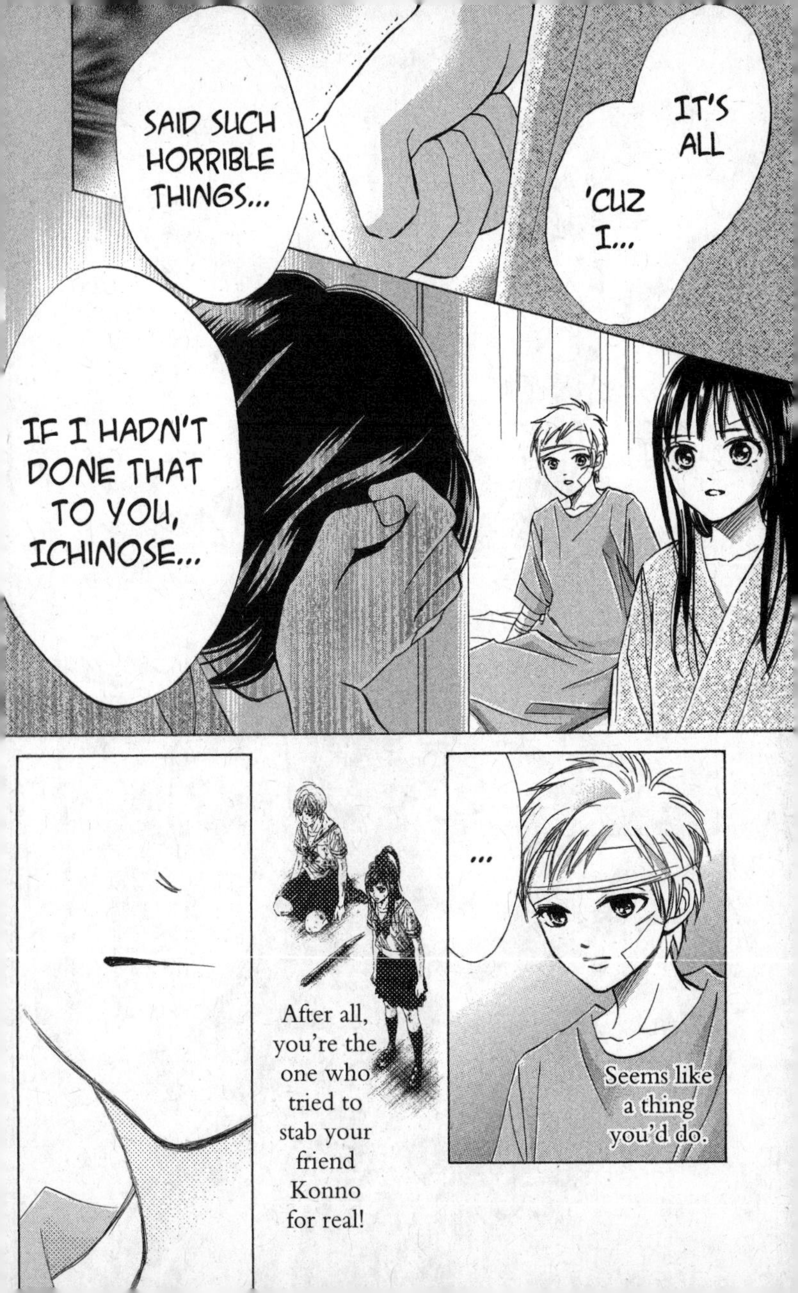
IT'S ALL 'CUZ I...
SAID SUCH HORRIBLE THINGS...
IF I HADN'T DONE THAT TO YOU, ICHINOSE...
...
Seems like a thing you'd do.
After all, you're the one who tried to stab your friend Konno for real!

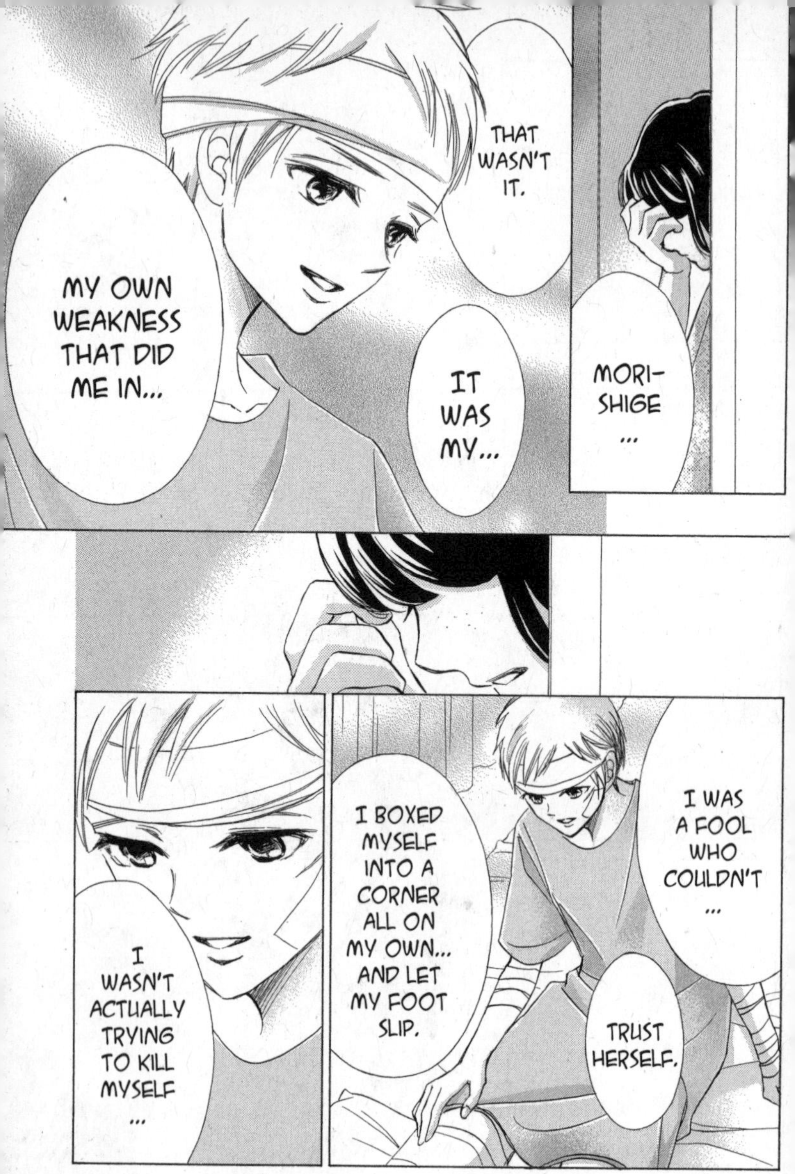
MORI-SHIGE ...
THAT WASN'T IT.
IT WAS MY...
MY OWN WEAKNESS THAT DID ME IN...
I WAS A FOOL WHO COULDN'T ...
TRUST HERSELF.
I BOXED MYSELF INTO A CORNER ALL ON MY OWN... AND LET MY FOOT SLIP.
I WASN'T ACTUALLY TRYING TO KILL MYSELF ...

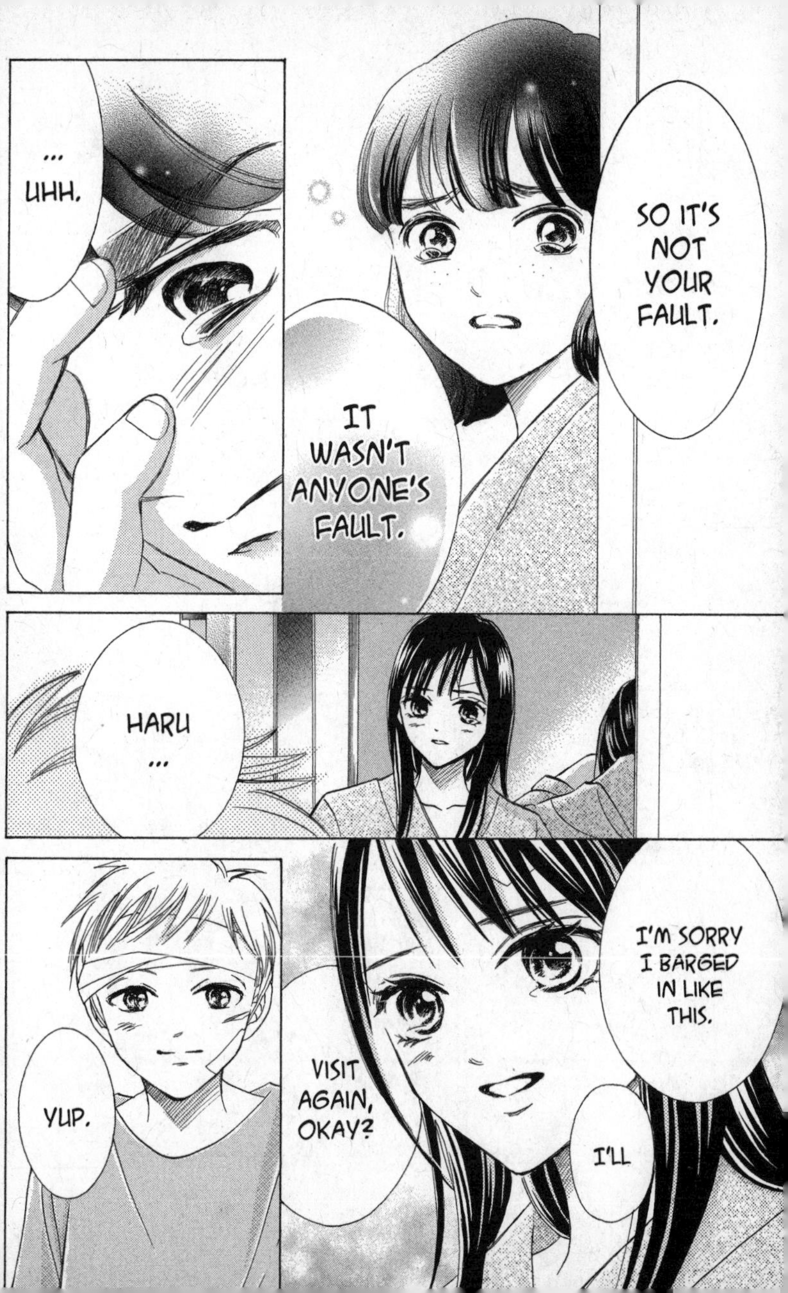
SO IT'S NOT YOUR FAULT.
IT WASN'T ANYONE'S FAULT.
... UHH.
HARU ...
I'M SORRY I BARGED IN LIKE THIS.
VISIT AGAIN, OKAY?
I'LL
YUP.

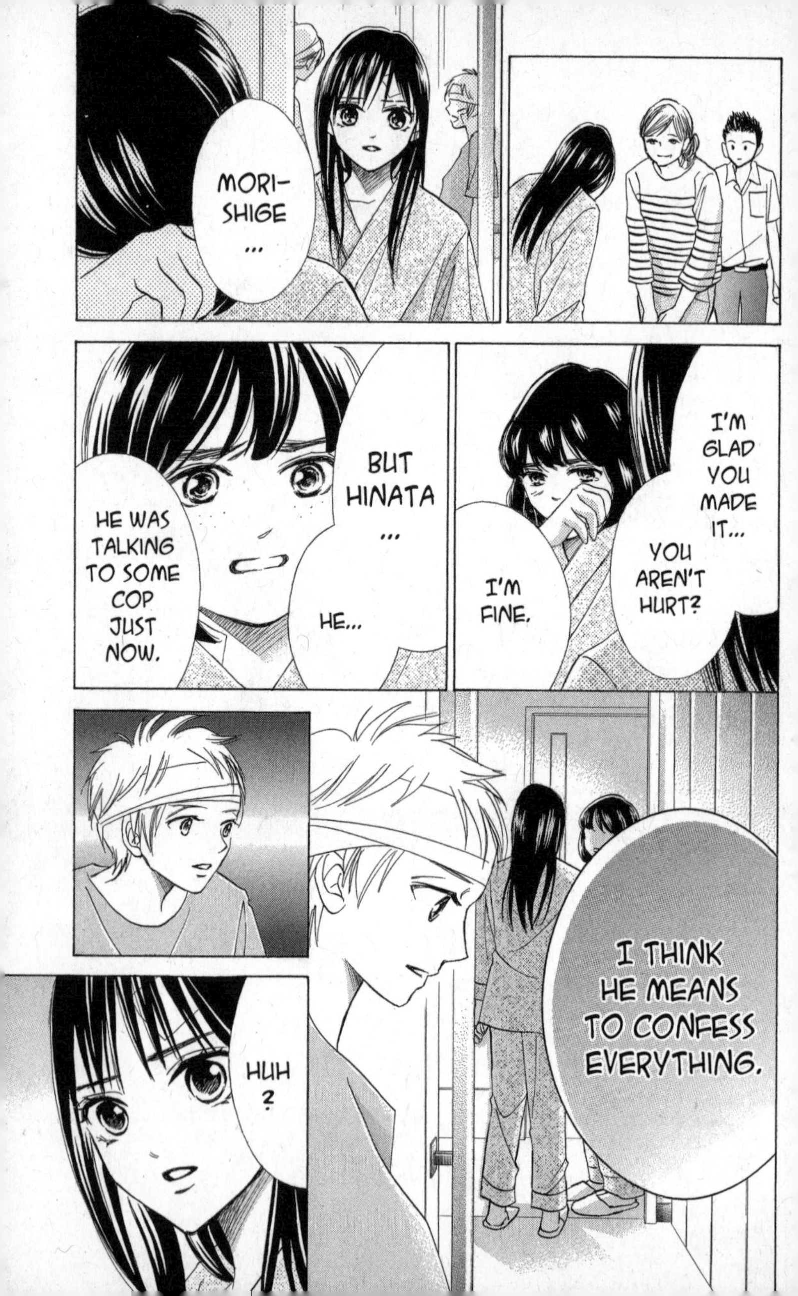
MORI-SHIGE ...
I'M GLAD YOU MADE IT...
YOU AREN'T HURT?
I'M FINE.
BUT HINATA ...
HE...
HE WAS TALKING TO SOME COP JUST NOW.
I THINK HE MEANS TO CONFESS EVERYTHING.
HUH ?

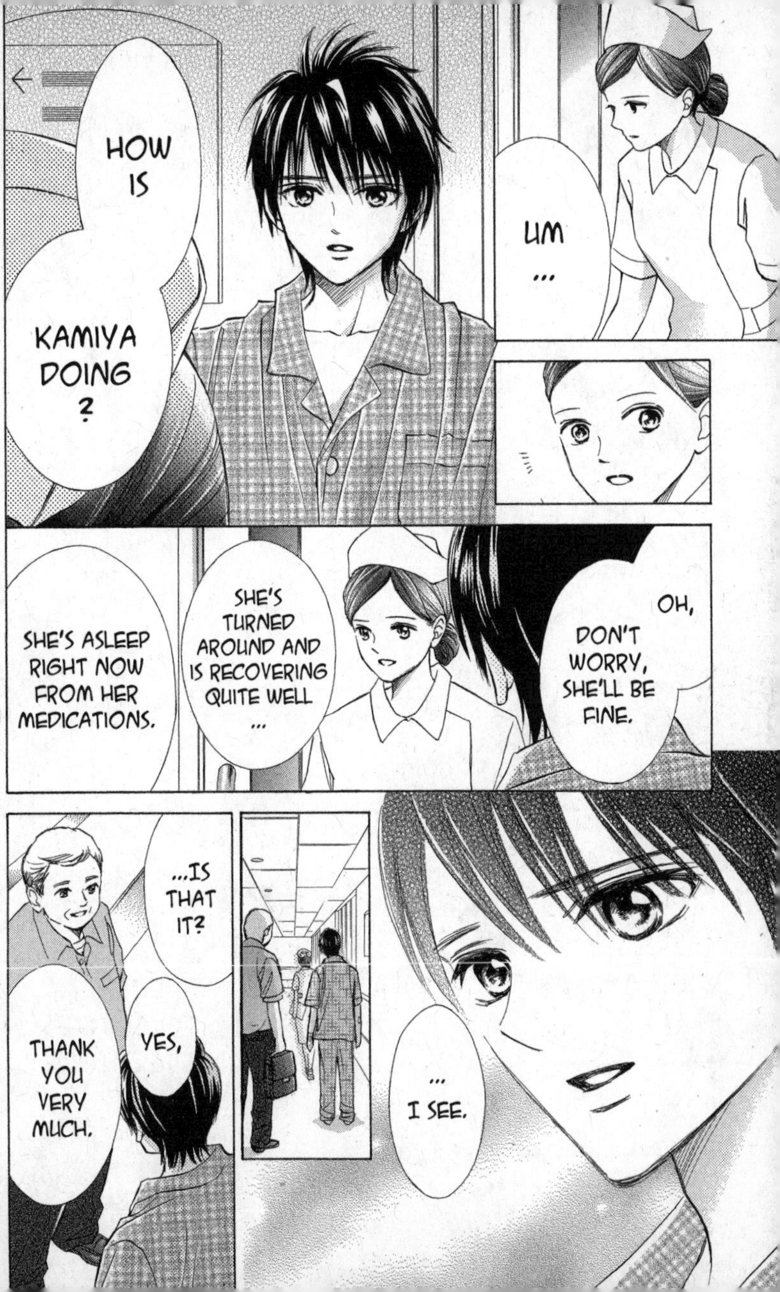
UM ...
HOW IS KAMIYA DOING ?
OH, DON'T WORRY, SHE'LL BE FINE.
SHE'S TURNED AROUND AND IS RECOVERING QUITE WELL ...
SHE'S ASLEEP RIGHT NOW FROM HER MEDICATIONS.
... I SEE.
...IS THAT IT?
YES,
THANK YOU VERY MUCH.

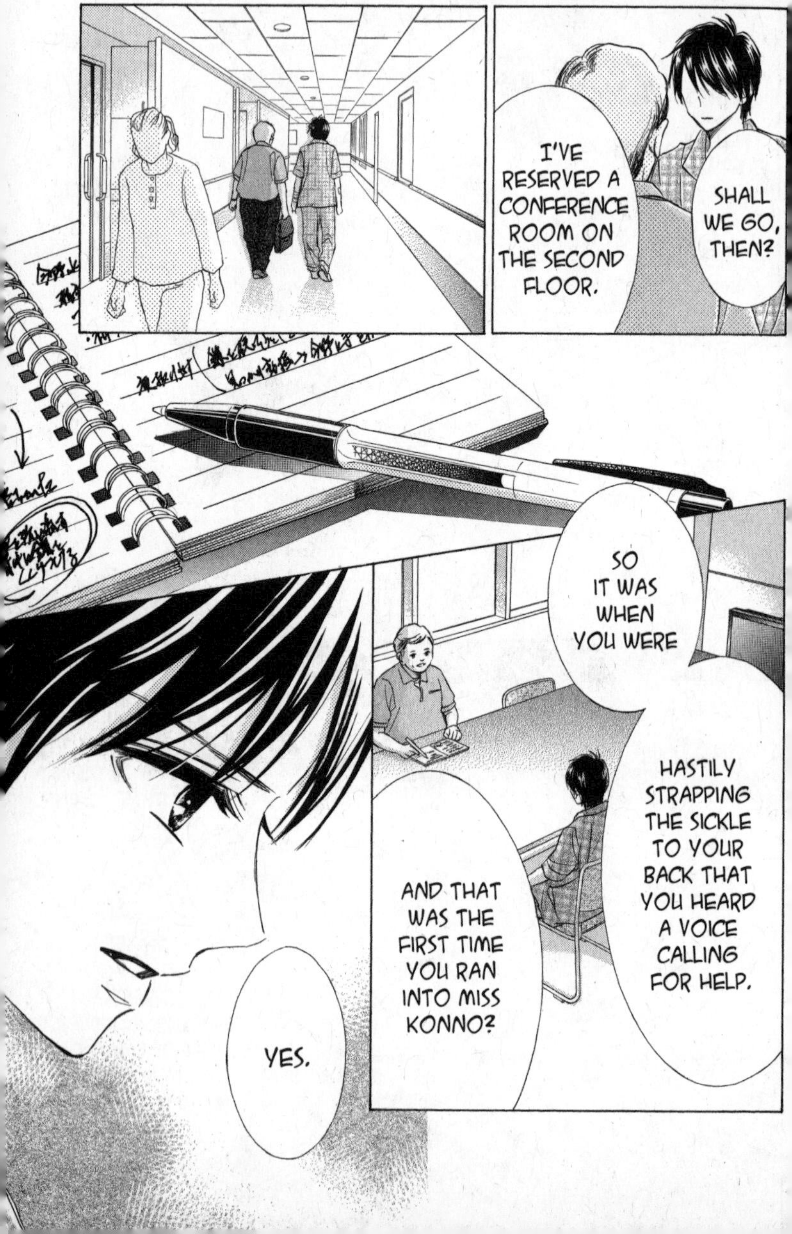
SHALL WE GO, THEN?
I'VE RESERVED A CONFERENCE ROOM ON THE SECOND FLOOR.
SO IT WAS WHEN YOU WERE
HASTILY STRAPPING THE SICKLE TO YOUR BACK THAT YOU HEARD A VOICE CALLING FOR HELP.
AND THAT WAS THE FIRST TIME YOU RAN INTO MISS KONNO?
YES.

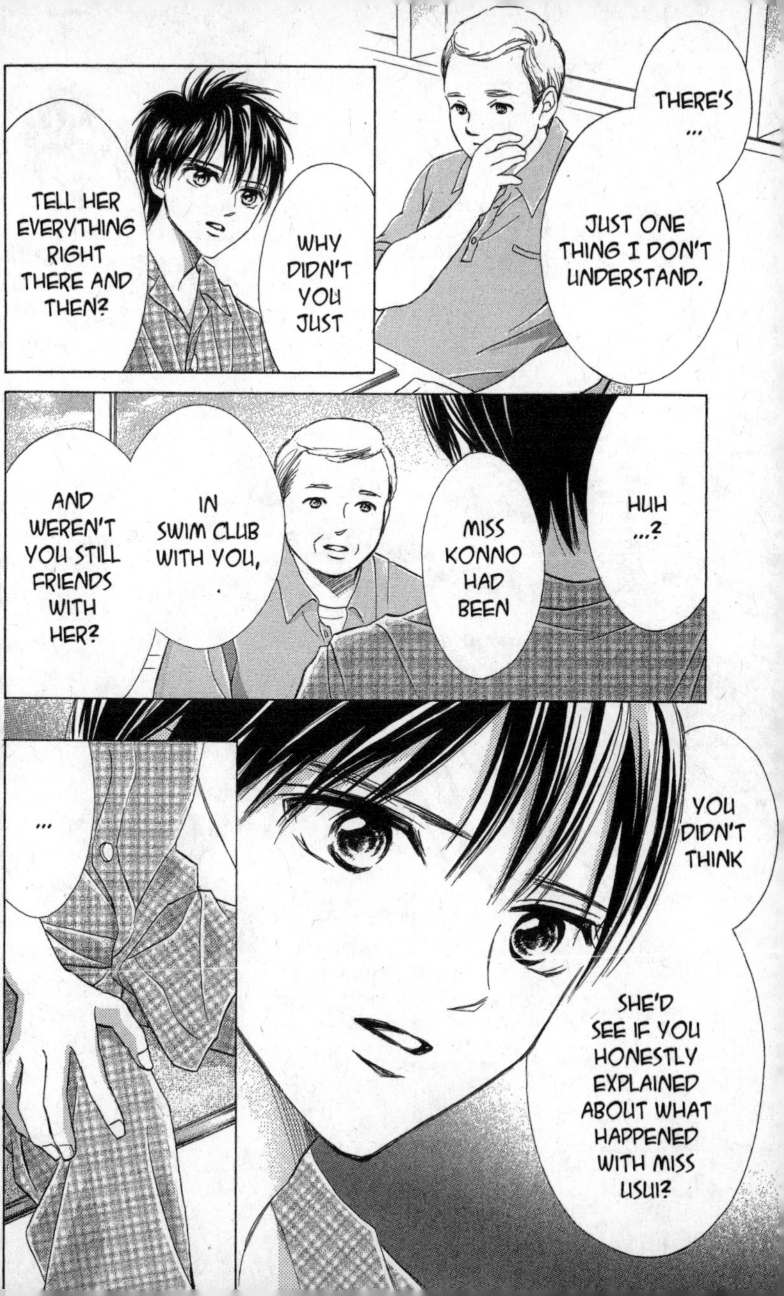
THERE'S ...
JUST ONE THING I DON'T UNDERSTAND.
WHY DIDN'T YOU JUST
TELL HER EVERYTHING RIGHT THERE AND THEN?
HUH ...?
MISS KONNO HAD BEEN
IN SWIM CLUB WITH YOU,
AND WEREN'T YOU STILL FRIENDS WITH HER?
YOU DIDN'T THINK
SHE'D SEE IF YOU HONESTLY EXPLAINED ABOUT WHAT HAPPENED WITH MISS USUI?
...

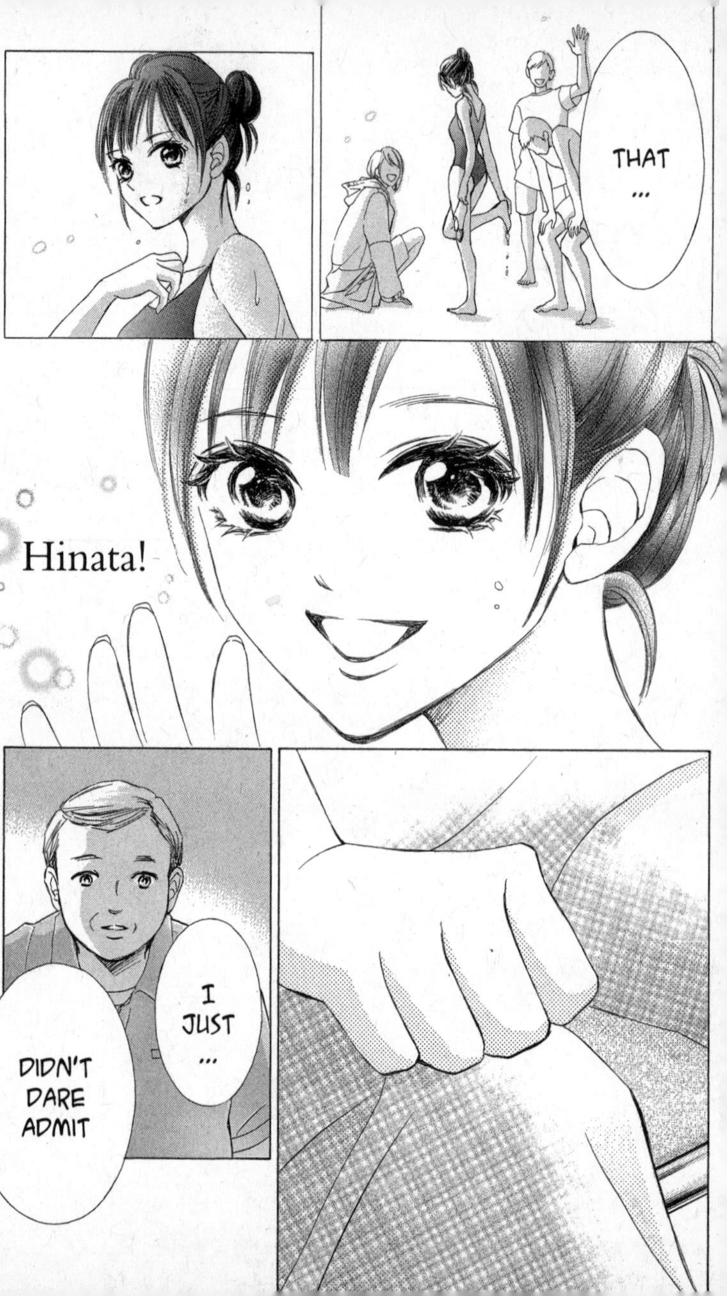
THAT ...
Hinata!
I JUST ...
DIDN'T DARE ADMIT

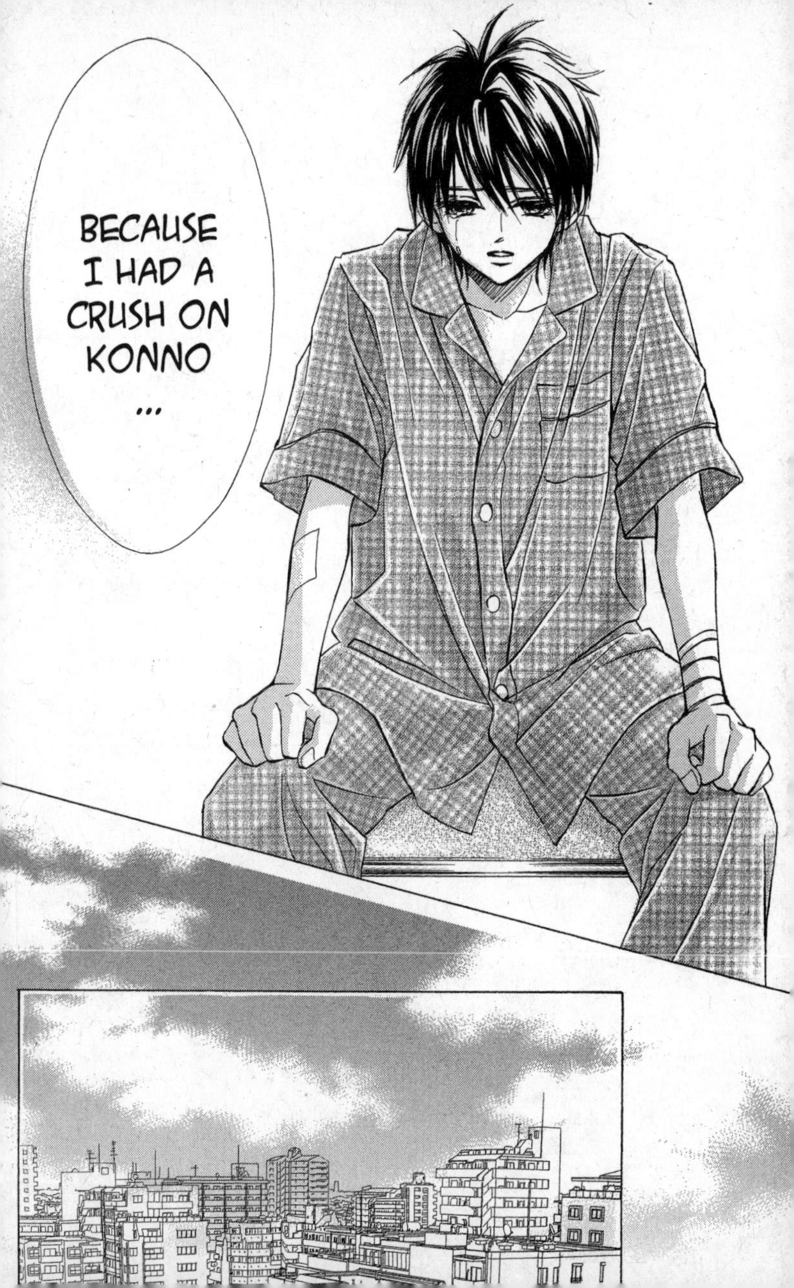
BECAUSE I HAD A CRUSH ON KONNO ...

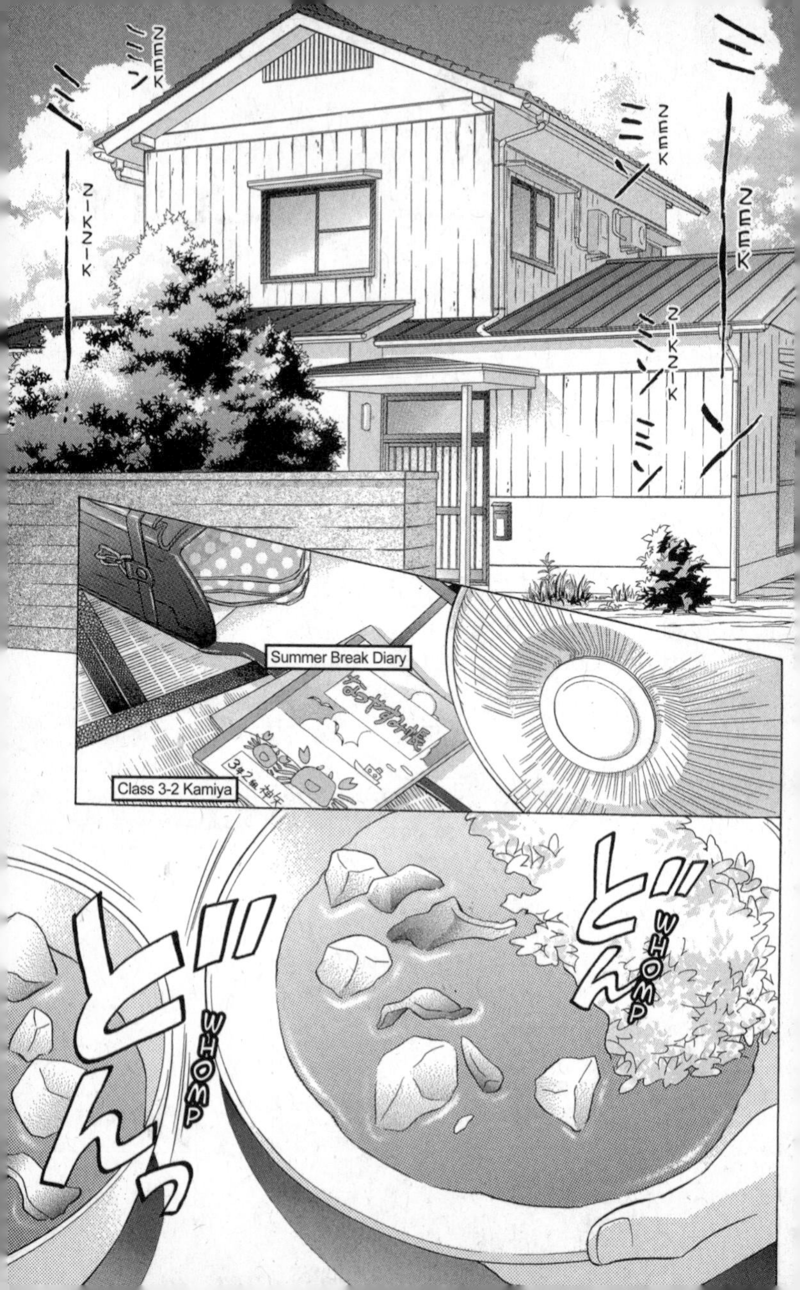
ZEEK
ZEEK
ZIKZIK
ZEEK
ZIKZIK
Summer Break Diary
Class 3-2 Kamiya
WHOMP
WHOMP

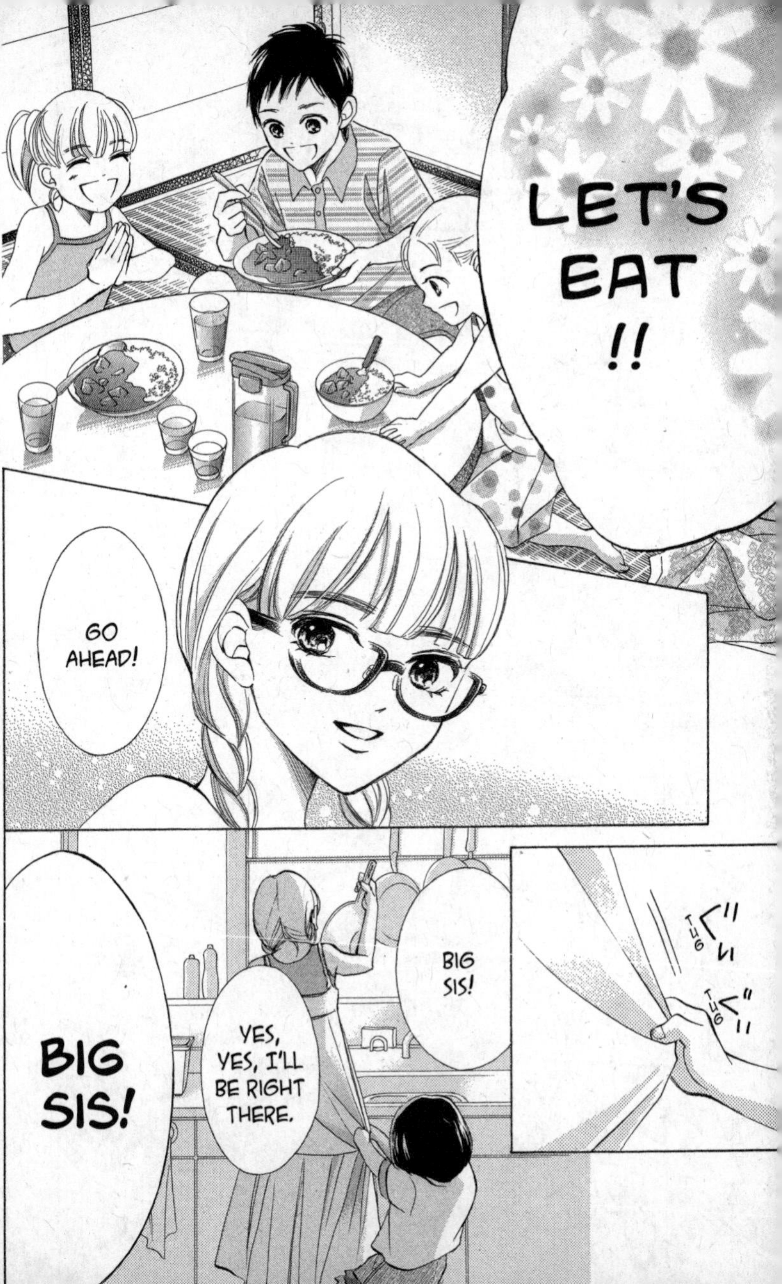
LET'S EAT !!
GO AHEAD!
TUG
TUG
BIG SIS!
BIG SIS!
YES, YES, I'LL BE RIGHT THERE.

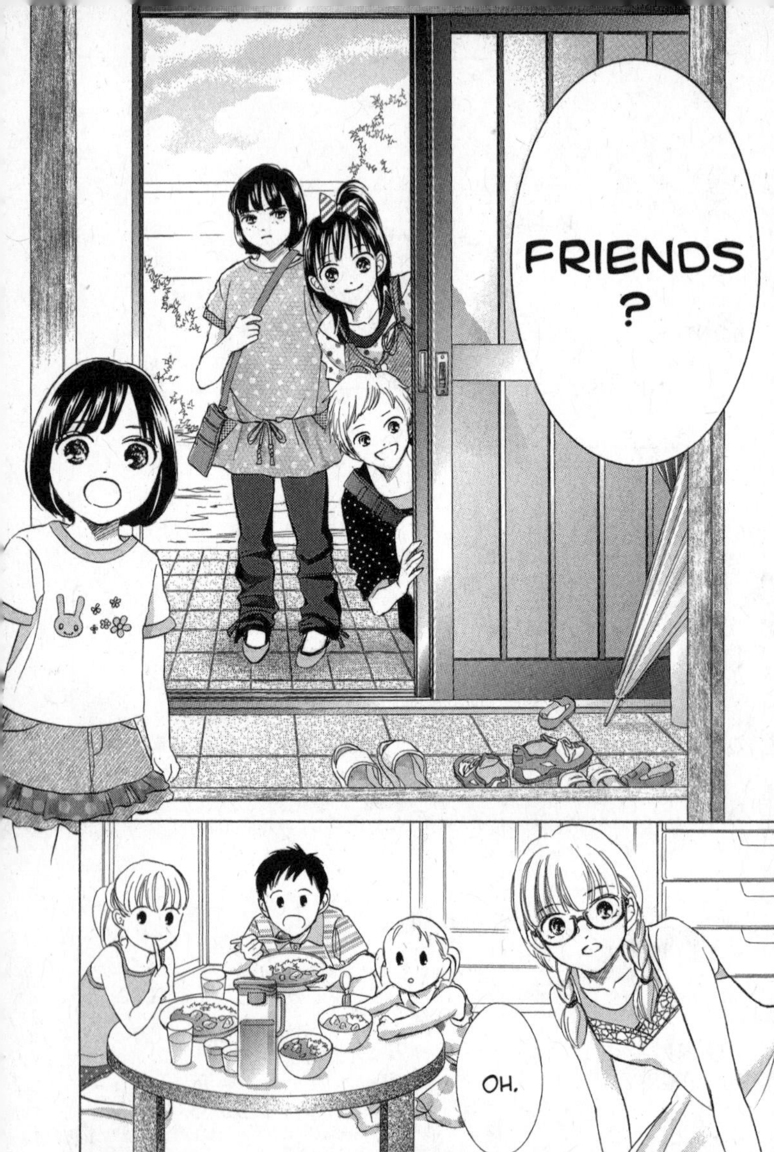
FRIENDS
?
OH.

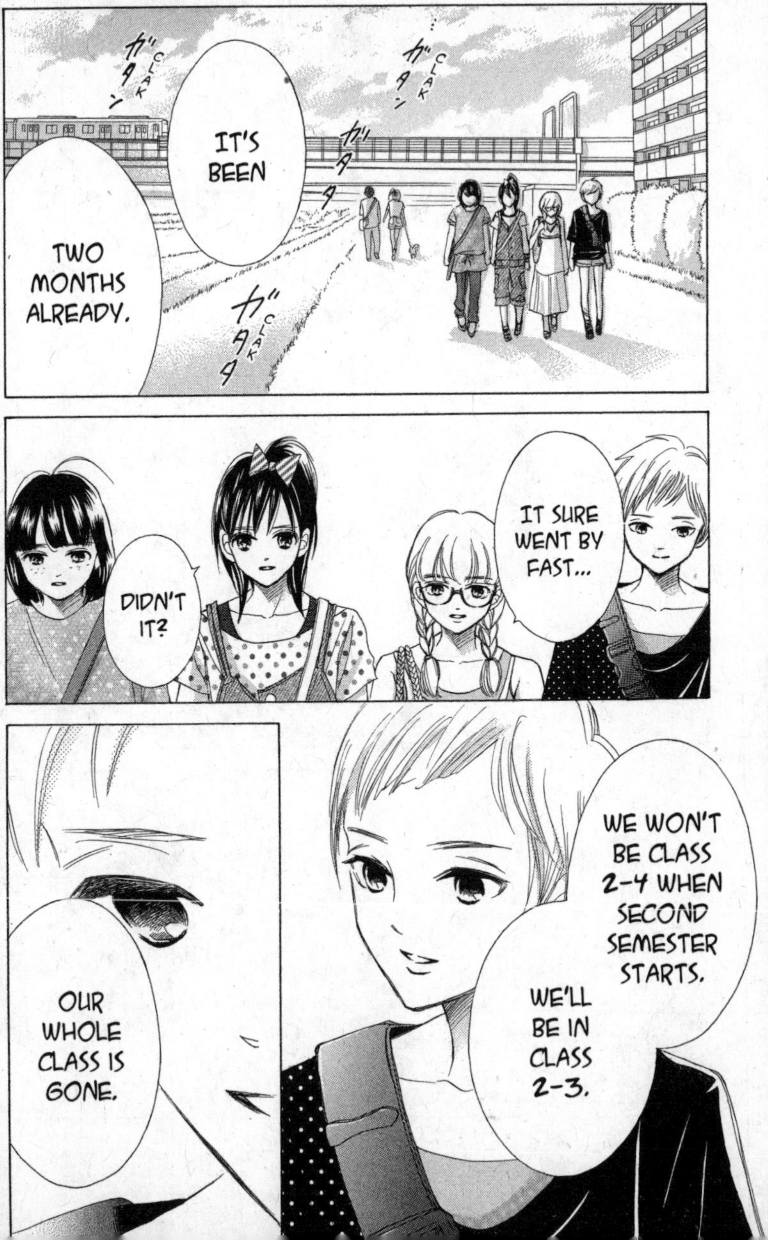
…ガタン
CLAK
ガタタ
IT'S BEEN
ガタン
CLAK
TWO MONTHS ALREADY.
ガタタ
CLAK
IT SURE WENT BY FAST...
DIDN'T IT?
WE WON'T BE CLASS 2-4 WHEN SECOND SEMESTER STARTS.
WE'LL BE IN CLASS 2-3.
OUR WHOLE CLASS IS GONE.

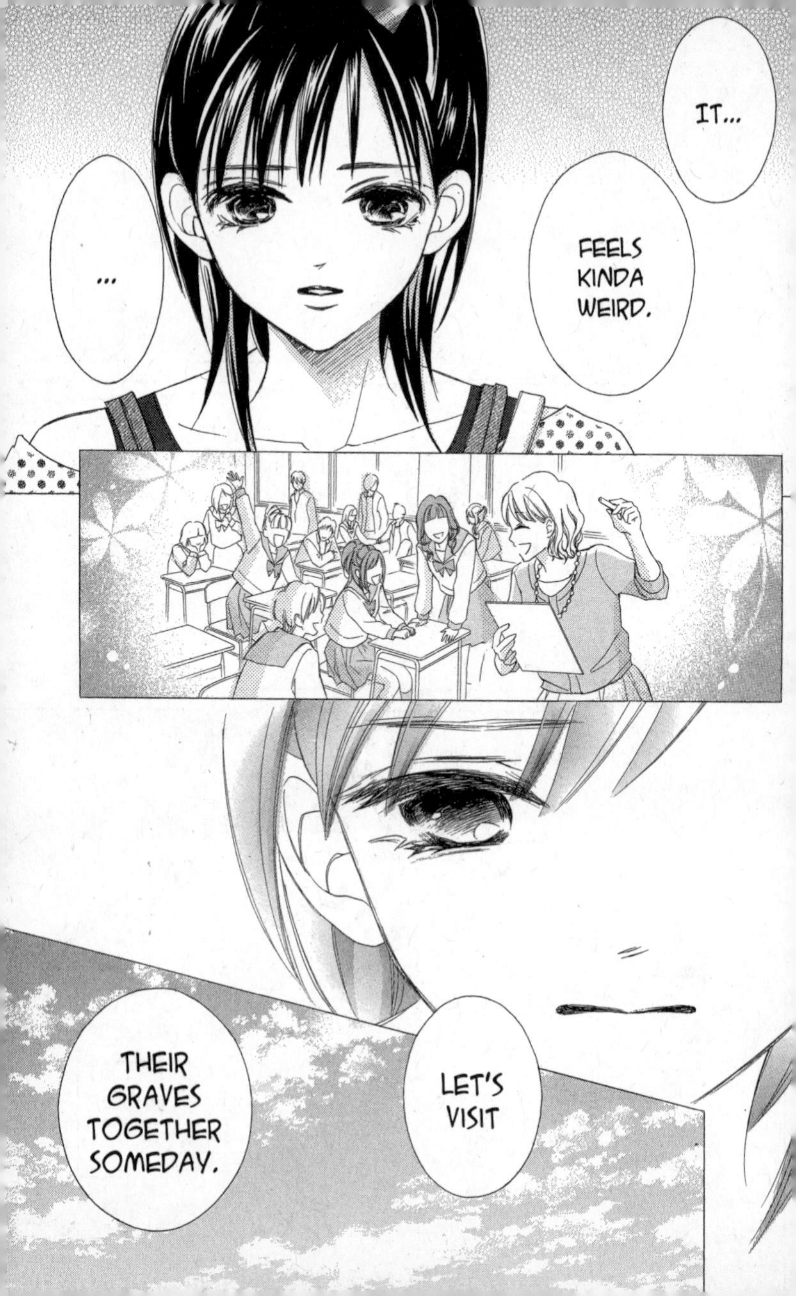
IT...
FEELS KINDA WEIRD.
...
LET'S VISIT
THEIR GRAVES TOGETHER SOMEDAY.

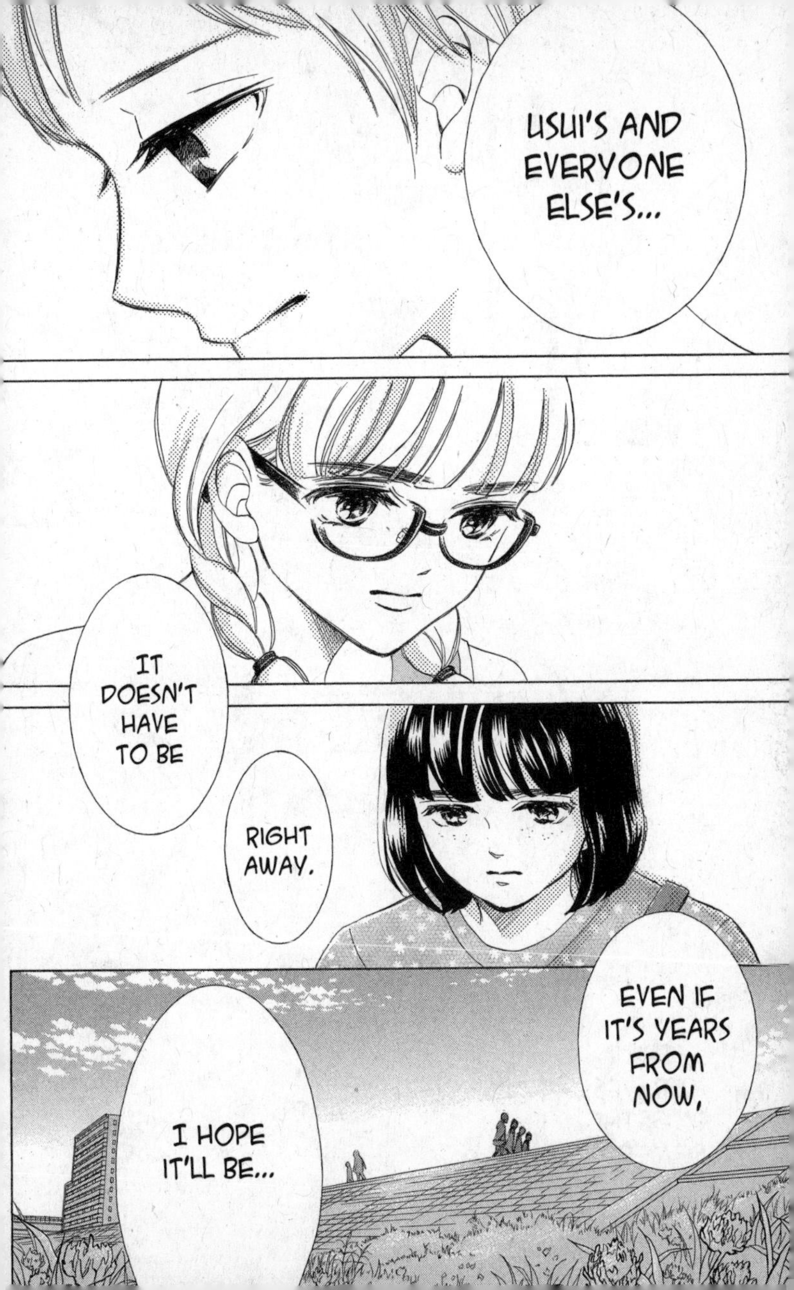
USUI'S AND EVERYONE ELSE'S...
IT DOESN'T HAVE TO BE
RIGHT AWAY.
EVEN IF IT'S YEARS FROM NOW,
I HOPE IT'LL BE...

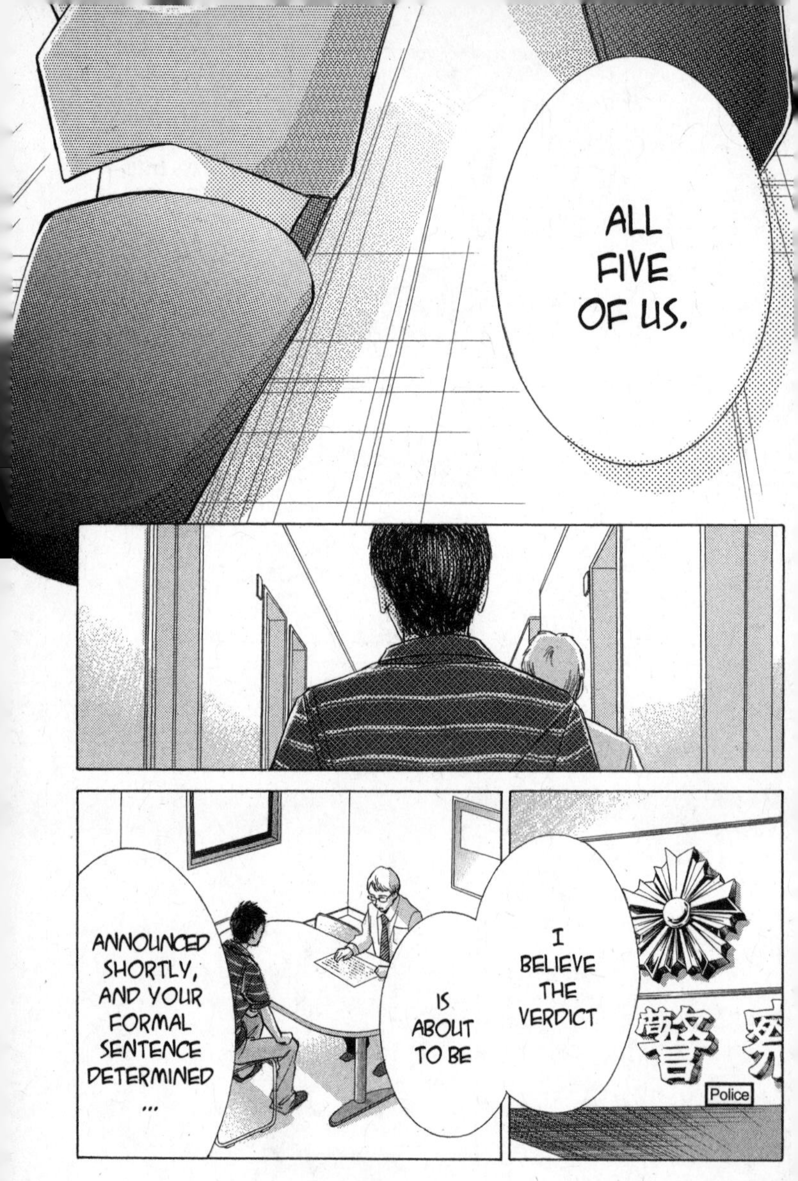
ALL FIVE OF US.
Police
I BELIEVE THE VERDICT
IS ABOUT TO BE
ANNOUNCED SHORTLY, AND YOUR FORMAL SENTENCE DETERMINED ...

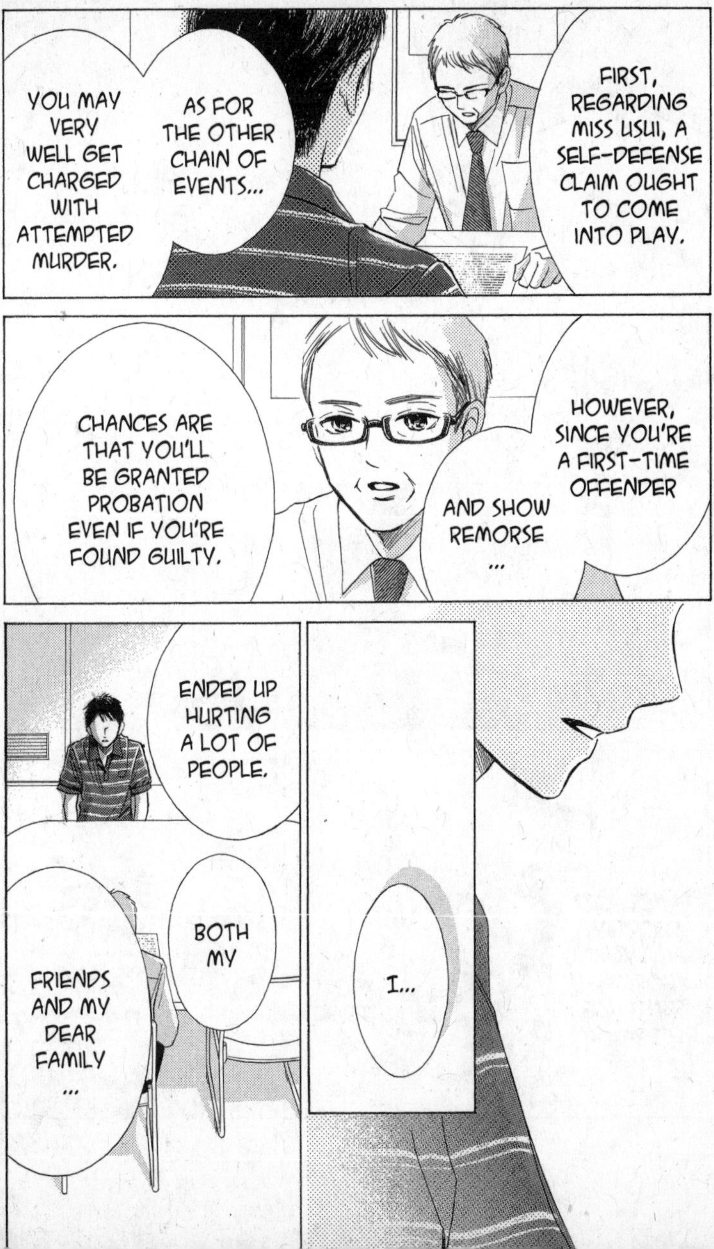
FIRST, REGARDING MISS USUI, A SELF-DEFENSE CLAIM OUGHT TO COME INTO PLAY.
AS FOR THE OTHER CHAIN OF EVENTS...
YOU MAY VERY WELL GET CHARGED WITH ATTEMPTED MURDER.
HOWEVER, SINCE YOU'RE A FIRST-TIME OFFENDER
AND SHOW REMORSE ...
CHANCES ARE THAT YOU'LL BE GRANTED PROBATION EVEN IF YOU'RE FOUND GUILTY.
I...
ENDED UP HURTING A LOT OF PEOPLE.
BOTH MY
FRIENDS AND MY DEAR FAMILY ...

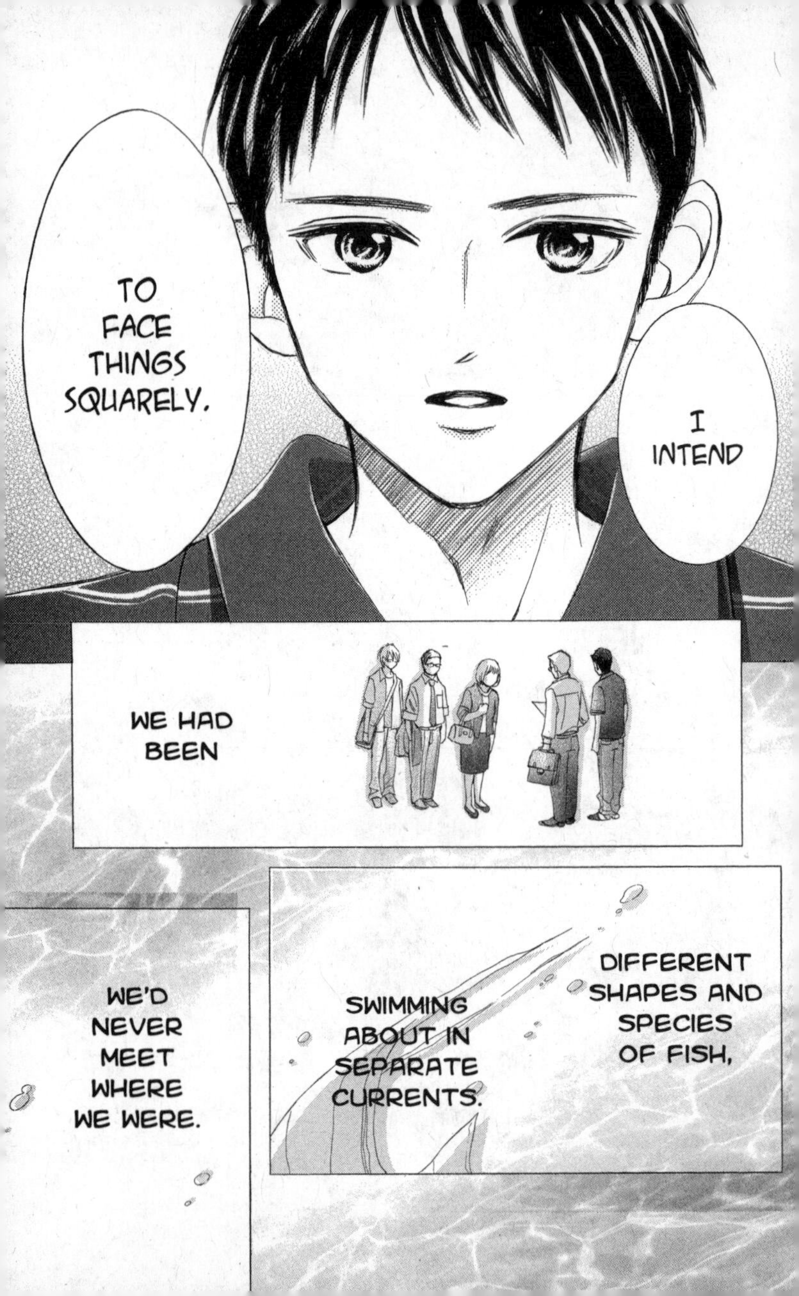
I INTEND
TO FACE THINGS SQUARELY.
WE HAD BEEN
DIFFERENT SHAPES AND SPECIES OF FISH,
SWIMMING ABOUT IN SEPARATE CURRENTS.
WE'D NEVER MEET WHERE WE WERE.

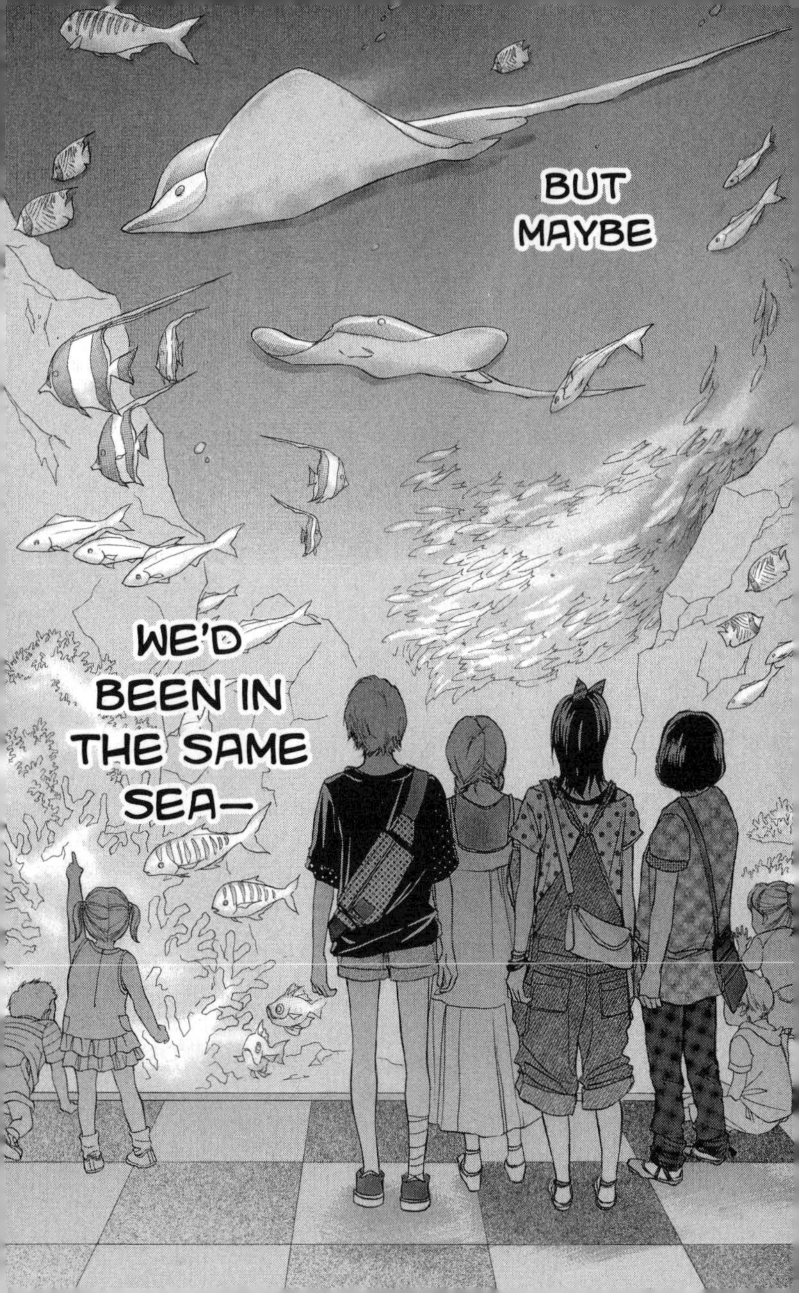
BUT MAYBE
WE'D BEEN IN THE SAME SEA—

YOU
DON'T
NEED
TO SWIM
WELL.

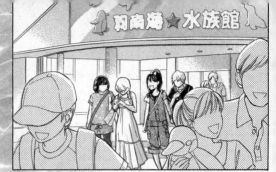

IT'S
NOT TO
FORGET
THAT
WE NOW
STEP
FORTH.

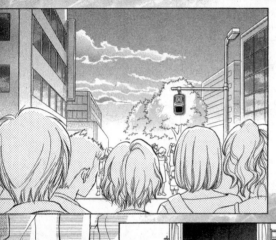

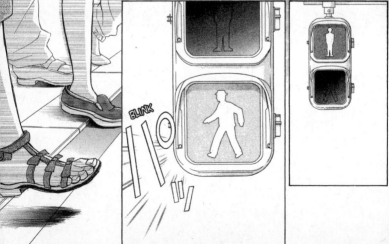

BLINK

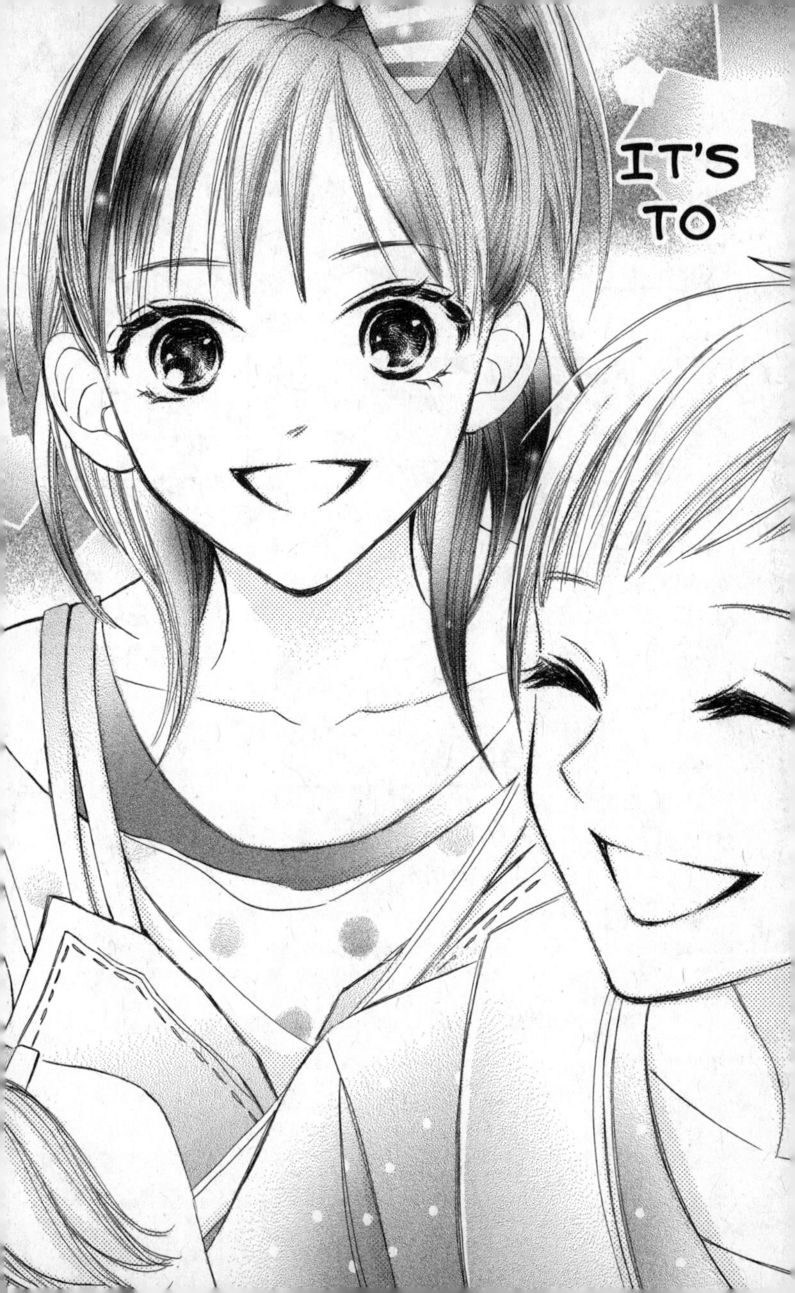
IT'S TO

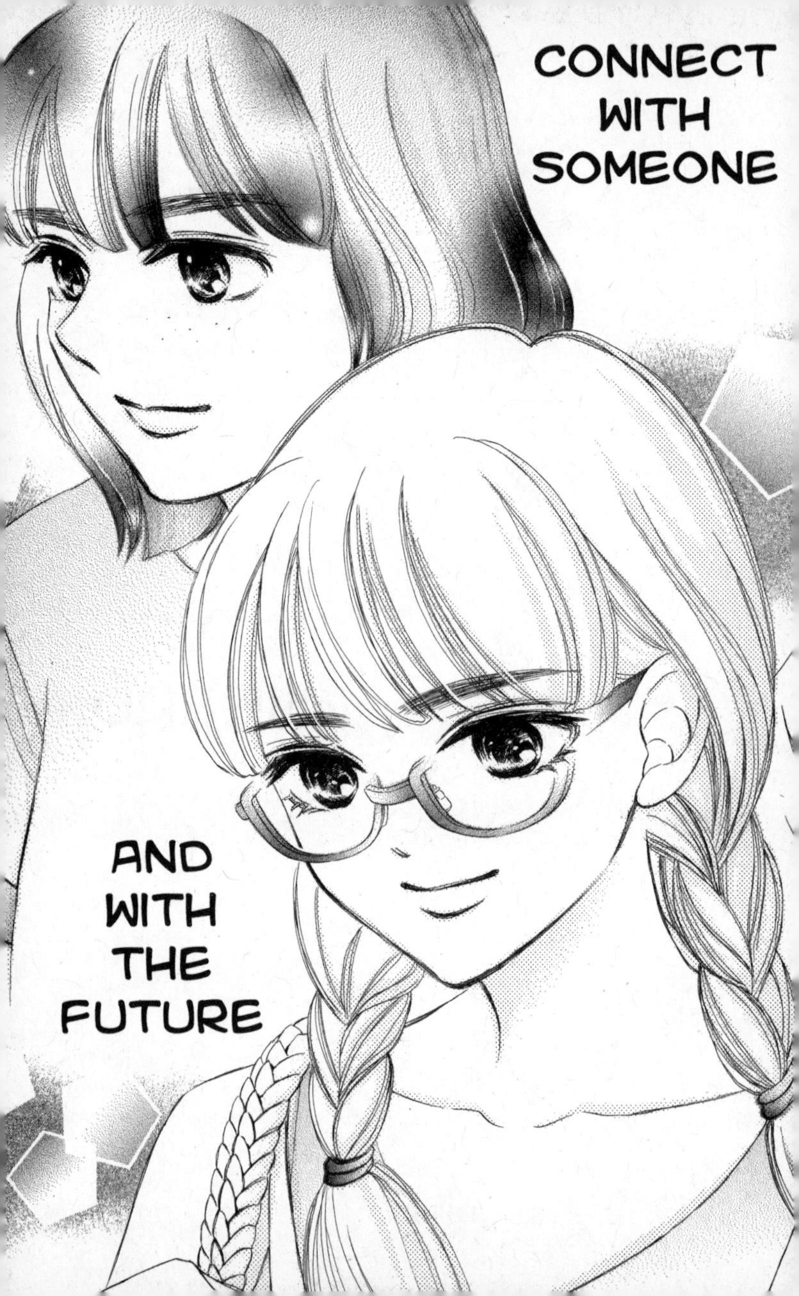
CONNECT WITH SOMEONE
AND WITH THE FUTURE

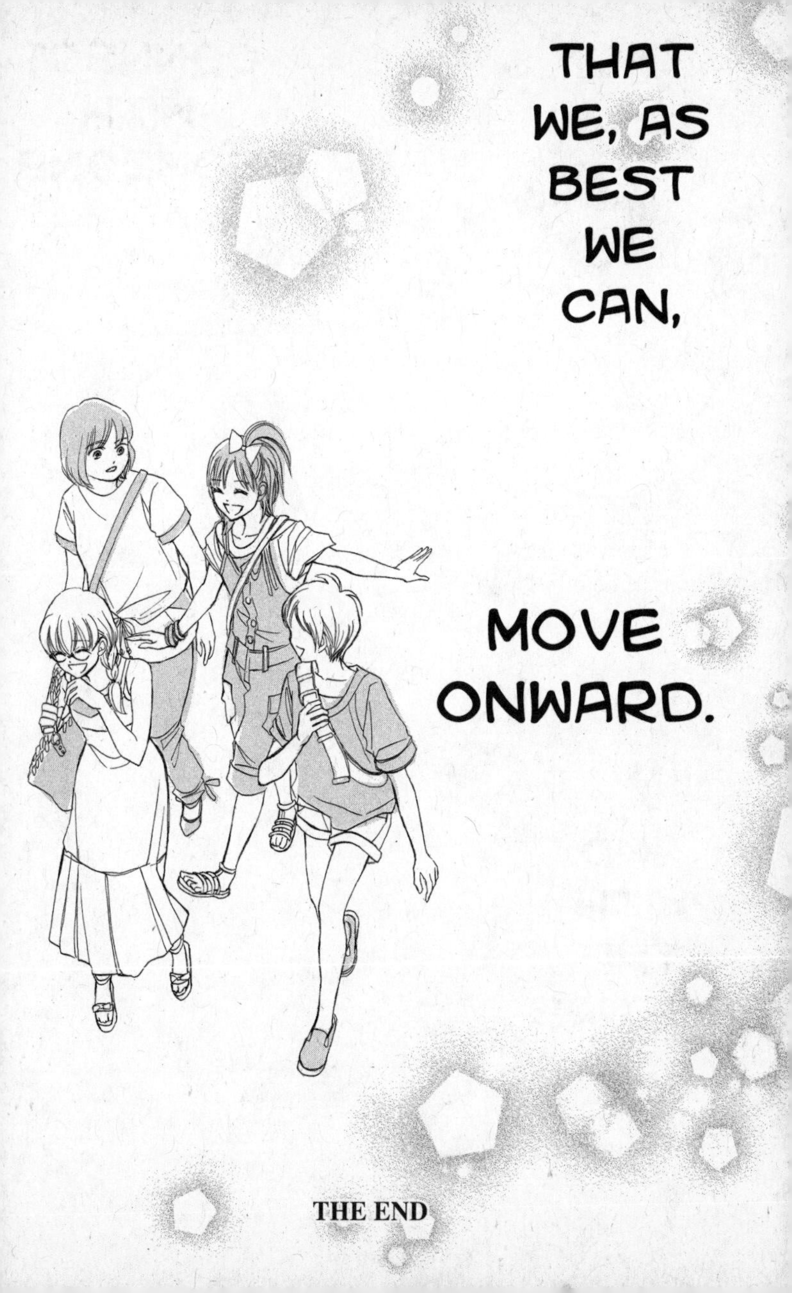
THAT WE, AS BEST WE CAN,
MOVE ONWARD.
THE END

L
I
M
I
T

...just a little bit more.

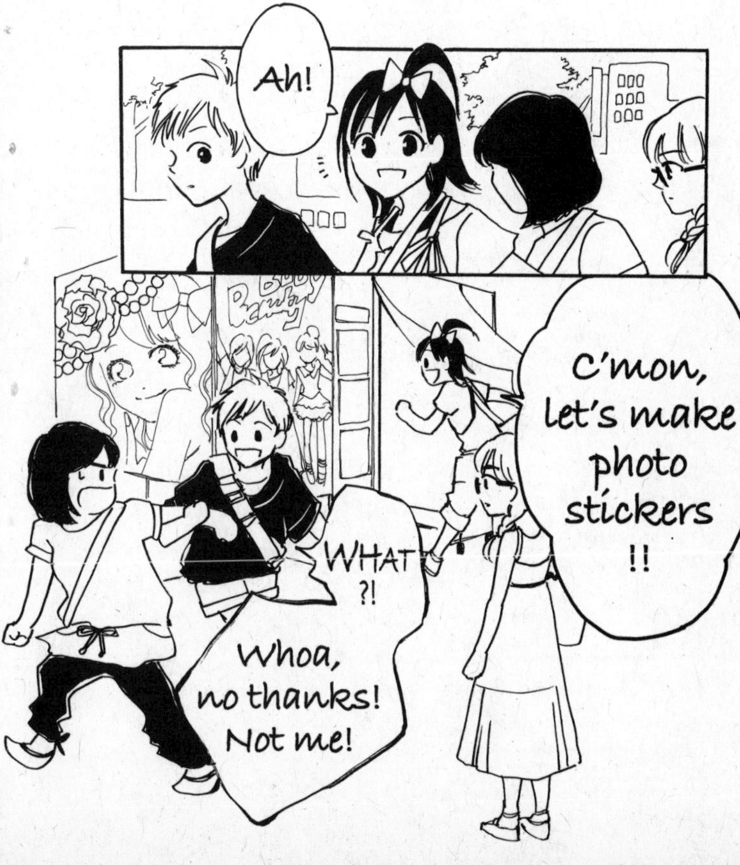
Ah!
C'mon, let's make photo stickers!!
WHAT?!
Whoa, no thanks! Not me!

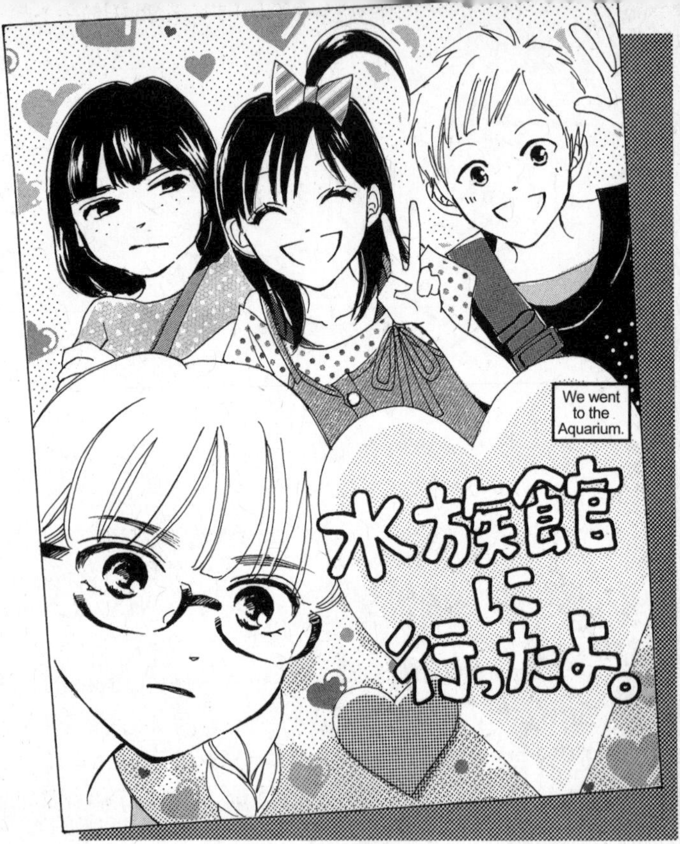
We went to the Aquarium.
水族館に行ったよ。

We had to retake it many times.

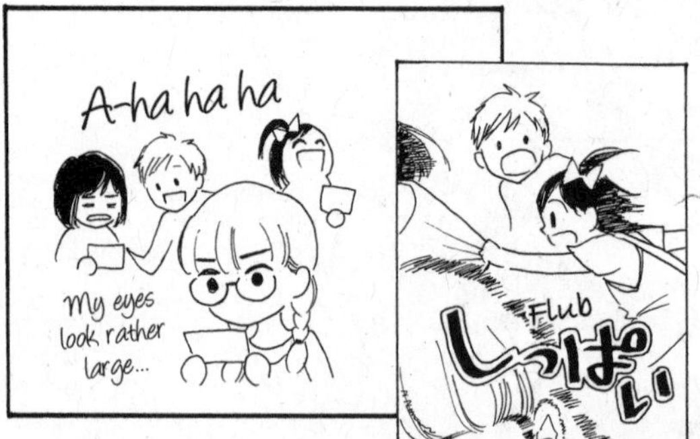
Flub
しっぱい
A-ha ha ha
My eyes look rather large...

Thank you

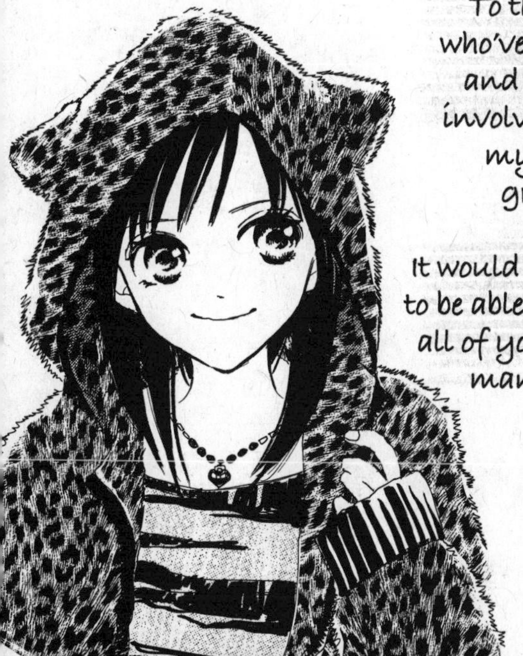

To those of you
who've read this far
and to everyone
involved in LIMIT,
my heartfelt
gratitude!

It would be my pleasure
to be able to connect with
all of you through my
manga again.
—Until then,

Keiko
Suenobu

2011.

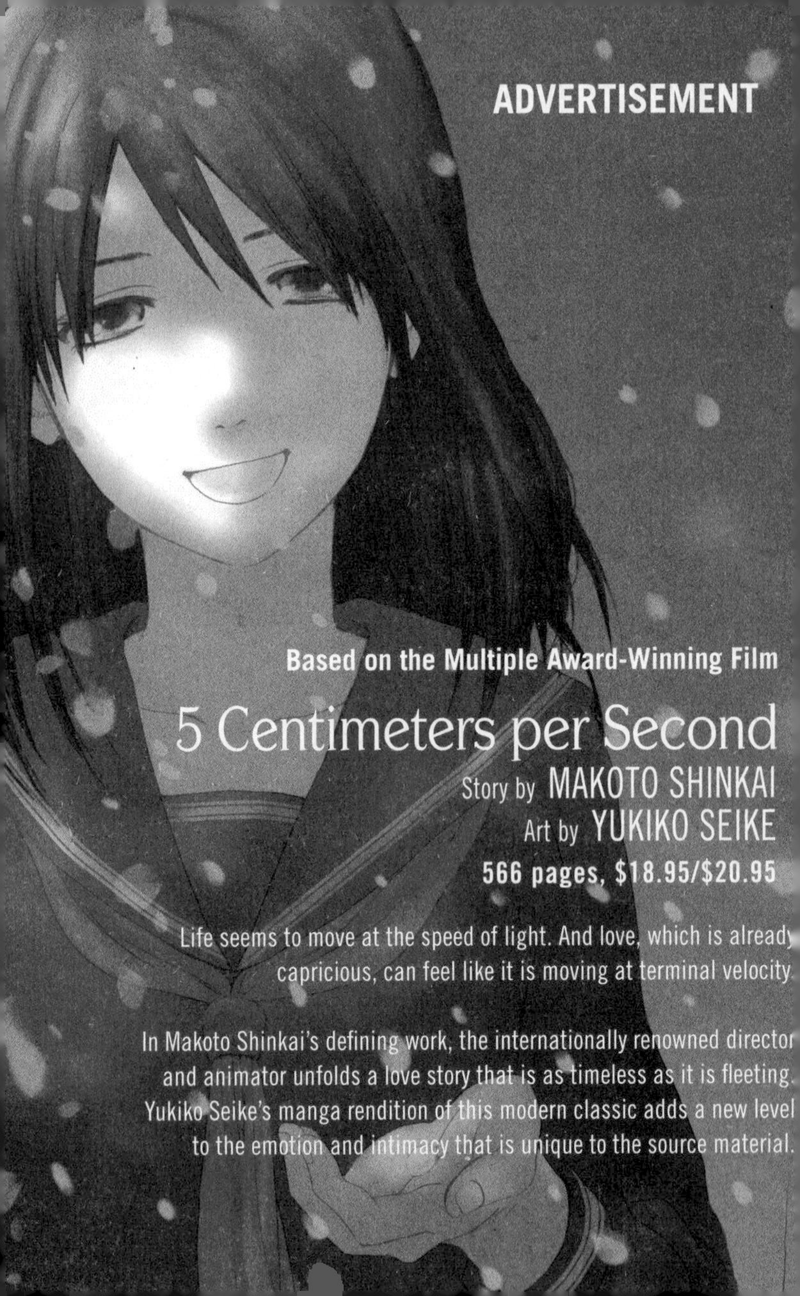
ADVERTISEMENT
Based on the Multiple Award-Winning Film
5 Centimeters per Second
Story by MAKOTO SHINKAI
Art by YUKIKO SEIKE
566 pages, $18.95/$20.95
Life seems to move at the speed of light. And love, which is already capricious, can feel like it is moving at terminal velocity.
In Makoto Shinkai's defining work, the internationally renowned director and animator unfolds a love story that is as timeless as it is fleeting. Yukiko Seike's manga rendition of this modern classic adds a new level to the emotion and intimacy that is unique to the source material.

LIMIT

Limit: Volume 6

Translation: Mari Morimoto
Production: Risa Cho
Tomoe Tsutsumi
Anthony Quintessenza

First published in Japan in 2011 by Kodansha, Ltd., Tokyo
Publication for this English edition arranged through Kodansha, Ltd., Tokyo
English language version produced by Vertical, Inc.

Translation provided by Vertical, Inc., 2013
Published by Vertical, Inc., New York

Originally published in Japanese as *Limit 6* by Kodansha, Ltd.
Limit first serialized in *Bessatsu Friend*, Kodansha, Ltd., 2009-2011

ISBN: 978-1-935654-84-1

Manufactured in the United States of America

First Edition

Vertical, Inc.
451 Park Avenue South
7th Floor
New York, NY 10016
www.vertical-inc.com